PSYCHOTHERAPY OF CHARACTER

*The **Play** of **Consciousness** in the **Theater** of the **Brain***

ROBERT A. BEREZIN, MD

Psychotherapy of Character: The Play of Consciousness in the Theater of the Brain

Published by Wheatmark®
1760 East River Road, Suite 145, Tucson, Arizona 85718 U.S.A.
www.wheatmark.com

ISBN: 978-1-60494-918-6 (paperback)
ISBN: 978-1-60494-941-4 (hardcover)
ISBN: 978-1-60494-942-1 (ebook)
LCCN: 2012956199

CONTENTS

Psychotherapy

On the Big Stage

INTRODUCTION

WHAT DO TINKER BELL, PHANTOM limbs, Scrooge, Genesis, Willie Loman, a schizophrenic delusion, Zeus, Grumpy (and his brothers), an incubus, Mozart's Requiem, *Eleanor Rigby*, your personality, Oz, *A Starry, Starry Night*, and flying in your dream last night have in common? They are the stuff of human consciousness. They have all emerged from the human imagination into our lives. They are fanciful, uplifting, sad, raunchy, dark, fun, scary, mysterious, and tragic. They embody different aspects of the human struggle, mystery, and wonder that have been present in all cultures throughout history. They encompass the richness and depth of the human story and, as such, the whole reach of human nature. And they represent what is inside of each and every one of us. Most important, they introduce the central theme of "The Play of Consciousness," the organization of human consciousness as a living drama in the theater of the brain.

The "play" is an entire representational world that consists of a cast of characters who relate together by feeling, as well as plots, set designs, and landscape. It is a unified field theory of human consciousness, which includes psychiatry, neuroscience, dreams, myths, religion, and art—all elements of the same thing. It derives from and is consonant with our child rearing and culture. The "play" encompasses the ineffable human mysteries—birth, death, and the disparity between our ordinary sense of self and our intimation of a deeper authenticity. It includes as well the dark side of our nature. And finally, it holds the key to the nature of beliefs in general. Human consciousness and human nature are one and the same. The creation of our inner play by the brain is the consummation of our Darwinian human evolution.

As a psychiatrist for the past forty years, my understanding of the play evolved in the context of my work with patients in the long-term psychotherapy of character. I bring the confluent themes of this book to life by telling the story of my patient, Eddie. We first meet Eddie at conception. From the beginning, he is a biological organism, adapting to his salient environment. The story moves to the development of his brain as an embryo and then on to fetal-Eddie, as his ongoing maternal environment is digested and established into his maturing cortex. This process accelerates after Eddie's birth, and at six weeks results in the first coalescence of his consciousness in the form of his rudimentary cortical play. The story continues on to the creation of his fully formed representational play at age three, composed of Eddie's foundational personas and their original scenario of relatedness. At this point, the book tells the story of Eddie's childhood and then his life as a teenager. Throughout his experience, the maturation of his consciousness continues in his developing brain. Eddie's character play forms from the collision of his nature with his nurture. It evolves as the actualities of responsiveness, deprivation, and abuse are digested by his individual genetic temperament in concert with the filter of his already established inner scenario. There are pernicious forces in Eddie's life that inform the writing of his inner play and give it a dark cast. The resultant damage to his play warps his character and intimate relationships and generates considerable suffering and alienation. The development of his personality and the consolidation of his maturing consciousness are actually one thing and inseparable. Eddie's play of consciousness is the central expression of the human genome. It is as relevant to the neuroscience and biology of consciousness and the brain as it is to my own field.

As a result of his suffering, Eddie ends up in my care. His narrative comes full circle with the story of his psychotherapy. Eddie's psychotherapy is an unchartered journey to trust and caring that encompasses the full depth and reach of his character. Eddie explores and mourns the pain of his deeply held characterological world through his genuine engagement with me. The very human process of therapy proceeds on the basis of boundaries, respect, and caring to ameliorate his suffering, and fosters the recovery of his authenticity and his capacity to love.

Eddie's psychotherapy is not a throwback to old-fashioned psychoanalytic therapy and its derivatives, which have been beset by considerable problems throughout the years. (Its practice suffered from dogmatic theories and miscast beliefs, which worked to the detriment of responsiveness to our patients.) Although my own roots are in psychoanalytic psychotherapy, I moved on to develop the psychotherapy of character as it is presented through Eddie's story. It is shown to be a specialized form of human engagement that repairs the damage to one's character by acting on the play of consciousness in the very way that it formed in the brain and consciousness in the first place. The psychotherapy of character is an art and a science that bridges the old divide between psychotherapy and the brain, and is at one with our core paradigm.

Over the course of my career, I have witnessed the rapid and tragic degeneration of psychiatry. Psychotherapy has become a lost practice. It is on the verge of extinction, no longer taught in most psychiatric residencies. Contemporary psychiatry has fallen under the sway of biological psychiatry, where patients no longer receive proper care. *Psychotherapy of Character: The Play of Consciousness in the Theater of the Brain* was written with an eye toward the recovery of my field. Biological psychiatry is the current incarnation of somatic psychiatry—insulin shock therapy, lobotomy, and electroconvulsive therapy—which views the cause of human suffering to be the brain itself, rather than the person. Its treatments have been to act directly on the brain—physically, electrically, or chemically. The current form of its doctrine is that problems come from genetic or developmental neurobiological disorders of the brain. And the prescribed treatments for its phantom brain diseases are psychoactive drugs. The cure for human struggle has been reduced to a pill, as if pharmaceuticals address the agency of human suffering. This has resulted in a destructive psychiatric drug epidemic, with psychiatric drug sales topping seventy billion dollars a year. Even worse, we are drugging a generation of our children with amphetamines and Prozac. Biological depression and its Prozac cure are now so firmly embraced by psychiatry and our culture at large that it seems preposterous to even suggest that it is an urban myth. The depth and scope of what it is to be human has been exiled by this dangerous and destructive practice. The source of human suffering—and our psychiatric conditions—is not now, nor has it ever been, a brain disease. It is purely human. Psychiatry is in crisis. And we, as a society, are in crisis. It is of the highest urgency to save psychiatry from itself and save society from today's psychiatry.

Psychotherapy of Character is a kind of professional memoir. My life's work has taught me that the real source of human suffering is not the brain. It is the person, the human being, in the context of damage to the play of consciousness. The art, the science, the discipline, and the wisdom of psychotherapy attend to this damage, not drugs. There are no miracles and no shortcuts. This book presents its paradigm as a positive alternative, with the hope that it will help the next generation take psychiatry in a constructive direction. In keeping with this, the story of Eddie is written as a narrative, not from a didactic academic orientation or format. The scientific elements are incorporated without footnotes to preserve the flow of the narrative. The *Play* encompasses the contemporary science of the brain and consciousness, while honoring the wisdom of the past and its grasp of the depth and complexity of the human condition. Woven throughout world history and all cultures is a rich mosaic of wisdom about the mysteries of human nature and human struggle. It has been part of our enterprise since the dawn of humanity. The past contains a valuable grasp of the ineffable, embedded in the knowledge and belief systems of its own time. Significant elements of this book were influenced by a distillation of knowledge from others, past and present, which I value without limit. The knowledge in this book is not a personal possession but a link in the ongoing chain of our collective understanding.

In today's very small world, we have the presence of exciting, yet confusing and conflicting, deeply held belief systems—religious, ideological, political, scientific, and technological. Human belief systems have always served the human quest in its efforts to grapple with the mysteries of life. At the same time, they offer the allure of false security and leave us subject to the hubris of "belief" itself. False or outmoded beliefs may give us short-term comfort, but are destructive to our well-being. They make us susceptible to Pied Pipers who promise salvation as they lead their followers off the cliffs; or Chicken Littles who intimidate people by preaching that the sky is falling; or purveyors of false knowledge who offer false hope, quick fixes, and magical solutions while creating slavery and blindness. A new and inclusive paradigm that is consonant with new knowledge and old wisdom is so important for psychiatry and society at large.

There is a prescient image in *The Mists of Avalon* by Marion Zimmer Bradley, a novel about the Arthurian legends. The story is told from the perspective of the priestess, Morgaine, protégé of Merlin. The title refers to an island in the middle of Lake Avalon. It is the repository of wisdom for the wizards and priestesses and is shrouded in the mists. Only those who possess wisdom are able to navigate through the mists to get to the island. It appears that over the years, the older wizards have been dying off. As their numbers diminish, fewer and fewer can find their way. Once they are all gone, Avalon will be lost in the mist forever. Human nature has not changed in the history of man and never will. We cannot afford to lose access to the Isle of Avalon. Finding our way is an ongoing process. *Psychotherapy of Character: The Play of Consciousness in the Theater of the Brain* is my view into the mist.

CONSCIOUSNESS

1

EDDIE'S DREAM
The Hidden Key

"IT WAS CLOUDY AND GLOOMY. *The forest was filled with darkness. A grotesque ogre was chasing me through a primordial forest. I was running down a dirt path surrounded by gnarled trees and overhanging vines. The misshapen giant took one step to my three. Fortunately, I was faster and more cunning. It was certain if he caught me, I'd be torn apart.*

"*The chase went on and on and on. There were several close calls and narrow escapes. I sped up to put some distance between us and got out of sight. I spied a tree with an enormous branch overhanging the path and climbed up. I positioned myself on the branch and prepared to pounce on the ogre when he came running by. I had with me a broomstick to be used as a spear. Soon enough, he lumbered up the path after me. Holding on to the branch, I swung down, kicked him with all my might, and knocked him over. I stood over him and clasped my hands together on the broomstick. I raised it above my head and plunged it through his chest into the earth.*

"At that point I awakened, my heart pounding out of my chest. I was sitting up in bed with my hands outstretched in front of me in the spearing position. The muscles of my hands and arms were taught and tense from the violence.

"I felt a surge of triumph, having killed him in hand-to-hand combat. I was so relieved to be safe from the monster. Despite the fact I sort of knew it was a dream, I was sure I had actually done it. In the next moment, I thought, *Oh my God, I've just killed someone. What kind of person am I? What's going to happen to me? Will I go to prison?*

"In a while, the lingering reality of the dream dissipated. It became more fully clear that it was just a dream. I noticed that the anxiety I had felt before I went to sleep had disappeared. And I felt enormous relief to just feel good again."

Eddie, the dreamer, was a quiet, studious, even-tempered senior in college. That afternoon he had an argument with his professor. Although the professor was in error, Eddie was forced to submit to his authority. For the rest of the evening he was subject to a nameless anxiety that he felt gnawing away in his chest. He had a hard time falling asleep that night.

How is it that Eddie went to bed and was awakened eight hours later by killing a monster in a dream? How did this alive drama get created? Where did this cast of characters, the landscape, set design, costumes, props, relationship, and plot come from? How is it that the dream felt completely real? How did he remember it to tell it to me in psychotherapy? In order to address these questions, we need to understand some things about sleep, dreaming, and Eddie.

During the day, we live our lives. We do what we do to survive, thrive, and prosper in our individual lives in the world. When we are awake, our consciousness is oriented through the five senses, our full neuromuscular enervation, and our internal organs. We are busy thinking, evaluating, planning, doing, feeling, and engaging.

We spend an entire third of our existence asleep. We are simply biological creatures, and sleep is a biological necessity. Sleep is a trance state. Actually, it is five different trance states. Each has specific wave patterns in the brain and particular functions. Likewise, wakefulness is a trance state as well, with its own wave pattern in the brain. The natural flow of consciousness is composed of these six shifting trance states of the brain-body. All six states serve the biological imperatives of the human organism. The brain, deprived of sleep, cannot process learning and will not produce its proteins. If totally deprived of sleep, we would become confused, hallucinate, and lose our sense of self. The absence of sleep for only a couple of weeks can even lead to death.

The function of sleep is to rest and restore the organism to be at its best to take on the challenges of living during the next day. During sleep, the muscles undergo rest and de-enervation. The biochemical waste products of muscle activity are eliminated and detoxified. Metabolically, all the organ systems do their night's work—digestion, detoxification, cleansing waste products, cellular repair, cell growth, immunological activity, etc.

A central arena for the work of sleep is for the rest and restoration of our consciousness. In order for consciousness to be at its best and open to take on tomorrow's challenges, it must digest and detoxify conflicts stirred during the previous day and recent past. This is the work of dreaming. The restorative processes of the organism during sleep operate in their appropriate contexts. With regard to cellular metabolism, digestion operates in the molecular realm. Emotional conflict, which operates in the realm of people and feeling, gets digested in its comparable world, a dream of people and feeling. The function of dreaming is consonant with the overall function of sleep—to restore the brain-body so it can be free and flexible to take on the next day in the most optimal way. Consequently, there is a special sleep state devoted to dreaming, REM sleep, whose function is to restore our consciousness. This trance state of sleep is the focus of our special attention.

In REM sleep, we are in a brain-body trance state. The attention of consciousness is withdrawn from reality. Consciousness is no longer oriented through the senses or the body. Consciousness recedes from our striated muscles, so we are in a state of paralysis. Muscle tone is at its lowest ebb. Likewise, it recedes significantly from our senses so that we are not oriented by reading reality. The eyes, no longer seeing the outside world, dart back and forth—with their *Rapid Eye Movements*—as we see a dream. If any of the senses gets stimulated beyond a certain threshold—a loud noise, a strong light, a strong touch, even a strong smell or taste—we shift trance states back to waking.

Consciousness, no longer operative in the theater of reality, now operates in a living theater of the brain, doing its sleep work. No longer tied to reality, the curtain is lifted on this inner theater. A drama, triggered by the events of the day, is now onstage. Untethered to reality, it writes its own play, giving us a window into the unadulterated nature of consciousness itself. Inner dramas triggered by the day's conflicts are the stuff of dreams.

It is through the enactments of the dream story that consciousness does its sleep work. Since dreams are about emotional conflicts, the feeling centers in the brain are central in the construction of all aspects of dream creation. Consciousness, in dreams, is not just a reductive brain rehash. Dreams are an alive, creative production of consciousness. Dream enactments take place in the living moment, as do the productions of waking consciousness.

It is also essential to realize that the actual work of a dream is enacted in sleep with no reference to wakefulness at all. Eddie's dream was not dreamed to be seen by awake Eddie—it was not a production to be shown in your local movie theater, on HBO, or on YouTube. It was purely intended to be shown on the brain's projection screen in sleep. The brain routinely does its REM sleep work unremembered.

With some difficulty, Eddie finally got to sleep that night. That is to say, he left his waking state with its beta brain waves. He did have some difficulty relaxing and allowing in alpha waves. Eddie finally shifted trance states into stage 1 sleep with its theta waves. Then he went to stage 2, where sleep spindles and K complexes appeared. Then he moved into stage 3 with its delta waves and gradually into stage 4 with increased delta waves. Then Eddie went back to stage 3, back to stage 2, and then on to REM sleep. This cycle—1, 2, 3, 4, 3, 2, REM—was repeated every ninety minutes all night long (REM sleep substituted for stage 1). As the cycles repeated, REM sleep got longer, and sleep stages 3 and 4 got shorter and shorter, and in the later cycles, they disappeared. Eventually, Eddie woke up; that is, he left the sleeping trance states and switched back to the beta brain waves of the waking trance state. And on and on he went, through the daily cycle.

Eddie awakened in his killing stance at 5:30 that morning. This was his fifth episode of dreaming that night, his fifth enactment of this conflict story. The previous four REM dreams took place but weren't remembered at all. (These full-out dramas go on multiple times a night, every night, unremembered, doing their work in the dark.)

We remember only a tiny fraction of dreams. Although remembered dreams are, in fact, useful in therapy, this is not their purpose or function. The happenstance that Eddie remembered this dream was an unintended by-product of his trance shift on awakening. If the purpose of dreams were for us to acquire information about our waking selves, remembering far less than 1 percent of them in some seemingly secret code would be woefully inefficient.

Since REM sleep is a trance state, we need to consider the nature of trance states. A trance state is a frame of consciousness within which we see an alive world. When we shift trance states, we enter a different world of consciousness. An ordinary example of trance shifting happens when we go to the movies. We go to a movie theater, park our car, wait in line, get our popcorn, and find a seat. Then the lights go down, and a movie is projected on the screen. This is when we shift from our regular waking trance to a movie trance.

As an art trance, a movie is a partial trance, where you still partially inhabit your regular consciousness. You are aware that you are in your seat, eating popcorn, and hoping there's no gum on your shoe. Meanwhile, you vicariously live the adventures on the screen. Although a movie is art and not real life, the feeling experience of the movie is real. As a representational illusion, it is "art-ifice." If it's a horror movie, you feel fear; with a comedy, you laugh; with a sad movie, you cry. When the movie is over, you shift trance states back to "real life." Sometimes, you may inhabit the feeling of the movie for hours after the movie ends. In this case, the trance shift back to regular consciousness is blurred, and you remain partially absorbed in the movie world you have just experienced. All art forms operate similarly. For example, when you see a painting, you become immersed in a partial visual trance and experience the human story as depicted by the art-ifice of the artist through symbolic forms on a canvas.

A dream is the experiential illusion of a world within the REM trance. The REM dream trance operates similarly to an art trance, with two important differences. A dream is not a two-dimensional art form like a painting but a kind of three-dimensional holographic movie with alive feeling. And the REM trance is a total trance state, not a partial art trance, where there is no awareness of being in a trance at all. While dreaming, there is no awareness of waking reality. There is no awareness outside its frame. Nothing else exists. As a full trance of consciousness, the dream experience just seems real and regular life.

In a total trance state, there is an intact boundary frame, with no perspective outside of it. The drawings of M. C. Escher illuminate this phenomenon. He draws fish moving in one direction and birds going in the other. If you focus on the fish, you see fish in the foreground. The birds constitute the background frame. They, as background, cannot be seen. Likewise, if you focus on the birds, you see birds in the foreground. And the fish now constitute the background frame, and they cannot be seen. You cannot see the birds and the fish at the same time. In other words, a figure seen in the foreground is only seen within the boundary of the background frame. Escher's use of the visual art-ifice of background and foreground frames operates like two total trance frames. Waking and REM sleep are full and separate trances of consciousness. Each operates as a total frame, within which you see its images. Consciousness in waking life is birds, and consciousness in dreams is fish. You cannot see birds and fish at the same time. Within each trance state, there is no awareness that the other even exists.

Eddie's dream simply felt real. He, as the persona Eddie, felt as real in the dream as when he was awake. The brain-body organization of consciousness creates an alive, real, feeling world within the frame of the dream trance. In his REM sleep trance, there was no awareness that he was dreaming. There was no awareness that there was such a thing as some other trance state, like wakefulness. The dream trance is experienced as simply living life. Consciousness is an ongoing fountain. It bubbles along all day in the trance of wakefulness and at night in the REM sleep trance. In the other sleep states, it rests.

In the morning, Eddie was awakened by the intensity of the dream drama itself. It was powerful enough to blur the transition between the REM trance and wakefulness. He sat up in bed. His muscles, under the auspices of the dream scenario, were no longer paralyzed and were enacting the dream murder. Adrenaline pumped through his body. He happened to remember this dream because of a blip in the transition between trance states. He was confused because the boundary between trance states was blurred.

Eddie, now awake, after having shifted from REM to the waking trance, temporarily believed that the murder he committed in the dream was real. He applied waking moral judgments to his dream actions. He feared literal real-life consequences. (This collision between Eddie's REM consciousness and waking consciousness might not be so confusing if humans were more like dolphins. In their sleep adaptation, only half of their brain sleeps at a time. The other half is awake. It would be interesting to know how dolphin dreams coexist with dolphin waking reality.)

Eddie's dream was a pure creation by his brain on the stage of his internal theater. His consciousness created a living illusion of an entire world. The dream, in this theater, had characters, a feeling relationship between them, a plot, and a landscape. The *dramatis personae* of this dream had two characters: Eddie and the ogre. The relationship between them was one of hate and malevolent intent, with a plot of pursuit and murder. Eddie and the ogre weren't just standing on an empty stage. There was a fully textured specific landscape, as if it were a daytime real world. Because this dream was completely created by Eddie's brain, it is clear that his brain is organized in such a way as to create all aspects of this entire illusion and make it feel real.

What else do we notice about the brain's creation of the dream world? A central feature of dreams is that they are always about personas. Sometimes dream characters may be recognized as people in our waking lives. Often, they are invented people with no literal reference to actual people in our lives. An emotional conflict that generates a dream in us is, by its nature, something that is disturbing to us. Since dreams operate in the service of restoring the well-being of the organism, dreams are always about our self and depict an image of self. The self is the subject of all dreams. Sometimes, our dream self is our current-day self; sometimes it's a younger version of our self;

sometimes the form of the self persona is as another person, either known to us or an invented dream character, both unrecognizable as our waking self.

It is very common for people in most cultures in history, including a lot of people in our own culture today, to believe that people seen in a dream are actually real. I wish to underline that all figures of self and others in dreams are persona representations, constructed by the brain. They are not real. If I have a dream, and an image of you is in it, my brain has created a representational image of you. It is not you. Likewise, if I dream of my dead grandfather, it is a representational image of him, created by my imagination in my consciousness. Even though he may feel very real, it is not an actual visitation from the dead. He is not there.

The two dream personas created by Eddie's brain in this dream are Eddie (the self persona) and the ogre. Eddie is small and physically powerless. He is in a state of fear and impotence. He cannot stop his sadistic pursuer. He possesses the superior attributes that he is quick and fast, physically and mentally. The ogre is a totally physically imposing persona. He is a giant on steroids—not someone to mess with. He is malevolent and unrelenting in his murderous intent. There clearly is no possibility of reasoning with him. The ogre is, of course, a synthetic dream figure, and Eddie hadn't actually tangled with one in reality. Likewise, the Eddie in the dream also is a synthetic dream figure of himself, created by his brain. "Eddie" is a representational image, like the ogre or my dead grandfather or you. Likewise, Eddie was not actually in a primordial forest outside of his sleeping body. He was in bed, asleep.

Eddie's brain created the images of both personas in this dream. Eddie and the ogre felt as real in the dream as Eddie does in real life. His brain created living, feeling images of people. It utilized its regular pathways to create these hallucinated illusions within the REM trance. These alive-seeming personas were created by webs of neuronal connections that loop all throughout the architecture of the brain—through the amygdala and the hippocampus, etc., the limbic feeling centers; the frontal lobes, the judgment center; the temporal lobes, the center of a sense of realness; the salient memory cortex; the various brain nuclei and ganglia; the body mapping centers, both cortical and subcortical, creating the presence of bodies; the auditory and thinking centers; and the vision centers to create the seen dream movie. The webs of these connected neurons create an activated brain map of neural constellations of webs of constellations that take form as images.

The organization of consciousness in the brain not only creates images of multiple alive personas but it creates feeling relationships between them. The feeling relatedness in Eddie's dream is one of sadomasochism. The ogre, a monomaniacal bully, hates Eddie. He is stalking Eddie in order to kill him. Eddie is in the masochistic position of this relationship. He is threatened, terrified, humiliated, and impotent. By his actions later in the dream, it is clear that the masochist in this relationship is also filled with hatred and murderous rage. The feeling centers clearly play an essential role in the feeling relationship between dream characters. The mappings that create feeling relationships are organized in the brain as the constellations of webs for the personas, plus webs that connect personas through feeling.

The entire dream landscape, the primordial forest, is, of course, a synthetic brain representation. This actual dreamscape is informed by the emotional feeling that generates the dream in the first place. Consciousness, orienting itself from the feeling centers of the brain, draws upon its patterns of patterns of patterns to create form, to create images. The way consciousness paints this scene is similar to an artist at his canvas. If an artist wishes to evoke a dark, brooding, dangerous mood, he might paint a landscape of primordial forest, with gnarled trees dripping with vines. Because the dream flows from this feeling state, the landscape creation arises from activated webs of neural mappings that are generated from these feelings. The landscape's correspondence with feeling, drawn by both the artist and the dreamer, derive from the same source, the pathway by which consciousness makes images. This is the "image-ination," the making of images. Every aspect of the dream is a synthetic construction by the image-ination in the theater of the brain. The dreamscape is shaped by correspondences with Eddie's internal feeling state. In this dream, the constellations give form to a dreamscape that resonates with an ominous and dangerous myth and fairy-tale landscape. This resonates with a scary transport into childhood.

The particular dream imagery also has correspondences with emotionally informed specific memory images from Eddie's past. When Eddie was troubled as a child, he often went to his grandmother's house and climbed the old apple tree in the backyard. Yes, this was a tree of gnarled branches with overhanging limbs. He would crawl out on the horizontal branches, as far as he could, to pluck off the apples for his grandmother's apple pie. He would bring a broomstick up into the tree with him to extend his reach so he could knock off ripe apples that were too high to reach. The apple tree was Eddie's protective refuge. Furthermore, in that tree he was daring, brave, competent, and resourceful.

The specific activated neural mappings looping around Eddie's memory cortex, guided by the feeling centers of his brain, created tree images resonant with feeling. On the one hand, there was the feeling of mythic, ominous danger, and on the other hand, the apple tree was a repository of refuge and strength. His image-ination created new and alive images that blended personal experiences with feelingful images. The gnarled limbs "dripping with vines" was a nice touch. In like fashion, the image of the ogre was drawn in a similar fashion as the landscape. The feeling of the ogre persona was what shaped his physical form. His form derived from the feeling of a huge, powerful, cruel, ugly bully. Here, too, the mappings were extensions of constellated images from the feeling centers.

Conflicts of the day are emotional conflicts, either about oneself or in relation to others. There are many potential conflictual issues that disturb people's well-being. The issues that may occupy the dream stage are combats, quests, challenges, boredoms, wishes, hopes, curiosities, pain, disappointments, sexual interests and stimulations, fantasies, competitions, fears, anxieties, cruelty, sadism, humiliations, sufferings, abuse, deprivations, traumas, envies, jealousies, sadnesses, and otherwise the full panoply of life's dramas, engagements, and relationship adventures. On this day, the conflict that stirred Eddie was one of humiliation by authority. It was to be the subject of his REM movie. Eddie's dream served his consciousness by digesting the humiliation by his professor through the dream story.

The immediate source of the problematic emotional conflict for Eddie was the argument with the professor that afternoon. Eddie was forced to submit to the stupidity of a man he did not respect. He was subject to being overpowered, bullied, and humiliated. There was nothing he could do about it. Eddie was clearly bothered by the incident. He kept thinking about the correctness of his argument and his frustration with this arbitrary professor. His evening anxiety just seemed to come out of the blue. It puzzled him, yet he couldn't shake it.

It is the actual dream story that enacts the digestive function of dreaming. The plot of the dream is not a rerun of a memory. Every dream is a new, alive creation. Consciousness does not have a rewind button. It is an ongoing stream in the present. The actual story of Eddie's dream was composed of two scenes. In the first, Eddie was in flight, running and running in a state of fear. If the ogre caught him, he'd be brutally killed. There were a number of episodes of close calls, where the giant almost captured him. Eddie barely escaped the danger. His advantage was in his being faster and quicker, but he was powerless to stop the menacing stalker. The dream pursuit happened over and over again — the jeopardy was ongoing.

In scene two, Eddie decided to fight. Being too small and weak, he couldn't take on the ogre directly. Here, his advantage was his superior mind. He developed and executed a strategy to kill the ogre. He then did so in full-out murderous fury. Fourteen hours after Eddie's argument with the professor, he awakened from this gruesome dream. How did a disagreement generate a dream where Eddie ran for his life and then committed murder? And where did the grounding for the dream plot come from?

This had to do with something that lay inside Eddie, an inner context. To get a sense of this context, I'll tell you something about Eddie's background. His father was an arrogant, self-involved, and cruel man. At home, he ruled the roost and was the dominant figure. Eddie spent his childhood hopelessly seeking his father's approval but to no avail. Father either ignored Eddie or diminished him.

PSYCHOTHERAPY OF CHARACTER

On the surface, his mother was deferential and catered to her humiliating husband. Behind the surface, she was actually cold, ungiving, and devaluing toward the father. Because Eddie's father had no interest in the children, they were left to his mother's designs. As problematic as Eddie's father was, his mother was actually worse. She was a cold and vicious woman. There was no moment of warmth in Eddie's entire childhood. She never hugged or kissed him—not ever, not even once.

Every day, she glared at Eddie with those cold eyes, beat him, and made him stand in the corner. She continuously told Eddie he was "bad" and deserved his punishments. Once, Mother threatened to send him to reform school, and for added spice, she dialed the phone as if calling the school. At other times she refused to speak to him or acknowledge his existence. She never relented from her onslaughts, nor did she acknowledge them, never mind apologize.

Socially, all of this was hidden. The family, with four high-achieving children, was well respected and admired. Occasionally, Eddie would turn to his father in despair about his mother. Father told him that he should understand and be the bigger person—this was just the way she was, so get over it.

By age four, Eddie had adapted to the beatings by devaluing his mother. Since he couldn't prevent her verbal attacks, he would mock and outsmart her by anticipating her well-worn words and say them back at her before she could finish her sentence. This further enraged her. He'd think to himself, *You're so stupid to go on screaming; I've just said it so obviously I know what you're going to say!* Mother's goal was to break him. He countered this by refusing to cry during the beating by numbing himself, physically and emotionally. This, of course, infuriated her and resulted in escalated violence. Since there was nothing he could do to stop it, he joined it—"Bring it on! Gimme your best shot! I don't care!"

The inner context for the dream, then, was a story that already existed inside Eddie. This story and inner world derived from Eddie's formative emotional experience with his mother and father. The emotional conflict with the professor resonated with this inner story. The surface of his inner story was the problematic relationship with his father. When Eddie sought approval from his professor, sure enough, his hopes were dashed once again. He was forced to submit to unresponsive disapproval from male authority.

More profoundly, the inner story of Eddie and his father telescoped to the more disturbing relationship with his mother. This was a world of physical and emotional sadism and violence. In fact, his father's humiliations were an extension of the core violations by his mother. Eddie's experience of his father was already filtered by what had come before. The relationship between Eddie and his mother was one of unadulterated sadomasochism. Mother related to Eddie by her sadistic and violent rage. As the masochistic object of this rage, Eddie was on the receiving end of unrelenting physical and emotional abuse, cruelty, humiliation, and threat. He was helpless, impotent, and intimidated.

The fight with the professor elicited this inner context, where Eddie was subject to a humiliating victimizer who had all the power. The dream story unfolded and was written through this prism. A dream is not a documentary of past experience. Eddie's dream was not a literal replay of the trauma of Mother's beatings and humiliation. But clearly, the drama of Eddie and Mommy Dearest was the foundation of the dream.

From the humiliation by the professor, Eddie's consciousness, in the dream, drew from the qualities of his mother to create the stalking, sadistic, murderous ogre. We know that in real life, Eddie's mother was not a misshapen male giant. This was, however, a dream persona of her. (The ogre's form was created from the feeling of his mother in a similar fashion as it created the dreamscape.) Likewise, Eddie wasn't depicted as a little boy. The proportions between an adult and a child are the same as between a giant and an adult. The Eddie dream character was clearly a portrayal of Eddie in his plight as a little boy. The plot of this dream enacted and grappled with the inner drama of Eddie and his mother. Consciousness put them out there on the dream stage.

The first scene of the dream was an accurate rendering of life with Mother. Eddie was unable to prevent the beatings and humiliations. He fought with what he had at his disposal—his intelligence and his will. But because he was, in fact, too small, he could not protect himself from physical abuse, humiliation, and a sense of impotence. Eddie found ways to survive the ongoing stalking and beatings, but he could never really stay out of harm's way. His actual fighting solution was to remove himself from himself. He did so by removing himself from his own feelings by numbing and not caring. He became a fighter in a continuous war. But this war had to be fought as a guerilla war.

In scene two, Eddie surmounted the humiliation and enacted his true inner aggression toward Mother. Now, instead of being the humiliated, terrified, impotent one, Eddie rose up and turned the tables. He choose fight over flight. Through the dream plot, Eddie digested the professor's humiliation by doing to his ogre mother what he couldn't do in real life. He killed the relentlessly cruel monster. The actual legacy of his mother's abuse was that it left Eddie filled with murderous rage toward her. Since his plight was hopeless, because he was too small and weak, he had to stomach his own retaliatory rage. His masochistic adaptation of taunting, provoking, numbing, and not caring about himself had actually intensified her beatings and humiliations. This served to amplify the internal rage that he carried inside. Not only did this result in the wish to stop her, but to do to her what she did to him, plus a little extra. The masochistic position is actually maso-sadism. He was filled with a rage that was proportional to her rage.

The argument with the professor had triggered this inner context. The drama of sadistic mother and maso-sadistic Eddie was inside all along. The dream gave form to this inner drama as the context for doing the work of detoxifying the day's conflict. In the dream, Eddie triumphed in the fight, and the conflict was resolved. The murder reversed Eddie's feeling of impotence that came from his failed attempts to defeat his ogre-mother. The dream creation of the broomstick as the murder weapon was drawn from two "feeling" sources: (1) The broomstick Eddie had used in the apple tree was stored as a positive memory image. It resonated with feelings of competence, courage, and triumph. (2) The murder-by-broomstick was an image of a violent penetration. In this story, the impotent humiliation was reversed, and Eddie's anxiety abated.

There are many dreams where the dream plot fails to resolve the stirred conflicts. In these cases, we have nightmares and anxiety dreams. Eddie, in fact, had a recurring nightmare that was triggered by the Manson family home invasion. In these dreams, he was in his parents' house, and he would receive a threatening phone call or note. In his fear, he called the police for protection. A plain-clothes detective then came to the door. Eddie didn't trust him, so he asked to see the officer's badge. When shown the badge, he was still wary. Eddie feared this was the intruder pretending to be a policeman. Eddie then insisted on seeing a uniformed policeman before he would open the door. Next, a uniformed cop arrived, but Eddie didn't trust him either, fearing it was the killer in a fake uniform. Then he became concerned that the locks on the door might not be locked, and the killer could open the door, or maybe the locks wouldn't hold, and the killer would burst in—the murderous intruder was going to get him.

This was an anxiety dream of the same inner story. The intruder was his sadistic mother. The internal drama was her unrelenting attacks. His suspiciousness was an accurate rendering that his mother was the dangerous violator from whom he could not escape. The very person who should have been Eddie's protector was the violator, the person from whom he could not protect himself. These dreams didn't end with relief but in anxiety on awakening.

There is an additional implication about consciousness and memory that we can take from recurring dreams. Once a dream—with its characters, imagery, relationship, and plot—is seen, it too goes into memory. These images are available for future dreams to draw upon. Consciousness in dreams can draw not only from waking experience, but from dream experience as well. Recurring dreams may actually reuse previous dream plots, images, or dream personas. Imaginary houses and rooms from a dream may be inhabited again in later dreams.

Here is an example of a patient's recurring dream throughout three years of therapy. Barbara was a very intelligent, charming, and engaging young woman, but there was a subtle emotional removal and distance about her. As it turned out, she didn't trust anybody in an intimate way—she came by this honestly from her formative past.

She took it for granted that to have a warm and trusting relationship was dangerous and absurd. She learned to protect herself from emotional injury by staying emotionally distant. Therapy came to be the bumpy journey toward a trusting emotional closeness between her and me. Over the course of the three years, she had a series of dreams.

Early on in the therapy, she had the following dream: "*I was living in a one-room house in the woods. It was a nicely decorated room, filled with plenty of good books and comfortable chairs. There weren't any windows, and there was no door. Everything was still and quiet and okay. I felt safe and content in my room. I had everything I could need. There seemed to be some danger in the woods outside, but I was safely sealed in. Nothing could get in, and I had no interest in going outside.*"

As the therapy proceeded, she had a second installment of this dream: "*I was in my house in the woods.*" It was the same house as in the earlier dream—no windows, no door, comfortable, safe. "*I sensed the presence of someone outside in the woods. I had no interest in what was going on out there. I felt secure, reading in my chair.*"

Six months later, we had installment three. This time, "*it was the exact same situation—same house, same scene—but there was a giant wrecking ball hanging quietly outside the house. It was very still and of no particular concern. I was content to be reading in my chair.*"

Months later came a new version. Everything was the same. Same house, same room. She again was reading. "*There was now a gaping hole in the side of the house. I could see the wrecking ball hanging silently out there. I wasn't scared that the ball had crashed through the wall. The hole didn't really concern me. I noticed it. I was oddly glad it was there. I had no inclination to go outside. And I felt no danger of something coming in. It was just there, and I continued on, comfortable in my chair.*"

The therapy journey toward emotional closeness continued. "*I had the dream. I climbed out through the hole and stood there right next to the house. I just stayed there and surveyed the woods. I felt okay.*

"I had the dream again. *This time, I began wandering farther from the house. I felt comfortable enough to be out there. I sensed the presence of a man out there. I was scared, so I went back to the house.*"

In the subsequent dream, "*I saw the man. So I stayed in the shadows, watching him. He wasn't anybody I recognized. I didn't want him to see me, so I stayed out of sight."*

In the final version of the dream, toward the end of the therapy, she said, *"I wandered a fair ways from the house and watched the man from the shadows. This time, I really wanted to talk to him. I was a little scared. I stepped out of the shadows. I felt good."*

Barbara's original dream depicted her state of emotional isolation and removal from intimate emotional contact with others. It did so via a representation of a one-room house with no entry and no exit. No one could get in, and she couldn't get out. All the way through the therapy, the literal physical scenario of the dream repeated itself. She kept inhabiting this same symbolic representation of her emotional situation. Each new version of the dream was a kind of status update on her emotional situation in the therapy with me. It reflected her gradual movement in the journey toward emotional closeness, intimacy, and trust. Each dream was a timely and accurate rendering of where she was in her journey toward intimacy. After she found her way in the therapy, Barbara translated her new capacity for intimacy into taking the same leap in her social life. Over time, as a result of her emotional availablity, she developed a solid realtionship which culminated in a marriage

Eddie's ogre dream teaches us that consciousness, as created by the organization of the brain, takes form as an image of a world filled with ongoing life. Specifically, the brain mappings are organized to produce a three-dimensional play, images of personas; feeling relatedness between them; an alive, action storyline; and an entire landscape that replicates the world. The world of consciousness in the dream is clearly an illusion, not actually happening in reality. It is a hallucination created by the brain.

We have seen that Eddie's dream was in the service of the sleep work of the REM trance. The "play" of Eddie and the ogre served to dissapate his anxiety state that had been triggered by his fight with his bullying professor. It did this through a new enactment of an old story that already existed in Eddie's brain. However, the dream was not just a repeated remembrance but a new and alive play of consciousness in the living moment. This story used activated memory to give form to an internal drama drawn from Eddie's formative past that utilized the inner story of Eddie and his mother. It didn't just spring from nowhere. It was there, organized in his brain mappings. As such it turned out to be useful in his psychotherapy, because it gave us a window into his inner drama, his internal characters and their problematic relationships.

"Eddie and the ogre" exited stage left from his REM trance that night. As Homer says in *The Odyssey*, "dawn showed its rosy fingers through the early mists." Now in the morning sunlight the curtain rises on "Eddie and the ogre" lurking silently in his waking trance.

2

THE CHARACTEROLOGICAL DRAMA IN THE WAKING TRANCE

IF I STAND ON THE dock at my Maine lake and look back at the shoreline, I see gentle waves rippling along the surface of the water. As I look down through the waves, I see a group of brownish-tan rocks at the shallow lake bottom. These rocks are irregularly shaped, solid, oval forms. I see rocks underwater. If I force myself to pay attention to my literal perceptions, everything changes. In fact, there are no solid lines outlining the circumference of the rocks at all. There are actually a series of broken lines, fragmented by the moving, wavy water surface. Likewise, I don't see solid stone forms. There are fragmented moving blocks of color and shadow and light. The surface itself becomes an ever-changing array of light reflecting off the angles of the moving ripples.

In addition, my eye actually takes in this literal information upside down and backwards. Yet out of these perceptions, my brain creates an image of rocks underwater. It knows from memory of past experience that rocks are solid bounded stones on the lake floor. It anticipates and comprehends that they have solid form with intact circumferences, with an accurate orientation of up and down and left and right. What I see is not what I actually perceive. It is an image created by my brain, projected onto the lake bottom. I simply experience this mentally imposed idea of what I see—I assume I am seeing intact rocks. I have no awareness that I am seeing a projected illusion of consciousness. I simply take for granted that I believe what I see. I am unaware that I am in fact seeing what I believe. If I were to paint this scene as solid rocks under squiggly waves, it would not look right. If I re-created the literal perceptions on the canvas, it would look like a lake bottom, and the viewer would see rocks underwater.

In our waking life, we ordinarily assume the world we experience is real and actual. However, like in a dream, it, too, is an illusion of consciousness created by the brain. The difference in the waking trance is that now external reality is the projection screen of our mentally created illusions, not the dream screen of the brain. The function and orientation of waking consciousness is to read reality through the senses and to deal with the world around us. The brain constructs its "rocks underwater" illusions in the following manner: It takes in literal sensory perceptions, which are fed into webs of neuronal connections that hook into a set of circuits that are already established in the cortex. The images we see are drawn from these cortical maps, not from direct sensory experience. This is called top-down (cortical) processing. It is the mode by which the brain creates its own images of the world. What we actually see is a hologram movie superimposed on reality, created by the brain.

To illuminate top-down processing, let us look at the phenomenon of phantom limbs. After an arm is amputated, the amputee may continue to see, feel, and have pain in the arm that is no longer there. How does this happen? Developmentally, as a baby, the amputee had organized and integrated the sensory and movement experience of his arm in his cortex. This had established a sensory and motor neuronal mapping of the arm. Thereafter, sensory and motor input from the arms link to these existing cortical arm maps.

My image of my arm, my feeling of my arm, and my experience of my arm come from this cortical mapping. The direct sensory input from my peripheral arm nerves triggers my top-down cortical arm. My actual experience of my arm does not come from a direct peripheral nerve processing of my arm. This is ordinary top-down processing—the way the brain is organized. However, when an arm is amputated, the previously established cortical mapping is not amputated. It continues to exist timelessly in the cortex. This cortical mapping continues to project the presence of the arm, even after the actual arm itself and its peripheral nerves are gone. Consequently, the amputee feels (and often literally sees) his missing arm that is clearly a pure illusion of the brain. The phenomenon of a phantom limb is a pure enactment of top-down cortical processing.

Let's get back to Eddie. One day, as Eddie was walking on campus, he approached an old friend he hadn't seen for quite a while. The friend gave him a big smile. Eddie returned the smile and said, "My, how fit you are looking these days." The friend felt flattered by this nice, warm greeting from Eddie. Sounds good, right? Unfortunately, there's more here than meets the eye. The story behind the story is that Eddie actually assumed his old friend had noticed that he, Eddie, had gained ten pounds since they'd last seen each other. Eddie believed his friend's initial smile was a mocking comment on his own weight gain—that this guy was laughing at him. Eddie's strategy to counter the ridicule was to get the attention off himself. To protect himself, he initiated a compliment about his friend's appearance. What seemed like a nice interaction on the surface was actually a mask for something entirely else.

The actual scenario that Eddie perceived and experienced was that his friend was a shaming judge. Behind the surface of this nice interaction, Eddie actually experienced a mini-sadomasochistic drama. The persona of the attacking judge was projected onto his friend, while the persona who was the object of ridicule was projected onto himself. In his inner scenario, this was an attack by a sadistic figure, toward Eddie, the object of attack. And Eddie was the deserving recipient of the shame judgment. The relationship between these two figures is one of sadistic attack dished out and attack received, masochistically. Does any of this sound familiar?

In this mini-enactment of a small moment of daily life, we see that Eddie was living a form of the same inner drama that was his dream. The presence of these figures, their relationship, and the drama itself was established in Eddie's cortex. His sense of self was as the masochistic persona—bad, shame-based, defective. His adversary was the sadistic persona, the judge-humiliator—you know, Mommy Dearest. They relate through attack, the attack of sadistic aggression. The inner drama of these two personas and their sadomasochistic relationship were inside Eddie. Eddie had no awareness that he was projecting these internal personas onto himself and his friend. In his experience, this was what was going on, period. Eddie had no idea that it wasn't actually happening.

When we see top-down processing in "rocks underwater," it is a simple and emotionally neutral rendering of the landscape. The world of self and others is far more complicated. The brain is organized to configure the inner drama in the cortex, with its cast of characters and their relationships to deal with the emotional world. This drama is the source of cortical top-down processing for the emotional realm. The emotional realm requires judgment through feeling to navigate its waters. The guiding element of the inner drama is emotional.

In Eddie's case, the sadomasochistic drama of Eddie and his mother was the central scenario that was mapped in his cortex. I call this drama of Eddie and Mommy Dearest the characterological drama of consciousness. His inner drama was created by his formative emotional world with Mother. It comprised his top-down context to anticipate, experience, and deal with the emotional realm. Once established in the cortex, the play is what Eddie saw as his emotional "rocks underwater." When Eddie's old friend gave him a smile of caring, he saw an illusion from his phantom drama. He saw a smile of ridicule—his mother's smile.

The characterological drama operates differently in the trance of waking life than it does in REM sleep. In REM sleep, the drama is the overt subject of dreaming. There, it is on stage and seen. In waking life, the inner drama functions invisibly. It is not on stage and is not seen. It is the hidden context, the prism through which we experience the emotional realities of self and others. It informs the meaning of our emotional experience. The panoply of thoughts and feeling states that comprise our day do not just exist as stand-alone items in a vacuum. They are filtered through the inner play through top-down processing. The characterological play is structured in the brain to serve these ends. The idea that feeling states exist as if they have no inner context misses how consciousness is organized and functions from our cortical networks.

Eddie simply experienced his invisible inner drama, projected onto his friend and him, just as we see rocks underwater. This is a relatively small and benign example of ordinary top-down processing, seeing what is believed. Eddie projected his mother's smile onto his smiling friend. To Eddie, it was simply so.

What transpired during Eddie's more loaded argument with the professor, when overt sadomasochism was actually in play? There was the same disparity between his conscious awareness and his invisible play, only amplified. Similarly, his internal drama was not seen, felt, or known. Yet it was happening. During and after the argument with the professor, Eddie was aware only of a content disagreement. He thought his professor was stupid and unreasonable. This is what he ruminated about. However, this intellectual disagreement was the vehicle for activating the battle between his inner personas. The sadomasochistic aggression of his hidden cortical play was activated by the argument in a powerful way. Yet Eddie had no awareness of being filled with impotent rage. If he had been asked, he would have denied any anger at all. Eddie was unaware that his activated phantom drama was intensely percolating throughout the discussion and into the evening.

The tell, however, was his anxiety. The characterological play was present and operating as invisible top-down processing during his fight with the professor. The ongoing fighting between Eddie's internal personas—the sadomasochistic battle—occupied a tremendous amount of his brain activity. Inside Eddie's invisible brain theater, the personas were fighting, just as if they were in an actual battle in physical reality. This fierce and consuming battle was a steady state of murderous rage between them. Eddie's anxiety didn't come out of the blue at all. It was generated by the masked, intense, sadomasochistic war of his internal play. If there had been no impotent rage in his "Eddie" persona, there would have been no anxiety.

His dream work in sleep was to detoxify this activated conflict. When Eddie went to sleep, the war between "Eddie and the ogre" took form on his dream stage. There, the battle was overtly waged, where it culminated in the stabbing murder. He did to the ogre—his professor, his father, his ogre mother—what he couldn't do in life. It was the impotent rage from the activated characterological play that generated this dream of murder. And when the Eddie persona rose up and killed the ogre, he was triumphant. Consequently, when the fight was settled in Eddie's favor, the anxiety evaporated.

We'll look at one more facet of Eddie's world to illuminate the presence and centrality of the ongoing top-down characterological drama in his cortex. When Eddie was a boy, he insisted on sleeping with a night-light on. When his bedroom was dark, Captain Hook was in his closet. And Eddie was terrified. When the light was on, Hook was gone, and Eddie was safe. What was this about? How could a flick of a light switch make so much difference?

Peter Pan lived in Neverland, where there was no passage of time. Peter had superpowers—he could fly and fight, and he was extremely quick. However, timeless residence in Neverland wasn't peaceful. It was actually endless war. Peter was eternally stalked by the evil Captain Hook. Hook was particularly menacing—there was that hook that replaced the hand that Peter cut off and fed to the alligator. Hook was consumed by the wish to kill Peter. It's worth noting that the alligator was, in turn, stalking Hook. Hook was subject to the same kind of threat that he inflicted on Peter. The Peter Pan story is a timeless fantasy. (Once established, our characterological dramas exist outside of time.). It is relevant that the alligator, who was pursuing Hook, who was pursing Peter, represented time itself, through the ticking of the clock that it had swallowed. Time, in reality, ticks on. Actual living, which exists in time, is haunted by the ongoing presence of our timeless internal fantasies.

The form given to the bogeyman in Eddie's closet was Captain Hook, who had become a figure in Eddie's "image-ination." Eddie took the Peter Pan story into his inner world, with him as Peter and Mommy Dearest as Hook. Consequently, Captain Hook, created by J. M. Barrie's imagination, became a figure in Eddie's inner drama. In fact, Hook is the same figure as the ogre in the dream. It's not surprising that Eddie attached himself to the images and plot of this story.

The Peter Pan story is consonant with Eddie's own inner drama. The images of the sadomasochism between Peter and Hook are sword play, knives, dismemberment, cruelty, stalking, and killing. As the *Puer Eternis* (the eternal boy), Peter has power and conquers his fear of the cruel, dangerous, humiliating Hook. Peter dismembers, torments, and seeks to kill him.

When the lights were off, the bogeyman popped right into Eddie's closet. It's worth noting that Hook was in the closet, as opposed to being actually visually seen. Figures of the characterological drama are always invisible in waking consciousness, even in the darkness. The darkness did transport Eddie into his inner living theater when he was no longer tied to reality by his visual sense. When the lights were shut off, the figure of Hook came on the stage and Eddie's cortical theater was projected into the closet. His presence was palpable and scary. Eddie knew that Hook was lurking in there.

Hook's menacing presence was very real to Eddie. Hook was there in the closet, and Hook was gonna get him. Cognitively, Eddie knew that Hook was just a character in a story and not real. Yet this piece of intellectual knowledge didn't diminish the terror of Hook's presence. This inner story was more emotionally impactful than reality itself.

We can see that the drama was right below the surface. By flicking the night-light on, Eddie could keep the figure of his internal drama at bay. His visual sense in the light reoriented his consciousness back to reality. In the darkness, with just the flick of a switch, Hook returned. Where was Hook when the light was on? He disappeared from the closet, back into the invisible internal play. With the light off, Hook came right back. The characterological drama of consciousness is always—timelessly—there. It is always in play, as the cortical top-down play.

In summary, the characterological drama of consciousness comes from the early formative experience with Mother and Father. It gets established in the cortex via the neuronal mappings of personas and their emotional relatedness. Once in place, the inner drama serves as the top-down processing of the emotional life of self and other. It is the prism through which we experience our emotional life. The inner drama is invisible, but present and ongoing. The feeling relatedness between personas in the drama is actively in play and happening in the brain. We saw that occur in an ordinary moment of everyday life. When Eddie's friend smiled at him, he unwittingly saw and reacted to his mother's ridiculing smile, the activiated top-down processed projection—Eddie saw a cruel and humiliating figure. It did not actually come from his friend. This was his "rocks underwater" belief.

In addition, we saw via the more loaded emotional incident with the professor that the internal feeling state between personas was much more intensively activated. The sadistic aggression of the internal play intensified sufficiently to create a psychiatric symptom: anxiety. It then generated a dream. The emotional state of our feeling self is predicated on these internal personas and their feeling relatedness. The characterological drama of conscousness operates in a cortical top-down fashion in both our sleeping and waking trances.

How does the characterological drama actually get written in the brain?

3

"The Play's the Thing"
In the Theater of the Brain

Eddie's characterological drama was mapped and established in his cortex. It functioned twenty-four hours a day. When awake, it invisibly guided his emotional life and determined his relatedness to others and himself. At night, it informed the visible play of his dreams. In general, top-down processing is the cortical brain function that simplifies and makes possible our ability to perform the complexities of moment-to-moment living. It would be too unwieldy for the brain to analyze the whole host of information from the senses and body nerves anew and connect it with our motor abilities, along with our intention, every moment. You wouldn't be able to lift a spoon to your mouth, never mind balance a strawberry on it, or encompass your intention, or have a cohered sense of "you." The cortex establishes a way to do all of this, with as little an expenditure of time, effort, and attention as possible. It does so by top-down processing, which creates symbolic form out of huge amounts of information.

When Eddie was in junior high school, he learned to play the guitar. As a beginner, he had mastered the easy chords—E and A. He wanted to expand his repertoire to B7, which is a much more challenging hand position. It required total attention to separate his fingers in a precise way in order to hold down the strings within certain frets. When first attempted, he couldn't do it. He had to slowly place each finger in the right place. The muscles didn't feel like they could get there, hold the position, or get sound out of the string. And it hurt. It required seconds to finalize the correct hand position. Each finger needed to be placed individually. Eddie thought to himself, *Damn, I'll never get this.* As he continued to play B7, leave it, and come back to it again, it got a little easier. He finally quit that practice session. After a night's sleep, he tried it again, but he still didn't have it. He kept working on that B7. Full conscious attention was still required to get his fingers correctly onto the frets. The sound was coming out better. But it was still slow getting there. The chord was not, as yet, usable.

After three days of working at it, Eddie could finally play B7. His fingers didn't hurt anymore, and he had better coordination for the hand position. His hand now operated as a whole unit, without much conscious effort. He no longer had to think about it. He had mastered the chord. It now joined his growing repertoire of chords. To the consternation of his brother and sisters, he rocked out "Peggy Sue" for hours. "You know I ... lo-o-ove you, girl" was still a little prolonged, but that didn't hold him back.

Eddie's experience of repeated efforts created a cortical map of the B7 hand position. The neuromuscular experience of his hand and fingers created a web of neuronal connections glued together by neuronal memory. Electrochemical processes take place within synapses between neurons that establish a permanent electrical pathway connection. This took place throughout the millions of connecting neurons that created the B7 map in Eddie's cortex. Once this neuron memory (the linkage between neurons) got established in the sensory and motor areas of the cortex for his fingers and hand, it became available to be activated as one B7 unit. The cortical map then became accessible for top-down processing—playing the chord.

When Eddie was learning B7, the lion's share of his conscious attention was focused on getting his hand on the strings so the chord would work. His attention was so focused and absorbed, there wasn't much left over for anything else. This focus created a B7 neuromuscular mini-trance. Of course, this was a partial trance, as his attention still could wander into thinking about other things, or the pain in his fingers, or that he had an itch. Once the B7 map got established and incorporated, the focus of the attention of consciousness

was freed up to be available elsewhere. It now required only minimal conscious attention to play B7, because it was cortically mapped
and simply drawn upon as one top-down unit. The trance was no
longer required. Playing the chord was on automatic pilot. His attention was now available for guitar playing and "Peggy Sue." Eddie's
experience of mastering B7 is a model for how all cortical maps get
established.

B7 is not just a stand-alone map in the cortex. It is connected to
much more extensive cortical mappings. Its neuronal connections
radiate outward with linkages to the mappings of the auditory center, for sound; the already established music maps, for incorporating
B7 into music; the visual and thinking centers, to monitor the guitar
playing; the vocal and verbal centers for singing; the total body sensory and motor centers, for holding the guitar and strumming with
the other hand, etc.; the feeling centers, as music is feeling; and to
the core mapping of Eddie himself, in order for the whole package
to derive from his intention. This entire mega-map was activated in
order for Eddie to play "Peggy Sue."

Cortical neuronal circuits create levels of order by creating patterns of coherence. They simplify the world into bite-sized pieces.
As a result of the cortical map of B7 and the more extensive musical
maps, Eddie did not have to process all the individual information
of touch, muscle coordination, guitar playing, singing, music, feeling, and intention separately. He could just play "Peggy Sue." When
doing so, he activated the fuller cortical mapping, and went into a
guitar playing-singing-music-"Peggy Sue" trance. The whole package was an enactment of top-down processing.

Eddie had one last problem with B7. As it turned out, the hand
position he initially used was scrunched up and awkward. It was
okay when used with simple chords such as E and A. But when his
playing got more advanced, it was hard to get in and out of B7 from
more difficult chords. To fix this problem, he needed a new hand position that was open and not constricted. He decided to change his B7
hand position. In order to do so, he first had to force himself stop to
using his previously scrunched up hand position. In addition, he had
to give his full conscious attention, once again, to holding his fingers

and hand differently. This took him back to muscular pain, clumsiness, slowness, inability, and frustration, just as it did the first time but not quite as bad. This was required for him to establish a new and different neuromuscular B7 map into his cortex. Soon enough, he got it.

Eddie first had to disuse the old map. Then he enacted the process of evolving a new one with new neuromuscular experience, creating new brain mappings. The mappings of B7 would then get incorporated into the broader circuits of playing the guitar. This exemplifies what was involved in changing the cortical mappings for B7, and by extension, how change itself transpires in consciousness. It involves disuse, relinquishing, loss, and new experience to create a new top-down form. Then top-down processing operates by using the new form that is established.

The brain is control central for the organism and, as such, serves its thriving and functioning. It is a living physical organ of the body. It is body. Its architecture is body. Its cells, the neurons, their shape and function are body. Its electrochemical properties are physical body. The very shape of the brain, the sequences of its growth and development, as well as the synaptic connections between neurons and their biochemical processes, are laid out and created by our genetic code. The mechanisms of neuronal memory itself come from orderly coded metabolic, electro-chemical genetic processes. The architecture of the neuronal connections all throughout the different parts of the brain are likewise programmed by the human genome.

The foundation and ongoing anchor of the cortex is its inviolable connection with the subcortical brain and body, which it serves. The core of the brain is the subcortical brain, which regulates body maintenance. It integrates and manages smooth muscle, the body organs, and the autonomic nervous system. The source of all information that comes into the cortex comes bottom up, through the subcortical brain, body nerves, hormones, and the senses. The operations of consciousness, however, flow top down from our cortex. As we shall see later, our essence does not. The level of order that creates our actual being flows from information from the early limbic-cortical brain, our body representations, and the subcortical brain.

The cortex gives order and coherence to information by unifying huge quantities of bits of information into more encompassing form. This follows from the remembered ordered way its neuron channels electrochemically link up, one to another. Two neurons get permanently linked by chemical processes that get established in the synapses (spaces) between them. This allows an activated electrochemical current to travel along an established pathway of connected neurons like an electric wire. These permanent, intact electrochemical circuits create neuronal memory. Single units of information get linked into patterns. A web of neuron (memory-glued) circuits constitutes a pattern of information. These webs link up with other webs to create larger webs. These webs of webs of webs create larger webs that map all throughout the architecture of the cortex.

The multiplication of these circuits creates a pyramid of order. Sensory information from the five senses and their neuronal impulses are at the bottom of the pyramid. Those are simple units of information. These patterns get linked to other patterns and become higher-level units of information. As these patterns get connected into larger and more elaborate patterns, they create higher-level units of information. The top layers of the pyramid, arising from the high-end cortical maps, create the symbolic forms that are used in top-down processing.

The brain has additional ways of linking maps of information to much higher levels of order, over and above the straightforward pyramids of order. Since many neurons can connect into one synapse, multiple neuronal circuits hook into one another, not just two. So multiple circuits of neurons get linked. This multiplies the patterns of circuits connecting to circuits even more. And finally, there are ganglions of neurons called brain nuclei, which operate as hubs to massively increase the connectivity of neuronal circuits, creating additional webs of connections, radiating outwards. This creates a higher level of order and unifies additional patterns into constellations of patterns, creating larger patterns. These huge networks of neuronal circuits link together to create the architecture of mappings that establishes high-end cortical maps. To make it even more complicated, the various neurotransmitters of connection qualitatively color the resultant symbolic forms.

When higher levels of order take form, they are increasingly abstracted from the original information and take symbolic form. Let's take language as an example. Language is a high level of order that a child develops at anywhere from one to three years old. Consider the word "swim." It represents and stands for the complex activity and experience of swimming. However, from the word "swim," I don't get wet, I don't kick my feet, I can't get splashed, and I don't need a towel. It reduces the whole thing to a four-letter word. The circuits of circuits that map "swim" are the operational unit that creates the word. "Swim" is an abstraction for a huge complex of information that allows me to communicate, in shorthand, to you.

The word "swim" is an abstracted symbol, not the thing. Once a symbolic representation is established, it becomes the prism through which we see. It is at a considerable remove from the actual experience of swimming. Once the cortical mapping for "swim" is established, the lower levels of order that comprise the host of things that swimming is, are then automatically bypassed. Language operates similarly to the top-down projected image of "rocks underwater," which bypassed the lower levels of order—wavy broken lines, glimmering lights, and shifting colors.

This pyramid of order allows the cortex to organize and assimilate incredibly large amounts of information very quickly and efficiently. Language allows us to talk. However, keep in mind that language can be quite misleading. As we shall see later, there is a price to be paid for this cortical representational shorthand. Symbolic forms, taken as reality, are at variance with the actuality they represent.

The cortical process of creating form and functional order out of an incredible mass of information is extraordinarily efficient. The pyramid of order, created by reducing information into patterns, operates exponentially. Here's a simple example of exponential expansion. Let's say you ripped this page out of this book. If you were to fold it in half fifty-nine times, its thickness would reach the sun. Don't worry; you can't physically do it—but you can do the math. Start with the thickness of one page—1/300 of an inch—and double it fifty-nine times. This results in 1,767,744,000,000,000 thicknesses of paper in a stack that will extend for ninety-three million miles.

The brain works exponentially in reverse. It gives form and order to large quantities of pieces of information by reducing them exponentially. Let's say the brain is inundated with 1,767,744,000,000,000 pieces of information of which to make sense. It operates by linking bits together. Units of two bits linked together create 883,872,000,000,000 patterns of two units. By repeating this process and linking together two-bit patterns with other two-bit patterns, we now have 441,936,000,000,000 patterns of four bits. If this process was repeated just fifty-nine times, it would create one coherent form out of all those units of information.

The brain creates order by encompassing, associating, and reducing incredible amounts of complex and diverse information into bite-sized pieces. It does so by integrating associated maps of lower levels of symbolic form, which in turn were created by integrating associated maps of lower levels of symbolic form. These webs of connected neurons create brain maps of associations of constellations that create the shorthand of functional, coherent, symbolic form. The information at the top of the pyramid takes form as the images and emotional states that are used for its top-down processing.

I certainly do not know how this leaps into actual mental experience. But I do know one essential modality of brain that plays a role: projection. When I see "rocks underwater," I see a projection of a cortical image onto the floor of the lake. Here, the projection screen is the lake bottom, through a visual projection. Projection is an intrinsic property of cortical functioning. And projection always has a projection screen. Rocks underwater has the lake floor as a projection screen. B7 has the hand muscles as its projection screen. The projection screen for Eddie's dream was the theater of the brain itself. As I type on my computer, my simple experience of touching the keyboard is entirely a brain-created projection of consciousness. My actual experience is that I touch and tap and feel the keys. The synthetic circuit goes from the sensing nerves in my fingertips to my cortical maps and back to computer keys as a projection screen for touch. In fact the nerve impulse actually reaches my brain a beat after the actual contact takes place. My experience of touching the keys is a cortical top-down projection. I take for granted that I actually feel these keys. But this is not actually so. It is a illusory experience of synthetic cortical projection. It's obvious to us, as outside observers, that when Eddie's hand was holding the broomstick in his dream, the whole thing was a cortical projection and not actually real. My experience of my hand on the keyboard is no less so.

A second intrinsic property of cortical top-down projection is that the cortical illusion is taken to be what is real. For sure, the function of "projections as real" is an essential adaptation that allows the organism's images to correspond effectively to the reality in which it lives. Projection onto a projection screen is an intrinsic property of cortical top-down processing. In fact, our experience is purely brain-created projective illusion at all times, in waking as well as sleeping. We never experience anything outside of brain-created experience. We do not experience reality directly at all. There is no such thing. It is impossible. We only experience the projections of our consciousness. And these are the images and feelings of top-down cortical creations.

We saw how the cortical map of B7 came from the interplay of neuromuscular experience syncing with neuronal pathways. Together, they create the cortical map for B7, embedding it into maps of sound, music, guitar, feeling, and Eddie's intention. All cortical mapping arises this way—the impacts of experience on the available brain pathways. The high end B7 mapping is a relatively simple one. At the top of the brain's pyramid is the highest level of order of all: the characterological drama. We aren't talking about a guitar chord anymore. It, like B7, is projected onto our living experience as a top-down cortical projection.

When we consider the evolution of the human species, what makes us human is not defined by the unique human functions, such as opposable thumbs, abstract thinking, reasoning, or computational abilities—those are good. The defining feature of our species is the synthetic "play" of human consciousness. The evolution of the structure and function of the limbic-cortical brain is at one with the creation of the play. The morphology, organized structures, and pathways of complex neuronal webs throughout its architecture create the patterns of patterns of patterns that enable the characterological drama. This is the cortical processing that allows for the meaning and coherence of our moment-to-moment functioning in life. The creation of images of personas, their emotional relatedness, and life plots—the full range of tragedy and comedy—is the drama. It constitutes the top-down processing of our individual selves and our emotional and relationship life. The coherence of human consciousness is the highest level of order of the human genome. We walk around all day long, each of us, in this brain-body synthetic bubble of consciousness, our genetic endowment.

The characterological drama of human consciousness is our adaptation to and is consonant with living the human life—the life of the individual and relatedness to others. It encompasses our surviving, our child rearing, our imagination, and our culture. It allows us to function as the individual and social animals we are. It creates the meaning landscape of human experience. This landscape encompasses the symbolic representations of human experience—self, others, relationship, and drama—in myths, narratives, literature, art, nursery rhymes, songs, movies, hieroglyphics, plays, belief systems, dance, journalism, cave paintings, fashion, religious incantations, and theologies.

How does the drama of consciousness operate in our daily life?

4

REFLECTIONS ON HUMAN CONSCIOUSNESS IN EVERYDAY LIFE

IN ORDINARY LIVING WE DON'T break down the illusion. We have no awareness at all that we are living a neurological illusion of reality. It's all just taken as real. As the Beatles said, "Ob-la-di, ob-la-da, life goes on brah. La-la how the life goes on."

One day Eddie's sister called him on the phone at his dorm. Even though she didn't identify herself, Eddie knew it was Clara just by the sound of her voice. Her "Hi, Eddie" was enough. Out of the seven billion people in the world, his auditory consciousness processed the unique timbre and tone qualities of her voice through the distortions of a low-tech electronic device—the phone—with just two words. His brain created the living persona of Clara in his mind's eye. He felt immediately comforted to hear from his favorite sister, especially as he had been feeling a little homesick.

They'd been chatting for a few minutes when she mentioned something about her dog. Something was wrong here. Eddie was confused. Clara didn't have a dog. Actually, his other sister Margie had one. Oops! This wasn't Clara. It was Margie. Margie's voice was very similar to Clara's. He scrambled for a moment and realized it had been Margie all along. He was somewhat crestfallen, because they weren't nearly as close. He didn't want to let on that he thought he was talking to Clara, because he was embarrassed and didn't want to hurt Margie's feelings. He hid his mistake, as well as his disappointment, and went on with the conversation. It seemed like he got away with it, as Margie didn't seem to notice anything.

What does Eddie's temporary confusion illuminate for us? At first glance, it seems like a simple case of mistaken identity. Under ordinary circumstances when talking to someone, that person is seen. The visual sense works together with the auditory to create the proper persona image. Auditory processing unlike visual processing does not go back to the source of its waves as its projection screen. Instead it links to an image in the mind's eye, normally informed by the visual. If Eddie had not been on the phone but had seen Margie with his eyes, he would not have confused her with Clara. The visual pathway would have been in force. It would have begun with light waves reflecting off Margie. He would have taken in her upside-down reflection in his retina, and it would have traveled up his optic nerve to the visual centers and their cortical connections. He would have activated the Margie persona. Then the image created in Eddie's brain would have been re-projected back onto Margie as its projection screen to complete the loop. Eddie would not have been subject to auditory ambiguity.

Without the input of Eddie's actual eye, he saw Clara in his mind's eye. On the telephone, the projection screen for the sound of his sister's voice was the persona image of Clara, created by his image-ination in the theater of his mind. When the mention of her dog didn't correspond to the believed Eddie/Clara world, the seamless fantasy broke. He became confused until his brain settled on a more accurate story.

When Eddie realized it was Margie, more went on than a simple correction of the incorrect Clara persona to the accurate Margie persona. The salient issue is that because of the persona confusion, Eddie had activated the wrong mappings, and the wrong limbic-cortical play. He had activated the Eddie/Clara play. As a result, his conversation was filled with the feelings of his relationship with Clara. His homesickness and longing for emotional holding were soothed by his immersion in the Clara top-down processed drama. The "Hi, Eddie," had generated this comforting experience for several minutes. With the correction, she was gone. Eddie shifted from an immersion in the top-down cortical drama of Eddie/Clara to an immersion in the top-down cortical drama of Eddie/Margie, with the accompanying meaning of his problematic relationship with Margie. Eddie went from one story illusion to another story illusion, albeit an accurate one.

Neither the incorrect nor the correct cortical play was a direct experience or enactment of reality. In both cases he was inhabiting an invisible top-down play. It is the nature of the trance of consciousness that Eddie's experience, in both plays, just seemed real. Eddie's confusion reveals that we do not live in or experience reality directly. We inhabit the mapped scenarios of our invisible top-down cortical plays of our consciousness. We live in our limbic-cortical illusions, unbeknownst to us, all the time. Our feelings of relatedness are generated from our plays. They are not a simple, direct, external state of feeling between two people in reality.

When I say that Eddie lived this drama in his mind's eye, notice the visual reference—mind's eye. Human image-ination is significantly visual, consonant with the prominent visual areas of our cortex. This is how the human cortex is anatomically constructed. The anatomy of our cortex is biologically determined, as it is with all species. We are not outside the flow of nature. Our unique human consciousness reflects our specific cortical anatomy, which follows from our genome.

The genome for other species constructs in them a species unique cortical architecture and consequently a unique consciousness. For example, the olfactory cortex in dogs is far more prominent than it is in humans. And their sense of smell is millions of times more sensitive than ours. My dog knows me by my smell as the top-down processed Bobby-smell persona. She knows me, and her emotional responses to me are in olfactory consciousness. People often assume that their dog carries a visual image of them in its mind, as humans do. This is wrong and is a projection of human consciousness onto a dog. A visual image of me is not her primary reference. And further, olfactory consciousness is more proximal and inherently connected to feeling, which is also consonant with dog nature. I don't really know what my dog's olfactory universe is like, but I know it's not like my primarily visual one.

We have just seen that both Clara and Margie were Eddie's cortical projections. Likewise, the Eddie that he knows as himself is a cortical projection of "Eddie." Similarly, the Eddie that I know is a cortical projection of mine, projected onto him. The people of Eddie's consciousness, your consciousness, and my consciousness are composed of the cortical top-down personas of our plays. And it is natural to simply take for granted that what we see is the real thing itself.

Let us use a different example to illuminate that the personas we know as ourselves and others are synthetic cortical representations. Eddie was an excellent mimic. He could imitate other people's voices and sound just like them. He could do a great imitation of Keith Richards of the Rolling Stones. He was able to nail the accent and the voice. Not only that, when doing so, Eddie used phrases and a vocabulary that was very Keith. In fact, his face transformed and looked like Keith's face. He hunched exactly as Keith stands. He wasn't just copying sentences he'd heard. He would improvise and play out imaginary scenes in the Keith character. He would act the way Keith would act, with his attitude and gestures. It was very funny and a little eerie. It felt like Keith was there. When he finished, Keith was gone, and Eddie was back. He looked like Eddie, sounded like Eddie, spoke like Eddie, and acted like Eddie.

What was going on here? Eddie hadn't memorized a Keith Richards vocabulary, analyzed his speech pattern, done vocal exercises to retrain his vocal chords, altered his facial expression in the mirror, or practiced standing differently. He hadn't written a script and committed it to memory. Voice mimicry was a feature of a larger phenomenon. Eddie was talking and acting and thinking and feeling as a different person in a new and alive situation. It was as if he was channeling Keith Richards's persona and body, as a whole.

Eddie took in Keith's persona receptively, where it was mapped in his limbic cortex. It was mapped all throughout Eddie's cortex, including Keith's body postures, his emotional attitudes, his accent, his verbal attitudes, his language, his facial attitude, his characteristic mind-set, and his musical singularity. His brain organized a coherent, alive Keith persona, which encompassed Keith's mind, his body, his personality, his feelings, and his attitudes. Once mapped, "Keith" was incorporated into plays and was available for top-down processing. We all do this as a matter of course. The fact that you might have Keith Richards in a dream reflects this routine receptive process.

However, as a mimic, Eddie had the art ability to utilize this mapped persona of Keith expressively. This was not a superficial imitation. Eddie gave the directorship of his own body-mind-feeling-organism to the Keith persona mappings, rather than the Eddie circuits. Eddie morphed into the Keith character by inhabiting his internalized Keith persona and play. Consequently, this controlled his vocal-chord tension, as well as the specific usage of his mouth and tongue musculature for the production of speech. It also drew from the auditory and speech centers for accent and vocabulary, the feeling centers for attitude and feeling, and the body centers for specific postural coherence and facial expression. Facial expression is very complicated. To recreate Keith's standing facial expression cannot be done as a conscious imitation any more than a fake smile can simulate a real smile. Facial expression, like a real smile, employs the involuntary facial muscles, not just the voluntary ones. The involuntary facial muscles are activated by autonomic nerves, which are generated from one's genuine feeling state and attitude.

Eddie could even do Keith guitar playing—his sound, his style. Of course, the guitar playing was more of a guitar caricature. Eddie couldn't really play a full-out Keith Richards's guitar because he was Eddie, not Keith. He could only play to the limits of his own talent.

To enter the Keith character, Eddie entered the synesthesia from any one point. He had just to start the voice, or feel an attitude, or start the face, and bang, he was there. Once there, Eddie's image-ination was given over to the Keith persona. He entered a Keith trance and switched away from his regular Eddie persona into Keith. It was not a studied imitation of Keith from the outside. Eddie went into Keith from the inside. His "Keith" was an alive character responding to life in the living moment. Like all art trances, this was only partial. Eddie's actual persona, albeit not fully inhabited, coexisted alongside it.

Obviously, the Keith persona lacked the depth of mapping of his regular Eddie persona. However, it is a demonstration that Eddie has the high level of symbolic order of this "other" persona in his cortical mappings. Most of us do not have this particular full-blown talent, although we can do it a little. Even though most of us can't enter into personas of others and channel them as Eddie could, they are routinely there in our cortical dramas. All of us receptively map other people.

In fact, there is a psychiatric character world that utilizes the mimic's expressive capacity—so-called multiple personalities. These patients create and enter an "other" persona to disconnect themselves in their consciousness from their regular self, to protect themselves from the pain of particular kinds of abuse.

Eddie's capacity for mimicry flowed from the organized mappings of personas in his cortex. Mimicry is the expressive form of synthetic persona image-ination. All personas—self and others—are mapped in the cortex on this high-end level of mappings of body-mind-feeling. Obviously, our persona of self is the most extensively mapped. Our most intimate relationships are more extensively mapped than more superficial ones. Our formative relationships are more deeply held and known. "Keith" was quite superficial, compared to the mappings of Eddie himself, or Clara, or Margie, or his mother. Our limbic-cortical image-ination generates top-down processed, alive representations of other people. These receptive mappings of others gives them a full vitality. These mappings are how we know ourselves and others.

Our actual experience is derived entirely from our consciousness. Its persona representations comprise the cortical dramas of our lives. If I have a dream of you, it is my cortical representational persona of you. It may look like you, act like you, sound like you, talk like you, think like you, and feel as you do, but it's not you. You didn't leave your body in the middle of the night and pop into my dream, although it may well feel like you were there. This is all there is, whether in waking life, in our dreams, in our fantasies, or in our art. It is a basic adaptational aspect of brain function to make its illusory images feel and seem real. It would not be functional or adaptive, if you were being attacked by a tiger, for example, to wonder if it was real or an hallucination.

Eddie's mimicry was a form of art. Art is a partial trance through which he expressively projected a human story—art is art-ifice. The synthetic ability of his expressive image-ination allowed him, within the frames of his art form, to project human drama. My receptive imagination took in his drama through the frame of the art form.

All communication vehicles are art—speaking, writing, music, painting, dance, theater, and design. Communication and art are one and the same thing. Art frames are high-end levels of symbolic codes. The particular structure of the symbolic codes differs for each art form. Art forms, as frames of experience, are not visible. They produce the experience, through art-ifice, of direct communication. Each art form utilizes a partial trance and specific codes for the communication of the human narrative.

The human narrative is composed of people in story—in relationship, in solitude, in activity, in thinking, and in feeling states. The stuff of the human story is universal to all of us. If you and I share the specific symbolic codes of an art form, I can go into a partial trance and transmit a story from my image-ination expressively. And you can go into a partial trance to take it in receptively, and feel it, and experience it.

I travel around in the shifting trance states of my bubble of consciousness, and you travel around in yours. The actual boundary between us is total and impenetrable. There is no such thing as a magical direct transmission of thoughts from one person to another. Communication between us only and always transpires through art forms. This is the vehicle that allows my image-ination to reach your image-ination, despite our total separateness.

One of the most enthralling stage plays I've ever seen was a one-woman show in New York, *The Syringa Tree*. Pamela Gien, the writer-actress played fifteen different characters on an empty stage. There were no stage props. She transformed, in front of my eyes, from a six-year-old girl, to an African nanny, to a Jewish doctor father, a Boer girlfriend, a pregnant black African girl, a revolutionary, and a South African soldier. From my seat in the theater, I saw all the different characters interacting with each other as the whole play unfolded. I saw the syringa tree itself on the African vista, the whole landscape, the houses, the costumes, and the characters. For two hours, I was in Africa. Everything was full and alive, as if it were a movie. The story of the play was incredibly powerful. I was emotionally moved for days after the performance. It's with me still. Her creation of the illusion of the characters, feeling, relationship, and tragedy, as well as the scenery and landscape, was mind-boggling.

Even so, ten minutes after it was over, I was back in ordinary reality out on the street. There I was, elbowing for a cab. It was a matter of course to transition from this powerful art illusion (created by the play of her remarkable expressive consciousness and my receptive consciousness), back to regular reality, and go on about my mundane business. How easily one takes for granted the remarkable states of the trances of consciousness—to move along from great art, to street survival, to dreams, to "What's for dinner?"

Each of us lives the personas and stories of our inner plays within our impenetrable bubble of consciousness. How in the world do I communicate the contents of this book to you? How do you make sense of what I write? Let's look at the writing and reading of this book as an example of an art form for communication. What processes are involved in our apparent mind meld? You are reading this book that I wrote from my image-ination. Both of us have established the high-end, symbolic language and reading/writing mappings in our cortexes for phonetic writing in English. I translate a bunch of ideas, images, and stories from my image-ination into a visual symbolic code of twenty-six letters. My work gets coded as these black symbols printed onto this white page. You visually take in this coded information and give it form by translating it back into ideas, images, and story by your image-ination.

The movie I express comes from within me. The movie you receive comes from within me. You recreate my movie in your consciousness. I project (throw outside of me) the contents of my consciousness, my image-ination, through the letter code onto this page. You introject (throw inside) the contents of my consciousness by giving form, through reading, to the code on your end. You go into a reading trance. You see and hear my movie. When you are reading, you are in a partial trance and are mostly unaware of the world around you. Your focused attention is absorbed in the reading world. Your process of reading is your receptive re-creation from my expressive creation. The formed images, ideas, and story you see and hear in your mind are created by your image-ination. You have given me the control, through the writing/reading code, for giving form to my content by your image-ination.

Phonetic writing of European languages uses very different cortical mappings from the ideogram writing of Asian languages. They are completely different codes. Phonetic writing, which combines combinations of twenty-six letter symbols, stands for units of sound (phonemes) to symbolize the sound of syllables and words—"fo-ne-tic ri-ting." The mappings for this symbolic code utilize correspondences between visual and auditory and language processing. Chinese and Japanese writing is very different. It uses ideograms composed of thousands of symbolic visual representations of the thing or concept themselves. Ideograms do not represent the sound of words, per se, in a particular language. They represent the image of a thing or the idea that has no reference to sound or language. The symbols are purely visual. The ideogram for girl is a symbolic picture of a girl. The ideogram for cat is a symbolic picture of a cat. Consequently, if Chinese ideograms were identical to Japanese ideograms (which they're not, although there is some overlap), then a Chinese author could write a book and it could be read by a Japanese reader. He would supply the language and sound of Japanese to these purely visual non-language-specific symbols. A Japanese reader could read the book of a Chinese writer, but the two of them could not talk to each other. We do something similar with our numeric symbols. Our numbers stand for the thing, not in a language. I see a "3," and it is "three." A Frenchman sees the same "3," and it is "trois."

Even if we share the symbolic code of phonetic writing, we don't all process reading in the same way, due to our genetics. Some readers process primarily through auditory pathways, while others do so primarily through visual pathways. To make sense of what he's reading, an auditory reader has to hear the sound of the words in his mind. Consequently, he requires silence and is bothered by background noise that interferes with listening to sound. He reads at the speed of sound—the speed of conversation. A visual reader will read primarily visually, and does not hear the sounds of the words in his mind. He can read happily with the TV and the stereo on in the background. He reads at the speed of light—the speed of movie visuals. In addition, the auditory reader is more naturally drawn to abstract ideas. If I write conceptually, he is at one with thinking about my ideas. The auditory reader is less comfortable with a detailed visual description. He has to work harder to force himself to "see" a description of visual images. On the other hand a primarily visual reader tends to be drawn more easily to see visual images. For instance, if I write about sitting at a lake, with the sunlight reflecting on the ripples of water coming through the pickerel weeds, as a black duck honks at her five ducklings swimming silently behind her, he will easily see this as a visual movie. He goes into a visual trance and sees the scene in his mind's eye. He will easily be transported from the reality of his reading chair to a lake in Maine. The visual reader, on the other hand has to work harder to put together and think abstractly about a group of abstract ideas.

Finally, how does the invisible cortical drama affect the way we perceive and deal with reality? How is it manifest and operative in our biochemical, neurological, hormonal, and synaptic physiology? And what are the implications for psychiatry? Let me address this through the following story told to me by my daughter, Lily.

Lily was at a party at a friend's house. The friend had two black cats that Lily knew quite well. Everybody was outside in the backyard for a barbecue. Lily's cell phone rang, and she went over to a far corner of the property for privacy and to get better reception. While she was talking, she spied one of the black cats in the bushes. She kneeled down, stretched out her hand and signaled the cat to come to her. It approached her. As it came out from under the bushes, she noticed a white patch of fur on the cat's head that continued right down its back and onto its tail. My daughter felt a sudden wave of fear without immediately knowing why. Then it hit her—skunk! With her heart beating fast, she turned and walked slowly away without getting sprayed.

Lily had been living in kitty world, one of her favorite worlds. Being partially preoccupied on the phone, she experienced "cat." The skunk, possibly rabid, did not behave like a wild animal. It came to her, much like a cat. The white stripe of fur was the visual trigger that didn't fit with a black cat. Lily remained in the kitty drama for a few moments before the discordant information registered. When the white stripe took on the meaning of skunk and its skunk-story meaning, she had a fear reaction. Then she fled. Notice that her fear reaction actually preceded her conscious recognition.

This wasn't just a correction of cat to skunk. It was a drama shift from kitty world to skunk world. From her immersion in kitty world, Lily was tender, warm, and maternal. Oxytocin and vasopressin were secreted from her hypothalamus, generating a feeling of love, tenderness, and warmth. Her autonomic nervous system created this mood state in the context of reading safety, trust, and love from her internal kitty world, triggered by seeing a cat.

When she saw the telltale white stripe, she shifted from kitty drama to skunk drama. In skunk world, she went in the other direction—into fight or flight. She went into a state of fear and, in this case, flight from danger. Her hypothalamus was stimulated to start the fight/flight response, secreting corticotropin-releasing hormone and stimulating the sympathetic nervous system. Her autonomic nervous system, through the vagus nerve, stimulated an increased heart rate. In concert with other brain nuclei, it stimulated the adrenals to secrete cortisol. This went back to the hippocampus and amygdala, the feeling centers. Her fight-or-flight response, with all its necessary aggression, followed. These reactions were regulated by neurotransmitters, particularly serotonin.

Here's the important point: both of Lily's responses—the tender response and the fight-or-flight response—*followed* from the meaning of two separate plays (kitty world and skunk world). The biochemical, hormonal, neurological processes were not the progenitor of her responses. They merely were the mechanisms that mediated and made manifest her response. Her response to reality was through a top-down processed story that was generated by her cortical mappings. The meaning from perceived sensory data was purely through an activated cortical play. This then determined the biological, biochemical, neurological, hormonal, muscle, thinking, and feeling responses that followed. It was a specific cortical story that determined her state of mind-body.

Neither animal was a stand-alone fact, independent of story. Each elicited a limbic-cortical drama—one for cat, one for skunk. The state of feeling response was consonant with the meaning of the internal story of each animal. The meaning of white stripe was skunk. The meaning of skunk was the skunk story—danger from overpowering olfactory assault, which Lily had previously experienced. If she had never heard of a skunk or didn't know its habits, she would not have been terrified of getting sprayed. She would not have generated a flight response. Likewise, Lily has a long history of kitty love. Her internal story of cats elicited the feeling states that comprise this story. It is the top-down cortical story that determined the biochemical, hormonal, and neurological responses. Each story reflected the mapping, first of kitty story and then of skunk story. The state of feeling and action response followed from the internal story of persona, plot, and feeling relatedness.

Lily's kitty and skunk worlds are relatively simple stories with an uncomplicated plot. How does this compare to the more central and powerful dramas, like Eddie's story of his ogre mother and him? We have seen that the primary story of Eddie's internal play was the relationship between "Mommy Dearest" and the object of her cruelty, Eddie. This cortical drama was ongoing in his consciousness, albeit invisibly. The ogre drama was the prism through which Eddie experienced the world. We have seen that this drama was sadomasochistic. It was not grounded in a loving engagement between a loving mother and Eddie's lovable Authentic-Being (which would have been analogous to Lily and the kitty). The currency of the ongoing sadomasochistic play was fighting anger between the two personas (analogous to Lily and the skunk). This story was deeply held. It was not a momentary enactment, like a skunk scare. Consequently, the fight of sadomasochism in Eddie's cortical world was a continuous steady state of war. There was an endless internal rage between his two personas.

Remember, Eddie did not consciously feel angry. The veins did not protrude from his neck, and his face was not red. Nonetheless, the sadomasochistic top-down drama of the fight between the mother persona and the Eddie persona was activated and present in the theater of Eddie's brain. Fighting anger between personas consumes serotonin. On an ongoing basis, the neurotransmitter serotonin fed the fight throughout the salient regions of his brain where these characters were mapped, particularly the feeling centers—the amygdala and the hippocampus. Unlike Lily's skunk response, which was a short burst and temporary, Eddie's perduring play was sucking up serotonin on an ongoing basis.

There are two essential points to keep in mind: First, Eddie's literal internal play was invisibly and constantly in operation inside him. And second, it is this actual story that determined what was activated in his brain-body circuits, including the activity of his neurotransmitters. Here's the way it works: As a neurotransmitter, serotonin regulates aggression in the mapped neuronal circuits for aggression. Aggression is not a dirty word. All of our functioning in daily life uses healthy aggression. Assertiveness and self-protection—our capacity for fight-or-flight—are necessary aggression that utilizes serotonin. However, the ongoing sadomasochistic war in Eddie's cortex between his mother persona and the Eddie persona is of a different order than the regular and routine aggression of daily life. This constant state of fighting, from the sadomasochistic play, is constantly feeding on and overtaxing the serotonin supply.

When a personality is subject to a steady state of war, at some point the supply of serotonin will cross a threshold and become depleted. At that point psychiatric symptoms are generated. Serotonin depletion is *not* the cause of psychiatric conditions; it is merely a mediator. It signifies two things. First, that the characterological world has actually been in an unsustainable state of internal war, and second, it is a signal that play has broken down. In the context of an ongoing problematic internal play, it is not a question of *if* but only *when* the system will get overtaxed.

The problematic plots of our cortical plays come from formative experiences of abuse and deprivation. They get elaborated in each of us in concert with the specifics of our temperaments. Temperament plays a major role in determining specific types of self-protective mechanisms that an individual employs to protect himself from pain. These self-protective mechanisms, in concert with deprivation and abuse, will determine the nature of symptoms when an individual's characterological world breaks down. The range of temperamental symptoms may be so-called depression, anxiety, phobic states, obsessional and compulsive states, or frank rage states. These symptoms are a signal that something is wrong. A characterological world with problematic fault lines will break down in characteristic ways.

Symptoms not only reflect that a characterological world has broken down but that the characterological world is problematic in the first place. It has structural damage that needs to be addressed. Symptoms are important indicators about the characterological world with which we are dealing. The issues of therapy are not about the signal that something is wrong but about the *something* that is wrong. The real work of therapy is with the characterological world, the self, and relatedness. As we will see later, symptom relief is not so difficult. Character is the heart of the matter.

If I am an auto mechanic, and you bring your car to me because the engine is overheating due to a cracked radiator, I can give your car symptom relief by feeding the radiator more fluid. This fix might work in the short run, but the structural problem has not been addressed. Just feeding the radiator will not fix the problem but will actually make it worse. There will be more leaks and more overheating and damage to the engine. As the auto mechanic, I had better understand the organization of the engine in order to address the real problem—a cracked radiator—and how and why that happened. I need to understand the real issues and not mask them.

Sadomasochism is the primary manifestation of problematic characterological reality. It is the ongoing war between two internal personas. Eddie's internal world is but one example of a problematic characterological world. There are many. Often, as with Eddie, the sadomasochism isn't recognizable.

Anger is the currency and intoxicant of sadomasochistic (S&M) relating. Anger is not a feeling or impulse that exists on its own. The anger is enacted between the two false but deeply held personas in the characterological play. Problematic plays are composed of these characters, living on a projection screen imposed on reality. The anger, in all its overt and subtle forms—whether a physical beating, resentment, envy, simple disdain, or self-criticism—is an enactment between these two characters.

In the absence of love between two Authentic-Beings, sadomasochism is the problematic solution to utter aloneness and emptiness. Hurting or being hurt and its accompanying anger gives the sensation of pseudo-vitality. Because S&M sensation feels real, one always becomes attached to this substitute relatedness. But it is a substitute that can never really work. As in frank S&M, the sensation ceases to be effective, and there has to be a constant escalation of attack to create the sensation of being alive. Built into this enactment is that the anger will continue to increase. The judge/sadist will punish the bad attackee but cannot be satiated. Feeding the internal fight escalates the war and generates greater hunger for more serotonin.

This sadomasochistic bond between internal personas is the primary human addiction, and serotonin is the abused substance. It underlies all the surface character addictions, such as alcoholism, drug addiction, gambling, dare-devilism, sexual addictions, frank sadomasochism, or sexual sadomasochism. It is the hidden force in all problematic character worlds, including narcissism and echoism.

People come to a therapist because they are suffering, due to the pain created by their symptoms. A psychiatric symptom is the signal that the sadomasochism of the cortical drama has crossed the threshold into serotonin depletion. Symptoms are the consequence of a diminished supply, like a fighting army whose supply lines have been cut off. Replenishing the serotonin allows the warring parties to fight on, escalating and fostering the internal war. Symptoms comprise the built-in crisis of problematic characterological worlds. "Crisis" in Chinese ideograms is drawn as the intersection of danger and opportunity. The patient's crisis provides an opportunity to address the real issue. The real issue is the problematic characterological play. Therapy is about dismantling the internal war and the recovery of the authentic self and the ability to love.

When a patient feels psychiatric symptoms, it is analogous to putting your hand on a hot stove. You receive a signal, which signifies harm. The temperature triggers a pain response that travels up your afferent nerves. You send an impulse down your efferent nerves to your muscles to get your hand out of there. I could treat this problem by injecting a drug to numb the pain nerves of your fingers. The upside to this solution is that it would take you out of pain and make you feel better. The downside is that you would keep your hand on the hot stove, feeling no pain. This solution would foster the pernicious situation and escalate the damage to your hand.

Here's the conventional fantasy about so-called depression and antidepressants: depression is a biochemical disease caused by a genetic insufficiency of the happiness substance, serotonin. Due to this disease of brain chemistry, you are genetically unable to produce enough of this happiness drug, so you feel "depressed." The treatment for this chemical "depression" would be to add in more joy juice—problem solved.

By pouring more serotonin (radiator fluid) into the synapses, one might (and this is a considerable *might*, at best) temporarily relieve the symptoms. Old antidepressants such as Elavil put more serotonin in the synapses. New antidepressants such as Prozac accomplish the same function by preventing the reuptake of serotonin in the synapses and creating a larger pool of serotonin on which to feed. However, what serotonin actually does is create a hardening of the self and an unconflicted selfishness. It intensifies an emotional hardening toward others. When fighting, you are hard and cruel. Your enemy is an "it," not a person. There is an attitude of coldness and hatred toward your adversary. This amplifies the emotional reality of the invisible sadomasochistic personas. The escalated hardness and coldness from adding in extra fuel for aggression is often experienced as feeling good. This is due to the fact that there is no *conflict* over hurtfulness. This has been numbed. To heal from cruelty, you have to feel the appropriate remorse and regret.

Real recovery is achieved by ending the war and allowing for the possibility of authenticity and love. Don't worry, a different cortical drama alters the chemical brain all by itself. The brain chemistry simply follows from the actuality of the internal drama. A drug fix, through a numbing psychogenic drug, estranges you from the possibility of change in your problematic play, and consequently from your best humanity and your best self.

Psychiatric symptoms are signals that need to be heard and felt to address the something that they signify. Adding serotonin to the system numbs out and overrides the signal. It is the sadomasochistic play in the theater of the brain that is the pernicious situation that damages the patient. This is what needs to be addressed. Our unique human story is the only subject of psychiatry — the cortical top-down characterological drama in the theater of the brain. The subject of our psychiatric endeavors is characterological reality and its perduring play.

How did Eddie's cortical drama become established in his brain? And what were the forces that shaped it? Before we move on to this we need to know something of his background.

Eddie was conceived during the Vietnam War, when his father was home on leave from the army. Father had been away for a year and was absent again for the following year. When Eddie was born, Mother was a young woman, home alone, already taking care of a three-year-old and a one-year-old. She didn't want another child, but the pregnancy was born of marital obligation, patriotic duty, and God's will. Two years later, she was to have a fourth child. We know that her background was considerably problematic. Her own mother, at some point, had a psychiatric hospitalization for paranoia. Her father was a workaholic, who built a successful business with his brother. There were rumors that he was sexually inappropriate with female employees and female relatives.

Mother was a pretty but an emotionally removed, cold woman.

She prided herself in her aesthetic appreciation of the arts—classical music and modern art. She kept an orderly and tidy house. Her general demeanor was one of pursed lips. She considered herself superior and special, such that nothing was quite good enough for her. She was highly critical about almost everything. Evidently, her husband was a disappointment to her, as she'd married beneath herself. And her children never measured up to the "exceptional" and talented children of others. There clearly was no intimacy with her husband or emotional closeness with anyone, including her children. She didn't have any friends. Her superficial social life was borrowed from her outgoing husband's social circle.

Father was an ambitious, arrogant man who made his way from humble beginnings. He was very successful in business. He married his wife as a trophy, and was consumed with impressing her and everyone else with his accomplishments. He had an intense involvement with his church, although its main function appeared to be self-aggrandizement. And this wasn't limited exclusively to his religion. It was the pervasive theme of his life. He had a very high IQ but a very low emotional IQ, with no idea about or any concern for the emotional well-being of anyone but himself. This, of course, included his children. In addition, he had an unacknowledged drinking problem. He was ashamed of his own parents due to their lower-class status. Consequently, Eddie barely knew his paternal grandparents and spent almost no time with them, even though they lived but a half hour away. Eddie's grandmother was a crusty, domineering woman, much like Eddie's father in personality. Eddie actually was somewhat frightened by her. His grandfather was removed and passive. He read the newspaper.

THE STORY
OF EDDIE

5

IN THE BEGINNING
Eddie Is Conceived; Life in the Womb

FOR INFANT-EDDIE TO BE FULLY cooked and ready to take out of the oven, we must set the timer to nine months. It all began when Eddie's mother released an egg from her ovary, one of the four hundred thousand she carried from birth. Eddie-egg then traveled from her abdominal cavity into a fallopian tube. Unless fertilization were to take place within the next twenty-four hours, Eddie-egg would wither and die.

As it happened, Mother had sexual intercourse with Eddie's father that night. Out of the sixty million sperm that entered and swam through Mother's vagina, cervix, uterus, and fallopian tube, it was Eddie-sperm that won the great race. It penetrated the membrane of Eddie-egg and injected its DNA. And so the DNA of those two meiotic cells hooked up, and we got Eddie—a one-celled living organism—a zygote.

Eddie' life began as a result of a membrane-boundary violation, the penetration of the Eddie-egg cell membrane. A boundary violation usually damages or kills an invaded cell or organism. There are only two exceptions to this in nature—when a sperm penetrates an egg to inject its DNA, and when a virus invades a cell to inject its DNA or RNA. (The viral DNA then takes over the cell's machinery to produce new viruses.) In contrast with the boundary violation that gave Eddie life, any violation of his boundary from then on would cause him damage. And unfortunately, as we will see, Eddie will be damaged by boundary violations within the year.

Eddie, as a zygote, was a biological organism and would remain so throughout his intrauterine transformations and for the rest of his life. As such he maintained himself as an alive organism within his intact cell membrane, and went about his cellular business. There is a set of processes that characterize how organisms function and interact with their environment that was fully present and operational in rudimentary and undifferentiated form in zygote-Eddie. To exemplify these central principles that are prototypical for biological life, we will turn to zygote-Eddie's distant cousin, a fellow one-celled organism, an ameba.

The ameba enacts its life functions, its *doings*, under the direction of its DNA. As *control central* its DNA effectively keeps the ameba going in its life and creates progeny. This carrier of order creates, gives form to, and directs the living organism. (Surprisingly, despite its simplicity, different strains of amebas have from one hundred to two hundred times more DNA than humans.) The ameba has a membrane boundary where it maintains an inner milieu. Within its boundary it is intrinsically alone. Its membrane not only separates the ameba from its sea environment, but it also connects it to that environment. It is contained within and related to its environment at all times.

The processes that the ameba manages at its membrane are essential for its living and thriving. There the ameba breathes, the ameba eats, the ameba excretes. For breathing, it transports O_2 across its membrane by osmosis from the sea into its internal milieu. (For future purposes, I will call this process *introjection*—"to throw inside.") Then it transports CO_2 back across its membrane from its inner milieu back out to sea. (I refer to this process as *projection*—"to throw outside."). For eating, the ameba engulfs and surrounds its prey by a membrane bubble. It projects enzymes into this bubble to digest its food. Then it introjects the nutritive molecules across its membrane into its internal milieu. There it synthesizes and creates new molecules—proteins, DNA, and others. The waste products are expelled back out to sea.

The DNA code not only operates the executive functions of the cell, but directs the ameba's other major work—it creates progeny. It propagates itself. Its DNA reproduces new generations of amebas by replicating itself and putting this code inside new ameba cell membranes that it manufactures. Hence, we have new amebas.

The life processes of the ameba, as a living organism, are distinguishable from inert and dead things. By virtue of being alive, the ameba "is." There is an "is-ness" to this living, surviving, propagating organism. This is a property of all living organisms. Now clearly, as the ameba has no brain, it does not have consciousness. It executes its functions automatically. It obviously doesn't think or feel or see. It doesn't plan or visualize, and it is not aware. It has no memory. The ameba clearly doesn't know itself. It just *is*. Yet its DNA executes its life functions in an orderly way, which direct the complexities of its living cellular operations. This "is-ness," which has no actual consciousness, is the rudimentary form of the *being* of an organism. When an ameba dies, it no longer exists as a living organism. It becomes just inert matter. It no longer "is"; it "was."

In the beginning zygote-Eddie was floating free in a fallopian sea. A membrane separated him from his fallopian environment, where he was inviolably alone. At the same time, it connected him to that environment. His initial work was the creation of progeny cells. But in this he differed from his ameba ancestor. When Zygote-Eddie replicated himself, under the direction of human DNA, his progeny cells adhered together, and he became a multicelled organism. And more importantly, he didn't just replicate similar cells. His progeny cells started morphing into different types of cells, creating various cell lines and organs. This is called *morphogenesis*—change in form, change in shape.

Morphogenesis is the most prodigious feature of the workings of Eddie's DNA. Morphogenesis will take place all throughout his life and will be at the center of our attention. Eddie was very, very busy morphing. In short order, this one-celled organism morphed into a multicelled trophoblast. Over the next five days trophoblast-Eddie traveled from the fallopian tube into Mother's uterus, and morphed into a blastocyst. At this point, when only a week old, blastocyst-Eddie secreted an enzyme that broke down the wall of his mother's uterus, where he embedded himself. This is *implantation*—blastocyst-Eddie was now adhered to his mother's uterine wall.

Implantation is the first great transformation in the relation between Eddie and his mother. This membrane connection between blastocyst-Eddie and the wall of his mother's uterus established a literal *attachment* between them. It is the beginning of an attachment that will remain, in one form or another, for the rest of their lives. The state of their attachment will shift in relation to the changing forms of Eddie's morphogenesis. This ongoing *dance of self and other* will unfold all the way to Eddie's adulthood and will be the second major focus of our attention.

Blastocyst-Eddie differentiated into two layers of cells. These cell lines would later become the different organs and tissues of his body. The inner layer, the endoderm, would morph into his intestinal system and the lungs. The outer layer would divide itself into two additional layers—a peripheral layer, the ectoderm; and a deeper layer, the mesoderm. The ectoderm would morph into his skin, his nervous system, and his sense organs—his eyes, ears, and nose. In turn, the mesoderm would morph into his bones, muscles, heart, and blood vessels.

At implantation, blastocyst-Eddie turned into an embryo. As such he began morphing furiously. At one point, embryo-Eddie was without a heart, and then one was beating. (The obstetrician heard it through his stethoscope.) In conjunction with his heart, he morphed some of his cells into a circulatory system and blood cells. Even though embryo-Eddie didn't really go through every stage of evolutionary history, in a rough sense he did recapitulate phylogeny. After beginning as an ameba, he morphed into an invertebrate. Then he grew a spine and became a fish. His gill arches would later morph into facial and throat muscles that would be used for talking in a couple of years. Then he turned into an amphibian. Eddie had a tail, and then it was gone. But he did get arms and legs. Primitive organ systems came and went and changed and migrated and got supplanted and reused. Brain tissues and nerves appeared and developed.

Meanwhile, back at the site of implantation, Eddie elaborated his attachment to his mother—the special membrane connectedness—by morphing a fetal placenta. His fetal placenta was, in fact, the other half of his body. He morphed a two-layered membrane that encircled him, the outer layer being the chorion and the inner layer, the amniotic sac—his fetal skin. This was filled with fluid to create an hospitable, protective environment. It provided shock-absorber protection, moisture, and maintained a constant temperature.

The site of attachment, where the fetal placenta adhered to the cells of the maternal placenta, was elaborated into Eddie's avenue for eating, breathing, and waste disposal. There, he morphed a mass of tiny blood vessels, which lay very close to the tiny blood vessels of the maternal placenta. At the placental attachment, food molecules and oxygen were transported from his mother's blood vessels to Eddie's. They were projected by mother and introjected by Eddie. Eddie's waste products and CO_2 were transported in the opposite direction. He projected them outside of him, where they were introjected and removed by the maternal placenta. Eddie and his mother retained membrane integrity at this attachment. He morphed an umbilical cord with two arteries and a vein, which connected the fetal placenta to the circulatory system of the rest of his body.

Mother's uterus was Eddie's total life-sustaining environment. This smooth-muscled internal organ was not mapped in her cortex. It was controlled purely by her subcortical brain. As a result, there was a constant seamless provision and responsiveness to Eddie by its autonomic and automatic operations. Her consciousness did not play a role in her maternal provision.

Likewise, Eddie was entirely contained inside his mother's womb. This began a legacy of *holding*, that like *attachment* would change form but continue for the rest of his life. His containment in the womb provided physical protection, proper temperature maintenance, and mobility (e.g., if there was danger from a lion, his mother would run away, and Eddie would go with her. Considerably later, Eddie would use his own legs, some time after he'd grown some.)

After two months of morphing furiously, Eddie approached more discernible human form. He was no longer an embryo recapitulating the history of life, he was now a fetus. As a fetus, his morphogenesis over the next seven months continued to be staggering. All of his internal organs materialized and developed. Fetal morphogenesis was geared toward the next major attachment transformation—life after birth. Eddie's morphogenesis was an enactment of body. He was body and nothing but body.

The most active locus of fetal morphogenesis was Eddie's brain. Throughout his entire seven-month fetal period, Eddie produced, on average, three million brain cells per minute. At peak times, his neural cell replication would take just an hour and a half! By adulthood, his brain would be composed of a trillion cells, a hundred billion of which would be neurons. Not surprisingly, half of Eddie's DNA was devoted to the development of his brain. His brain was body. His brain morphogenesis was body.

The morphogenesis of Eddie's fetal brain was extraordinary. Neural tissues developed from ectoderm cells. They morphed into the neural tube and then his primitive brain and peripheral nerves. These brain cells migrated and continued to differentiate into the various parts of his brain. The cells of his cortex aligned themselves through six orderly migrations, all sequenced from DNA directions. After these very active cell migrations, his individual neurons morphed further, sending out long axons and dendrites (receptor extensions) to hook up its trillions of connections to other neurons all throughout his cortex and all the way down his spinal column. These processes continued throughout his fetal development.

Then his neurons secreted myelin, a fatty tissue insulation sheath around his axons, which speed up nerve impulses up to a hundred times faster. (The pattern of myelinization would accompany the developing functionality of his maturing brain, and would continue on until Eddie was an adult. The frontal lobes, which process intention and coordinate feeling for judgment, would be the last part of the brain to myelinate. Eddie, as a college student, hadn't yet finished his frontal lobe myelinization when he began therapy with me.)

The final aspect of fetal-Eddie's brain development was the hooking up of connections between his cortical neurons via the synapses. Each dendrite may have as many as thirty thousand synapse connections that use a hundred possible neurotransmitters. The neuronal mapping all over his cortex and the rest of his brain utilized trillions upon trillions of synaptic connections. These synapses began to form in fetal-Eddie at about the fifth month of pregnancy. The neuronal mapping continued to establish itself throughout the rest of his intrauterine life.

Eddie's brain now took over as "control central" for directing his fetal life. His subcortical brain developed and established its operations. It managed and maintained his autonomic functions and his internal milieu—the regulation of every tissue, every organ, and all the smooth muscle in his body.

Eddie's extraordinarily complex and rapid morphogenesis took him from a one-celled organism through the various species of evolutionary history, all the way to a fully developed human infant. But morphogenesis was not just restricted to Eddie's embryonic and fetal stages. It would continue for the rest of his life, through his infancy, childhood, adolescence, adulthood, and old age. After birth, it would take place at a progressively slower rate, except for speeded-up transformational periods—at his puberty, and much later at involution. To the naked eye, Eddie's body as a child would appear to be unchanging and static. But it was actually in a continuous state of slow morphogenesis, too slow to be noticeable. If we could watch Eddie's transformations as a time-lapse movie, we could see the changes unfold. Eddie, at twenty-one, was seventy-two inches long and weighed in at 170 pounds. This is the same creature who once was twenty inches long and weighed in at eight pounds. This bald baby boy will soon have a head of brown hair, and then it'll be white hair, and finally Eddie will be bald once again.

Eddie's DNA directed a fetal morphogenesis that was species-specific—he wasn't going to mature into a sparrow or a schnauzer. His DNA was also specific in creating a unique individual—Eddie. His being was as unique as his fingerprint. If, during the intercourse of Eddie's conception, a different sperm out of the sixty million had won the great race, he would have been a different being—his gender, the features of his face, the color and texture of his hair, his athletic ability, his musical ability, his mimicry ability, his height, the shape of his teeth, his mathematical intelligence, his sense of direction, his aesthetic intelligence, the contours of his feet, the color of his eyes, whether he would be an auditory or visual reader, his temperament, his orientation toward inwardness or engagement with others, the smell of his head as a baby, and his balding pattern later. Eddie was an indivisible whole. His body, his brain organization, and his consciousness were all one. His unique being wasn't the sum of its parts. It simply was the whole organism itself—Eddie.

Fetal-Eddie had been held and protected inside the womb. His attachment at the placental membranes had provided full, seamless responsive provision. Within this safe harbor, Eddie had transformed from a zygote into a human baby in nine short months. His fetal work was done. Eddie was fully cooked. He was ready to come out of the oven. The timer was ringing.

However, with the next great shift in the dance of self and other—birth—things were about to change dramatically.

6

AND ON THE SECOND DAY
Eddie's Birth ... And the
Beginning of Consciousness

EDDIE'S MOTHER WAS UP ON a ladder, cleaning the kitchen ceiling, when her water broke. She was annoyed at the interruption—and the mess. The "water" splashing onto the floor was actually amniotic fluid composed of Eddie's urine. It had been contained within his fetal skin, the amniotic sac. His ruptured fetal skin was about to be shed, leaving his baby skin underneath.

Eddie's imminent birth would be the first of the two momentous transformations of this chapter. The second one, as we shall see, would be the birth of his consciousness, which would take place about six weeks later.

It was time. And Eddie would not be deterred. He had been morphing furiously toward this moment for nine months. His metamorphosis was complete. His respiratory system, his heart and circulatory system, his gastrointestinal system, and his evolving brain were all primed and ready to go. His mother's womb had been Eddie's total world for holding and provision. At birth, he would shed his fetal skin and sever his old attachments. Eddie would emerge as his new infant body. But he would not be left to his own devices. New and differentiated avenues of holding and attachment between him and his mother would be restored.

At birth, the bones in his head were not yet fused. His skull needed to be malleable to go through the narrow passageway of the birth canal. Bone fusion would wait until later. His pertinent neuromuscular systems had gotten prepared for mouth eating and were mapped in his brain for automatic suckling. His suckling muscles were in shape, five times stronger than adult jaw muscles. The very design of his infant face was contoured for breast-feeding, having morphed into its breast-suckling design—a squished-in chin and flattened nose.

Eddie's lungs were now ready for oxygen to cross the cell membrane at his alveoli for lung breathing. Fetal-Eddie had been busy dissolving the hyaline membrane, which had been covering his developing lung tissues, to allow for oxygen exchange. Soon, he would be breathing on his own, rather than from his old membrane hookup at the placenta.

His heart was likewise at the ready. It had been beating for months and circulating his blood. But his fetal cardiovascular system was different from a baby's. Fetal blood did not need to circulate through his inactive and immature lungs because it was getting oxygenated at the placenta. It just needed to be pumped directly throughout his body. Consequently, there was a hole in the wall between his right and left atria called the foramen ovale. This was a passageway for the blood to bypass his not-ready-for-prime-time lungs. Eddie had morphed a flap of heart tissue that was ready to seal off this foramen at his first breath. This then would allow the right side of the heart to pump the blood into his soon-to-be-opened lungs.

The fetal morphogenesis of Eddie's brain had been staggering. Cortical mapping for touch, vision, hearing, taste, and smell had already begun. He had been laying down tracks, myelinating, and attaching synapses in the sensory areas in preparation for life outside the womb. His sensory cortex was at the ready for utilizing his senses to map and give order to his new post-birth sensory experience of the world. Likewise, neuromuscular mappings for suckling and some basic arm and leg movements were in place.

(For the purposes of this discussion, we will temporarily take a detour from Eddie's actual life in order to illuminate the ordinary processes leading up to the creation of consciousness. Hence, we will treat Eddie as if he had been cared for by a good-enough mother. Later, this will be contrasted with his actual circumstances.)

Back to Mother—her contractions had begun. She and Eddie's father raced to the hospital, where the contractions grew more and more painful. Eventually, she couldn't take it anymore. She cried. She screamed, "I can't do this! Take me home, now! You did this to me!" The intense pain broke her will. But soon enough she pulled herself together and finished labor as a renewed and formidable woman. (She was broken emotionally during a phase of labor called transition. Transition pain isn't linked to a specific physiological uterine event. It is built into the process. Transition always happens. It always breaks the mother.) Finally, her contractions subsided. They had finished their work of opening the cervix and thinning its tissues. Suddenly Mother felt a tremendous urge to push.

The moment was at hand ... the top of a head surfaced ... then the head, with a face that no one had ever seen before. Shoulders emerged ... and Eddie slithered out, a glistening umbilical cord trailing behind. The cord was cut. With no oxygen, it was breathe or die. There was quiet in the delivery room, as all held their own breath, waiting ... Eddie cried. He breathed! They all breathed. There was laughter in the delivery room. For his entire life, Eddie's breathing had been placental-umbilical. He shifted to his newly operational diaphragm/lung system, and it worked. We know that egg-Eddie and sperm-Eddie had been alive cells. And Eddie was an alive organism as a zygote, embryo, and fetus. But his autonomous life as a baby did not begin until his first breath from his own lungs. Symmetrically, his autonomous life would end at his last breath.

Newborn Eddie was a little misshapen and funny-looking because his head had gotten crushed when it went through the bony passageway of Mother's birth canal. He had a hematoma on his forehead. Eddie was cleaned off, and very soon he was in Mother's arms.

Fetal-Eddie actually took the journey down the birth canal to the outside world in two trips. We have just seen part one. Soon after Eddie came out, Mother delivered the placental body. Despite the fact that throughout his entire life, his placenta had been the vehicle for his all-important attachment to his mother for protection and provision, from the obstetrical point of view, his soon-to-be-discarded placenta was already relegated to the status of "afterbirth."

While delivering the afterbirth, Mother's own placental tissues were torn away from her underlying endometrium, which ruptured her uterine blood vessels. She started to bleed. She put Eddie to her breast, where he began to suckle. This triggered Mother's pituitary to secrete oxytocin into her bloodstream. The oxytocin tightened up the smooth muscle of her uterus, which squeezed and closed off the ruptured blood vessels in the organ he had just vacated. Eddie's first feeding stopped his mother's bleeding. It helped restore the intactness of her boundary and saved her life.

Eddie's birth was painful and dangerous for both Eddie and his mother. One might ask the philosophical question, "Why is childbirth so painful?" Of course, there's no real answer. But this we know: birth was the first great boundary shift between Eddie and his mother in his journey to independent adult existence. Eddie went from containment and physical membrane attachment inside his mother to autonomous life outside her body, where new forms of attachment and holding would be established. For Mother, this emptying and the severing of membrane attachments took place in her uterus. This wrenching, monumental transition was physical. Consequently her pain was physical uterine pain deep inside her body. Mother's birth experience was one of physical pain and getting broken, followed by a sense of renewal and restoration.

Birth was the first enactment, and most major of the changes, in holding and attachment that will accompany every step of Eddie's growth to follow. Eddie will go on morphing. He will take control over new independent functions, while Mother will relinquish them and re-establish new avenues of attachment. The pain of labor and birth prefigures what will transpire at every step of Eddie's growth and differentiation. Childbirth is more than a metaphor for Mother's pain at separation and loss throughout the boundary shifts that lie ahead. It serves as a paradigm for what will take place in the ongoing dance of self and other. All of the transitions that lie ahead will prove to be disruptive and painful. From now on, as Eddie continues to grow and change, Mother's pain will be emotional.

It is as if, by the pain of childbirth, nature is saying to Mother, "Let me introduce you to child rearing. You've just come through the biggie. Childbirth foreshadows the pain of growth and loss that is to follow. This is the worst of it. The rest won't be quite as bad, with the possible exception of adolescence. Any questions?"

Birth itself, for Mother, wasn't just a membrane boundary transition. Mother had carried Eddie in her womb for nine months. She had been full with Eddie inside. Now she was empty of him. Soon she would hold him once again in her arms. There was an additional pain. It was not a physical pain: it was the emotional pain of loss. This would be so for each boundary transition throughout the rest of Eddie's development. For Mother to move on to a new attachment, she had to mourn the loss. Mourning is the vitamin of growth. If you have any questions about this, check out whether mothers are laughing or crying when they drop off their children on the first day of nursery school.

If we look into our time-lapse camera, we will see Eddie's morphogenesis take him from the womb to Mother's holding arms, and from her holding arms to off by himself. He rolled over. He sat. He crawled. He walked. He walked away, following his curiosity. He turned back to see Mother watching him. He saw that she was. He was carried in her holding gaze. He went off again, out of sight. He no longer needed to check in on her gaze. It was inside of him. He carried her, carrying him in her gaze. He carried her in his heart. She is still there.

At every step of Eddie's morphogenic growth, Mother would hold him once again in a new and differentiated way. Each boundary shift was accompanied by the pain of loss. She went from a full womb to an empty womb; from an empty womb to holding arms; from holding arms to empty arms; from empty arms to holding him in her gaze; from her gaze to Eddie out of sight and to Eddie held in her heart. He is still there.

A similar process would take place regarding the loss and re-establishment of their provision attachments. Eddie at Mother's breast fulfilled the first boundary shift between them for feeding and eating. This established a new form of membrane-membrane feeding. For all mammals, breast-feeding is a transitional stage, a halfway station, in the journey toward a more differentiated independence for eating. A new attachment circuit was established that looped through both of their bodies. Unlike with placental feeding, however, the membranes were now detachable. Eddie's mouth muscles suckled at Mother's areola. This stimulated her pituitary to release oxytocin, which we are already familiar with. It traveled through her blood to her breasts, where it triggered the milk ducts to empty into the milk sinuses. This is called the *letdown*. Eddie's jaw and tongue muscles expressed the milk (actually colostrum at this point) out of the milk sinuses into his mouth and down into his newly operational stomach and intestines. There he secreted enzymes to digest (i.e., break down) the colostrum into smaller molecules, which were transported across his intestinal membrane into his blood vessels. This process was similar to Eddie's food introjection so recently operational at his discarded placenta. The newly restored mammalian eating arrangement between them was still autonomic and automatic body processes for both Eddie and his mother. It was directed by their subcortical brains and operated without conscious cortical control.

The subsequent boundary shifts they established for eating would no longer be body membranes like the first one. Let us take out our time-lapse camera once again. We have just seen the shift from internal placental feeding to external breast-feeding. Eddie then shifted from the breast to bottles, to sipping cups, to drinking from a glass, to solid food, to being spoon-fed, to holding the spoon and feeding himself, to solid food cut by his mother, to cutting his own food. Mother's choreography was reciprocal. As Eddie continued to establish more independent internal control, she relinquished control and re-established a more external provision. Mother continued her later form of food provision by shopping for, paying for, and cooking his food until Eddie was on his own and provided for himself.

The most important arena of Eddie's morphogenesis continued to be his brain. As a newborn infant, Eddie's neuromuscular capacities were rapidly developing. A major focus of Eddie's morphogenesis was in the realm of gaining muscular control over his body. During this time, he coordinated his neck muscles to hold and turn his head. His arm coordination and grasp developed. The sensory and motor circuits were not random happenings but were in the service of developing internal control, in the service of his intention. All of this was mapped in his cortex. Higher and higher levels of cortical order were established. Sensory mappings were in process to create and organize representations of the outside world.

However, the most important aspect of Eddie's brain maturation, which is at the heart of our attention, are those mappings that flowed from his amygdala and limbic system. The function of fetal-Eddie's early amygdala and limbic system was to map his survival interactions with his maternal environment. This brain circuitry linked the body, hormones, subcortical brain, and the cortex—the amygdala for impulses of fear and pleasure; the hippocampus for gluing memories; the cingulate gyrus for attention and autonomic functions, such as heart rate and blood pressure; the hypothalamus for regulating the autonomic nervous system; and the thalamus, the relay station from the subcortex.

The morphogenesis of his limbic system had been progressive and ongoing throughout fetal/newborn Eddie's development. By the time he was born, these limbic circuits had matured and were sufficiently organized for his foundational appetites and rudimentary emotions of fear, anger, alarm, sadness, satisfaction, pleasure, hunger, and thirst. Eddie had been mapping his maternal attachment, responsiveness, and provision experience through his limbic system since early in fetal life.

Fetal-Eddie's womb environment had been automatic, and autonomic. As such it was seamlessly responsive. It was mapped through the warm and gentle pathways of oxytocin into his cortex (Lily and kitty world). However, his situation changed as a result of the tumult of birth, and thereafter life as a newborn was very different. Eddie's maternal environment was no longer seamlessly safe and responsive. Birth itself had cast Eddie into an unfamiliar state of major trauma, as well as life-or-death distress. Mother held newborn Eddie in her warm and tender arms and brought him to her breast. Eddie was held once again in a new way. He was quieted and soothed. He was intact. The holding and warmth previously supplied by the womb was re-established. The continuity of holding was unbroken. That oxytocin that Eddie's suckling stimulated not only let down his mother's milk and stopped her uterine bleeding: it would play one more important role in the relationship between Eddie and his mother. It also acted on her brain, where it stimulated the feelings of maternal love and tenderness. Eddie's own suckling amplified the tender love he received. The oxytocin did its job. The Eddie-Mother attachment was restored.

Infant Eddie's limbic system continued to map his new maternal environment into his cortex. But now things were somewhat different. His environment was no longer automatic. In this new world mini-disruptions were built in. When Eddie was startled by a loud noise, his arms and legs would flail. His heart pumped adrenaline, and he cried. This startle mapped a fight-or-flight response in his cortex (Lily and skunk world). He was restored by his mother's holding. Her responsive repair re-established, maintained, and mapped his well-being through oxytocin once again. (A well-delivered "boo" will elicit this startle effect in you and me as adults. We recover intactness by relying on our internal resources of self-soothing and self-holding, although an external hug helps.)

Eddie now felt hunger in his newly operational stomach. Hunger disrupted his sense of intactness and well-being. He cried. His cry was the call of distress. Mother responded. She brought him to her breast. Mouth to breast, Eddie hooked on and fed. Milk quieted the hunger. Mother's breast and her soft and tender arms stilled his distress. Eddie was whole and intact again. His well-being was maintained. All was reflected in his developing limbic-cortical mappings of experience.

Eddie's baby skin was his new membrane of attachment to Mother for the functions of holding, connection, and warmth. His skin experience of touch, holding, and warmth was actively mapped in subcortical as well as cortical circuits, mediated by the limbic system. Let's say Eddie was left in a cold room with insufficient clothing. This would generate distress, and he would lose his intactness. His limbic system would map this experience in his cortex. Alternatively, when dressed in warm, soft clothing, or with skin on skin, or the timely placement of a soft blanket, Eddie's limbic system would map it the other way.

Good-enough mothering repaired and restored Eddie's cohesion on an ongoing basis. Within Mother's responsive holding and care, Eddie flourished and thrived. I refer to it as "good enough," because there is no such thing as perfect responsiveness. It can't be, and it doesn't have to be. It only has to be good enough. Guided by maternal love, Mother remained the ongoing safe harbor of warmth and loving.

Eddie's morphogenic clock kept on ticking. It was time. One day when Eddie was six weeks old, Mother reached down into his cradle and picked him up to feed him. Something stirred in her chest. All of a sudden she was bursting with a feeling of tenderness and love. She looked at Eddie and he was looking at her. Something was different. She felt an actual feeling emanating from Eddie. It touched her. It was the feeling of Eddie.

During those six short weeks, Eddie's foundational appetites and rudimentary emotions had morphed to a sufficiently high level of order to crystallize into a feeling of tenderness and sweetness—the cohered *feeling of Eddie*. Yesterday there was no *feeling of Eddie*. And suddenly it was here. Yesterday, Eddie was simply an infant. Today, he is a human *being*. I refer to this *being, the feeling of Eddie,* as the *Authentic-Being*.

And so it began. Eddie's consciousness was born. His Authentic-Being was a persona in his rudimentary theater of consciousness. Eddie's Authentic-Being had no reference to an image of Eddie at all. It had no representational form. It was purely the feeling of his being. It was not knowable through the senses, thinking, or image-ination. It could not be seen. It was not an idea. It did not lend itself to being understood or comprehended. It would only touch and be touched by feeling. And it did. Morphogenesis had continued marching on. Eddie's Authentic-Being was a synthetic brain creation, which consolidated from sufficiently high levels of order in his limbic cortex.

A reader might say, "Six weeks? That sounds kind of arbitrary. What's so special about six weeks?" Simply put, six weeks is when it happened. The *feeling of Eddie* at that point was an actual presence. Prior to that, when Mother held Eddie in her arms, she did not actually feel anything from him. And then it happened. She was touched in feeling by his presence. This is the litmus test. Eddie was present

PSYCHOTHERAPY OF CHARACTER

as a feeling being. Mother had been predisposed to love Eddie at his birth, and she did. But now, with the presence of the feeling of Eddie, she fell in love with him. His feeling of tenderness and sweetness touched her, and her Authentic-Being and its feeling touched him. They resonated in feeling. Prior to this, mutual feeling was not possible.

Eddie's Authentic-Being was a persona in his rudimentary theater. And it didn't exist on its own. It arose in relation to an additional persona, the Loving Other. The mappings of Mother's responsive care in the womb, as well as her responsiveness during his first six weeks, consolidated into the feeling of a second persona. Likewise, the Loving Other was purely a feeling of a being and had no representational form. Eddie's theater coalesced with these two feelings of beings resonating together with loving feeling.

The coalescence of Eddie's consciousness was built into his ongoing morphogenic flow. It was no different from any of the other morphogenic transformations. At one point, embryo-Eddie had no heart, and then one day, he did. And it was beating. Likewise, baby Eddie had no Authentic-Being. And then one day, it was there—the feeling of Eddie. And you could feel him.

As we have seen, Mother's nurture up to this point was sufficiently holding and responsive. Neither abuse nor deprivation had come into play significantly. Consequently, Eddie's Authentic-Being was a direct creation of his nature, his genetic endowment, within the safe harbor of good-enough nurture. The unfolding of his morphogenesis created his Authentic-Being and his theater unadulterated by abuse or deprivation. Keep in mind that this extraordinary creation by his limbic cortex is just ordinary biology. It isn't unique to humans. You may notice its presence in kittens, puppies, and fawns.

Eddie's human-being life began with his birth in his theater of consciousness. He would inhabit his limbic-cortical theater and live through its synthetic illusions for the rest of his life. His Authentic-Being was his essential being and would remain so, inviolable, from now on. Likewise, it would be the basis of love, given and received, for the rest of his life. And it would underlie the more elaborated representational persona images of Eddie that future morphogenesis would create.

Prior to his consciousness, physical touch had been the exclusive avenue of holding between Eddie and his mother. With the beginning of consciousness, the resonant feelings of tenderness became the avenue of connection between them. This was the realm of feeling. The feeling of his Authentic-Being supplanted, and was the extension of, physical touch and holding. The very words that characterize feeling are lifted from the words for physical sensations. You physically *touch* me. Your feeling *touches* me. *Physical warmth* is comfort. *Emotional warmth* is comfort. *Sweetness* is the *taste* of mother's milk. *Sweetness* is the *feeling* of Eddie. *Tender* is a soft and delicate *texture*. *Tender* is a soft and delicate *feeling*. Physical softness is gentle to the *touch*. *Feeling* is softness itself.

When new and higher levels of cortical order supplant older forms of order, the earlier forms of established brain-body mappings remain intact and operative. Physical touch and its brain circuits are ongoing and retain enormous power. The body-brain mappings of physical touch remain present and operative throughout life. Touch generates powerful feelings in people of all ages and is an important component of intimacy and closeness. This can be emotionally confusing later in life, when physical touch without relationship love can easily be confused with loving. And even more important, sexuality, which is inherently connected to physical touch, can also be confused with loving closeness. In the absence of real intimacy, it is not love and can be misleading. Actual love is the feeling resonance between two Authentic-Beings.

The continuity of the seamless ongoing safe harbor for holding remained intact through the reattachment between Mother and Eddie after birth. The boundaries of connection then shifted at the birth of Eddie's consciousness. From then on, relatedness would proceed from his consciousness as feeling. The continuity of Eddie and Mother's attachment had been unbroken, and trust was maintained. It was in place from the beginning and continued on. Trust was not learned. It was the extension of the holding and responsiveness of the intact womb. It always was there—the chain was unbroken.

As we know, the preceding story of mothering during Eddie's first six weeks was not, in fact, Eddie's story. The reality of his post-birth maternal environment was quite different from our imaginary mother. Here is the real story ...

Eddie's mother was overwhelmed by Eddie's birth. She was already depleted by her two older children, especially a one-year-old who was still in diapers. She had no external resources—husband or family or friends. Most important, she didn't have any internal resources upon which to draw by dint of her own constricted and brittle personality. She had nothing to give to baby Eddie. It was her nature to carry on and meet her obligations dutifully, but with a resentful, cold discipline.

Eddie was bottle-fed. His mother delivered the cow milk to him every four hours, whether he was crying for it or not. She had read that "demand feeding" would spoil the baby. The four-hour schedule was the perfect solution. When he cried—ten minutes early, an hour early, two hours early—she let him cry it out in his crib. This was "good for him." Besides, she had so much to do, with the other children and all. She felt no inclination to pick him up and was relieved not to have to do so. The crying, however, was irritating.

In the matter of feeding, she was punctual. His sisters would be left to their own devices during his feedings. If one-year-old Clara needed to be changed, she had to wait. Mother boiled the glass bottles and plastic nipples. She heated the milk and measured the amount to be delivered. She followed the prescribed directions. Mother held Eddie on her lap with her stiff cold hands and held the bottle. His very need for attention depleted her. Her resentment was present in the brusqueness of her touch. She blamed Eddie for the out-of-control, noisy chaos of the other children who were waiting for her attention. She performed the feeding with stoic perfection and prided herself in a job well done—the perfect mother.

After he drained the bottle, Eddie would cry out from the gas pain of these molecules being broken down in his newly operational gastrointestinal system. The insistent crying would irritate Mother and throw her schedule off for the rest of her chores. Burping was an unpredictable process. The pounding for burps was a little too hard, but Eddie was keeping her from her appointed rounds. Occasionally, the fussing was too annoying, and she might give him a shake to quiet him down. When that didn't work, a slap would do the trick.

At best, the feeding was dutiful and mechanical. It was, in fact, cold and harsh, with some violence. Mother would rather be elsewhere. Eddie was busy mapping the actuality of this experience in his cortex under the direction of his limbic system. Survival, in this cold world, was associated with fight-or-flight and startle, not so much oxytocic warmth and gentleness.

With hunger, Eddie's sense of intactness and well-being was disrupted. When hungry, he cried. But he hadn't checked out the four-hour clock. He cried and cried and cried. There was no response. He was alone. There was nothing. His cries turned into screams of angry demand, screams of terror. His state of distress continued unabated. All of this was mapped through his limbic system. Sometimes, he would stop crying, much to his mother's satisfaction. This was not because all was well but because nothing was forthcoming. He gave up. It was hopeless. This was apathy. He didn't die. He just went on from there. It was mapped. Eventually, it was time for the next feeding. He was in brusque hands, harsh hands, cold hands, the nipple forced into his mouth, roughness—all of this was mapped. His attachments were inhospitable. His limbic system activated distress responses, and attachment was mapped accordingly. Trust, the continuity of responsiveness, was breeched. Distrust, unlike trust, was learned. It came from Mother's inhospitable environment, where her provision was insufficient, unreliable, unresponsive, depriving, and cruel.

Now, in terms of Eddie's experience leading up to the birth of consciousness, we have good news and bad news. First the good news. Fortunately for Eddie, his mother's problematic impacts, albeit very consequential, turned out to be insufficient to interfere with the coalescence of his Authentic-Being, as well as the Loving Other persona. The true measure of abuse and deprivation for these weeks had been insufficient to warp Eddie's original play. He came out of it okay, with an intact Authentic-Being and Loving Other.

How can that be? The evolution of Eddie's Authentic-Being took place throughout fetal life, as well as the beginning of infant life. The lion's share of the development of Eddie's consciousness was as a fetus. During this time, the limbic system mediated the actual experience of Eddie's womb-survival environment. As we have seen, holding and provision was totally body/membrane and completely automatic and responsive. Eddie's intactness and well-being were well maintained. Because there wasn't any deprivation, unresponsiveness, or abuse to speak of, there wasn't much fight-or-flight limbic mapping taking place. Consequently, during his developmental fetal life, Eddie's limbic cortex was mapped in a state of well-being in the context of warmth and responsiveness. This prefigured an intact Authentic-Being and Loving Other.

Likewise, as a newborn, Eddie continued on, for the most part, in a relatively similar fashion. Eddie's response to his maternal environment was still mostly subcortical and automatic body. We have just seen that his mother's provision was now, to some degree, subject to her character. Fortunately, her inhospitable care made only a partial contribution to his overall experience, and didn't override the core of his mappings.

Newborn Eddie's untoward maternal experience was certainly mapped. It cast a shadow on his Authentic-Being and Loving Other, creating an associated feeling tone of a dark and foreboding emotional landscape. But it was insufficient to seriously damage them. Despite his mother's treatment of Eddie, he did forge an intact Authentic-Being and Loving Other in the circuits of his limbic-cortical mappings.

It sometimes happens that when a mother's problematic character is too harmful during this period, it can damage the intactness of the forming Authentic-Being itself. This would leave the child subject to a psychotic dissolution during adolescence. Eddie's Authentic-Being was somewhat vulnerable but not enough to prefigure a psychosis. Thus, his Authentic-Being was safely formed and grounded in his intact theater of consciousness.

Now, for the bad news ... From now on, Mother's pernicious treatment of Eddie would affect his developing theater of consciousness in a major way. His limbic mapping of unadulterated deprivation and abuse will cause serious and substantial damage to the formation of his emerging representational self and the plays consolidating in his consciousness. As we will see, "as the twig is bent, so grows the tree."

7

AND ON THE THIRD DAY
Eddie's Story Takes a Dark Turn

EDDIE NOW HAD CONSCIOUSNESS. HIS astonishing morphogenesis from a zygote to a sentient being had taken place in just nine months and six weeks. If you held him in your arms, you would feel tenderness. He would relate to you, and you to him, through a resonance of feeling that emanated from his Authentic-Being. His rudimentary consciousness was organized as a theater, composed of his Authentic-Being and Loving Other personas relating together by a feeling of tenderness. Both personas had no representational form. Each was pure feeling, the feeling of a being. Now and for the rest of his life, Eddie would inhabit his theater of consciousness. The crystallization of his Authentic-Being in his limbic cortex created his initial sense of self. From now on, he would relate to the world and process his experience as this "self" in his brain.

Over the next two to three years, something even more astonishing would happen in Eddie's theater of consciousness. As his limbic system continued to map his interactions with his maternal-survival environment, higher and higher levels of order were becoming established in his cortex. Over time, this would be sufficient to create symbolic form and representational images. By virtue of this staggering morphogenesis, his rudimentary theater would be transformed into a fully representational theater—organized as plays; composed of plots, stage sets, and landscapes; with a *dramatis personae* of three-dimensional images of personas, who relate together with differentiated feelings. Eddie's "self" would no longer be formless but fully representational. The appearance of the formed symbolic images of Eddie's characterological drama emerge in parallel with language. They both reflect the same extremely high level of cortical order necessary to create symbolic form. In language, we have words and sentences. In the cortical theater, we have the limbic-mapped representational images of self and other, with coherent states of emotional relatedness.

Eddie's evolving play would now be written as his limbic system digested the actualities of his mother's nurture. To show how this takes place, I will tell three fictitious versions of the story of Eddie breast-feeding, each resulting in a very different play.

The First Version

One day when Eddie was four months old, a glistening white tooth crowned at his gumline. Mother discovered him with two fingers in his mouth, crying inconsolably. When Eddie cut his first tooth, it hurt. He didn't understand this dysphoric experience of unrelenting pain. It was new, disruptive, and untoward. As it broke the boundaries of comfort, Eddie's well-being was not maintained. Life was not seamless anymore. It was painful. Teething was a built-in morphogenic disruption.

Mother was upset by his distress and gave him a few teething rings to chew on. A frozen bagel seemed to work the best. She dabbed her fingers with whiskey and rubbed his inflamed gums. She held him tight. His distress was soothed. His intactness was restored and maintained.

Eddie morphed a mouthful of teeth. They would be used in the service of self-sufficiency — the chewing of solid food. Teeth also carry their legacy as a biting weapon. Chewing and biting are part of the natural chain of growth and maturation. With his new teeth, Eddie would explore their dimensions.

One morning when Eddie was breast feeding, he came up with a good idea. With a devilish gleam in his eye, he bit down ... hard. Mother screamed in pain. She pulled him off with a loud "no!" Eddie cried pathetically as if he were the one who had been bitten. Soon enough, the crying stopped and he was ready to continue his meal. Mother put him back on her breast. He fed for a while, and then he did it again. First the gleam, then the chomp, then the pain, Mother's rebuke ... and more pathetic crying.

With his powerful jaw and mouthful of teeth, it was built in that Eddie would bite. All breast-feeding babies do. His biting impulse was followed by his intention, and then he did it. Obviously, the bite violated the boundary of his mother's sensitive tissues. It hurt—a lot. Her sensitive breast tissue is a built-in differentiating boundary.

The bite sent Mother through the roof. She pulled away. Her "no!" was an effective rebuke. It drew a line between his bite and her breast. By this reproach, Mother said "no" to her boundary being violated. In fact, she actually said a "yes" in the service of honoring her boundary. This was not an object lesson for its own sake. She was not setting a limit to artificially control baby-Eddie for his own good. His biting hurt and could not be ignored. To be an effective reproach, it required considerable aggression on Mother's part. It successfully overpowered the aggression of his bite, and broke him out of his biting state of mind. By virtue of her sufficient reproach, she insisted on respect for her boundary.

What actually transpired in Mother? The pain of the bite was not fun. It violated her tender membranes. When bitten, it is human nature to want to bite back—plus a little extra. "An eye for an eye, and a tooth for a tooth" is built into all of us. Mother's retaliatory impulse didn't make her a bad person. The retaliation wish is, by definition, a sadistic impulse—the intent to inflict hurt. It is the natural response to an attack and was put into her by being bitten. Obviously, to attack back would not have been a good idea. In order for Mother to rebuke effectively, she had to accept the flash of her wish to retaliate without acting on it. She was then free to exercise the considerable aggression of her "no!"

Mother's rebuke was assertive aggression, not sadistic aggression. Nonetheless it was uncomfortable for her to sit with the high degree of aggression necessary to direct a rebuke toward her baby in the first place. In addition, the rebuke aggression is easily confused with the activated impulse of sadistic retaliation aggression, and gets blurred with it. The intensity of both is high. Then, after she delivered the rebuke, she was forced to witness Eddie's pathetic crying, as if she had beaten him. Fortunately, she didn't feel guilt or, at least, not too much guilt. Her minor conflict did not interfere with her rebuke.

Mother was then free to genuinely engage Eddie in a loving way again. Without an effective rebuke, this wouldn't have been possible. Mother's reproach allowed her to bring Eddie back close, physically and emotionally, in a real way. Reproach, etymologically, means "to bring back close." It said "no" to the bite, not to baby-Eddie. It restored her genuine availability for relatedness through love and tenderness. This encompasses the central dynamic of child raising—boundaries and love. Breast-feeding was such an important vehicle for these negotiations between Eddie and his mother. (As a note, I want to be clear that I am not saying that a bottle-fed baby cannot be well raised. Loving responsiveness can certainly be established between mother and child with bottle feeding.)

As Mother established and maintained her boundary, Eddie learned the dimensions of his biting impulse. It got established in proper proportion, place, and function. The bite served as a vehicle by which Mother and Eddie negotiated their boundaries, and differentiated good aggression from sadistic aggression. This fostered and allowed Eddie to harness and modulate his good aggression. Aggression is not a dirty word. Eddie's wherewithal to take on his future life challenges will come from the freedom to exercise his good aggression.

Through good-enough mothering, Eddie eventually respected Mother's boundary and stopped biting her. By re-establishing their boundaries, they were able to retain relatedness through love. Throughout, Eddie mapped his experience—the bites, the rebuke, and the restoration of being close again—into his cortex through his limbic system. Mother's good-enough provision of boundaries and love fostered Eddie's well-being. As a result, a boundary-respecting and loving inner play was written, a story of a good-enough self and a loving mother.

The Second Version

Let's say Mother has sadism in her character. Eddie gets that gleam in his eye and bites. Mother retaliates with a slap in the face. This little jerk bit her, and he got what's coming to him. She'll teach him not to bite! He bites again—this time a smack, the next time a good shake will do the trick, then another slap. Mother was unconflicted and untroubled by her behavior. Eddie was bad, and he deserved to be taught a lesson he wouldn't forget. And she was just the one to do it.

In fact Mother's slaps actually inflamed a retaliatory impulse inside Eddie. He briefly suppressed his inflamed rage out of fear, but it then exploded. He bit again. Mother escalated her punishment. She slapped him again. This generated a sadistic discharge and sadistic contact with Mother. After a few rounds, Eddie got intimidated and suppressed his stoked-up rage. He learned his lesson and stopped biting. He submitted and acted "good" on the surface. All was mapped.

The scenario that was written into Eddie's developing inner story was sadomasochism. Eddie's "self" persona was written as bad, and the persona of "other" was written as mad. Relatedness was on the basis of rage attack. To retain relatedness and discharge his built-up sadistic aggression, sadomasochism was the substitute avenue of engagement. It was mapped as such by his limbic system. There was no mapping of having been brought back close, in loving.

Version Three

Mother has a masochistic character. She feels guilty about all aggression, both sadistic and assertive. She considers all aggression to be sadistic. In order for her to be a good and loving person, she must control and deny any aggression. She believes that a rebuke would be cruel. With a gleam in his eye, Eddie bites. But Mother is conflicted about her retaliatory impulse. It is not acceptable for her to feel any aggression toward baby Eddie. Unfortunately, this interferes with the provision of an effective and responsive rebuke. Therefore, his bite will have no consequences. Mother establishes that it is okay

for Eddie to hurt her. The absence of a rebuke actually communi-
cates, "Bite away, no problem!" She'll just take it.

Baby-Eddie will not honor a maternal boundary that hasn't been
upheld by his mother. The absence of a rebuke actually fosters more
biting. As a result Mother takes it and takes it. Eventually, she can't
take it any longer. She explodes and lashes out. Then she feels guilty
about her explosion and vows never to do that again. Consequently,
she won't rebuke at the next bite. Once again, this will foster the delivery of more bites. The pattern will repeat. Eddie bites; Mother feels
increasingly guilty about her own sadistic impulses and takes the
abuse all the more.

Of equal importance is that, in order to suppress her anger,
Mother withdraws. It's not possible to ignore being hurt. Due to her
withdrawal, she ceases to be genuinely emotionally available. Even
though she may behave correctly and appropriately on the surface,
it is false, albeit well-meaning behavior. Emotional withdrawal is
at least as problematic as sadistic retaliation. It means that Mother
cannot and does not genuinely bring Eddie back close. This is to be
distinguished from her guilty, good, "should" behavior. As a result,
Eddie is subject to periods of emotional withdrawal, alternating with
unpredictable sadistic retaliations, while everything looks good on
the surface. Meanwhile, on his side, Eddie counters the absence of
connectedness by getting substitute and compensatory relatedness
through biting. He will seek her attention via sadism, not though loving relatedness. In addition, biting becomes an avenue of punishing
Mother for her withdrawal.

Fairly soon, Mother will stop breast-feeding because baby-Eddie
is "a biter." Her punishment is to sever the loving connection of the
breast-feeding itself. And because his impulse to bite has been fostered, Eddie is in agreement that he is a biter, that he is bad. This
is congruent with what his mother believes and carries about him.
These sadistic currents were mapped by Eddie's limbic system into
his cortex, thereby writing a sadomasochistic play, similar to the one
written in relation to the sadistic mother but from the opposite direction. Eddie is bad, mother is mad though smiling, and substitute
engagement is sadistic.

We have seen three ways that Eddie's internal story could have been written. In each case his limbic system digested his mother's actual provision into his foundational play. Under the best of circumstances, mothering cannot be perfect. The presence of a protective, warm, timely, soothing, holding, maternal provision will always be, to some degree, unreliable and unresponsive. All children have to deal with adversity. There is plenty of it built into life, and there can never be an idyllic paradise. There are always life circumstances in the family that will affect mothering to one degree or another—death, sickness, divorce, unavailability due to preoccupation with others, work, the arrival of new children, demands of older children, psychiatric conditions, alcohol or drug abuse, miscarriages, war, and so forth.

However, baby Eddie was a not super-fragile being who was easily damaged by simple untoward experience. As with all babies, Eddie was very resilient. It actually takes a lot to damage a baby. The regular processes of growth and change in life always create disruption, and the resultant distress is manageable with good-enough mothering. With good-enough loving, Eddie and Mother get through it together. On the other hand, Eddie certainly did not need extra adversity. It is not true that if it doesn't kill you, it makes you stronger. The impact of nurture on the writing of Eddie's internal play flowed from the character of his mother in concert with life's exigencies.

These three stories of breast-feeding and biting are prototypical of how the play gets written through the limbic filtering of Eddie's maternal experience—to show how it all works. Let us now get back to Eddie's real story as it informed the writing of his actual play.

The Real Story

When Eddie teethed, his insistent crying was irritating to his mother. She did the right things with the wrong spirit. She gave him baby aspirin and applied bourbon to his inflamed gums. When this didn't work, it led to a slap or a shake to quiet him down. Otherwise, he was left to his own devices. He was never held by a soft warm body nor comforted with tenderness.

We know that Eddie was bottle-fed. The doctor instructed his mother that bottle feeding was superior and more sanitary. And she could control for the correct dosage of milk. Besides, holding and tenderness were not her strong suit. As we know, his feeding was administered with brusque hands, harsh hands, cold hands. Mother found body contact disgusting and dirty. All this was limbically mapped.

With his new teeth, Eddie tried out his bite on the plastic nipple. Plastic has no pain nerves, and he could bite as hard and long and often as he wanted. Since Eddie didn't hurt his mother's sensitive tissues, he did not bump into a "no!" He didn't have to modulate his aggression. Consequently, there was no limit to his biting. (On the good side, it did spare him from Mother's potential sadistic retaliations.) This also was limbically mapped.

Because he was the recipient of his mother's cruelty on an ongoing basis anyway, Eddie was already filled with a suppressed retaliation rage looking for an outlet. Consequently, biting the plastic became an avenue of discharge for that rage. Unmodulated biting fostered and exacerbated biting. Not only that, biting into an inanimate object was not satisfying. The purpose of biting is to have an impact, to inflict pain. With no satisfaction of impact, an intensification of frustrated biting ensued. This meant that Eddie's anger discharge went nowhere and felt impotent. It was limbically mapped.

The absence of reciprocal interaction between Eddie and his mother had important repercussions. Biting became an avenue of impotent, sadistic rage that had no limit. There was no responsive modulation of aggression through which Eddie and his mother would be brought back close, never mind that closeness was decidedly lacking in the first place. All was mapped.

As Eddie grew older, each new thing replayed and extended what came before. To his mother, his diapers were the source of dirtiness and disgust. He was dirty and disgusting, and he inflicted it on her. The cut of his jaw and the shape of his body were ugly. She despised the sight of him. When he didn't speak in full sentences by age one, he was stupid and embarrassing to her. She knew of other babies who were already verbal. He was the ongoing object of ridicule and shame. It was mapped as such.

The central horror of Mother's nurture was the absence of maternal love. From the beginning, she did not respond to his Authentic-Being at all. He was an "it." There was no genuine feeling from her and no feeling for him. Eddie's very need for her love and care was an unwanted and an "unwant-able" intrusion that drained her. Mother did not touch or hold Eddie with tenderness and warmth. This absence created a deprivation. Eddie adapted to his unrequited need for love with tears of rage alternating with withdrawal into apathy. But his solutions to a cold and unresponsive world could not effectively protect him. His ongoing well-being remained in distress. All was mapped.

Mother's actual contact with Eddie was rough, hard, and cold, both physically and emotionally. His experience of relatedness was as the recipient of pain and attack. His need for love did not disappear. In the absence of a loving and respectful something, however, Eddie attached to the substitute form of relatedness—abuse. Later, he would develop a taste for it.

Mother operated from the top-down processing of her character drama from her own cortical theater. For her, baby-Eddie was the projection screen of her internal play. He was the "bad" persona whom she judged as deserving of her attacks. She was not at odds with her own cruelty. She was "good," and he got what he deserved. The projected images of Mother's consciousness became consonant with Eddie's consolidating internal story.

The abuse and neglect by Eddie's mother stands in stark contrast to the care of a good-enough mother. Responsiveness and tenderness of feeling would have provided a safe harbor for Eddie's Authentic-Being to be at the center of his thriving and developing self. She would have related from her Authentic-Being to his. Likewise, with sufficient maternal love, the developing image of "other" would be deeply infused with love and would carry that resonance. The capacity for love and authenticity, all throughout life, derives from a play forged by maternal love. As we know, this was not to be Eddie's fate.

Even before his formless Authentic-Being crystallized in his rudimentary theater, the limbic-cortical mappings of Eddie's early experience had taken a dark turn. Nonetheless, his Authentic-Being did cohere undamaged. But now, his mother's abuse and neglect led to a much more problematic outcome as his representational play crystallized. The unadulterated abusive and depriving maternal environment was limbically mapped into his maturing cortex and colored his specific representational personas of self and other.

Eddie's unique characterological self, as well as his fully representational play of consciousness, was formed. The basic story was written. It consolidated and took form as a textured and nuanced sadomasochistic drama. Eddie was bad. The persona of Mother was mad. She dished out sadistic punishment. He deserved it. The punishment fit the crime. There was no relatedness on the basis of respect and tenderness, only sadomasochism. His life from now on would be experienced through the cortical top-down prism of this persona play. This dark play of sadism, anger, badness, hatred, war, emptiness, and emotional isolation would continue to deepen and extend itself throughout his childhood.

When we add in what we already know of Eddie's future—the beatings and the banishment to the corner—we can see where things are going. His childhood solidified, confirmed, and deepened his established internal drama. His internal personas became the characters of Eddie's ogre dream at night and informed his invisible internal theater of consciousness during the day.

The final issue in the writing of Eddie's play is the role played by his temperament. How did it digest his problematic maternal provision to create his unique characterological self? And what happened to his Authentic-Being as his *bad* characterological self became the operational center of his identity?

8

AS THE CURTAIN RISES
Eddie's Play Is Written by His Brain

ONCE EDDIE'S RUDIMENTARY PLAY WAS established, things turned. He was now subject to his mother's character unbridled. She was in charge, and we have seen the cruelty of her treatment of Eddie. He was at her mercy for the full scope of maternal provision and responsiveness. His mother's damage was not minor league. She was a cold, paranoid, blaming sadist. We are familiar with Mother's physical abuse, intimidation, humiliation, criticizing attacks, coldness, shaming, blaming, and control. With the total absence of any loving touch, physically or emotionally, the only contact Eddie ever had consisted of physical and emotional beatings. His only available avenue of engagement was through sadomasochism.

The most harmful feature of Mother's abuse was deprivation itself. Eddie received no love from Mother at all. She never held him, touched him, kissed him, or told him that she loved him. She was emotionally removed and rejecting. In fact, as Eddie told me later, whenever his mother witnessed expressions of love in the world around her, she was overtly disgusted by it. She openly disparaged sweetness, tenderness, and loving as "sentimentality" for inferior people.

There were additional elements in Eddie's world of abuse. Eddie's father had no emotional involvement with Eddie. He was a purely self-involved narcissist. Nobody else existed for Eddie's father but himself. He was fundamentally not there. He was off working or involved with his own solipsism. When he was physically present, he demanded admiration. If he felt injured, he would viciously turn on the perpetrator. Father abandoned Eddie to his wife and did not protect him from her, though he knew what was going on. "Better you than me" was the attitude. Eddie told me during his psychotherapy that when he was in high school, he turned to his father in desperation over his mother. His father said, "There's nothing I can do. You need to understand her and make the best of it." Then he said, "She's not so cold," and as proof, he proceeded to tell Eddie what great sex he had with her.

And then there was Eddie's oldest sister Margie. She was as selfish and self-absorbed as her father. She was concerned only with what Eddie could do for her—serve her and admire her. In addition, she showed herself to be manipulative and controlling. She didn't care about Eddie. The sum total of Eddie's experience of nurture was abuse. He was subject to the four elements of abuse—the absence of love, unrelenting sadism, the paranoid projection of him as bad, and pure self-involvement by his mother, father, and sister. Nobody was involved with lovable Eddie or saw him as such.

A major component of child rearing is protection from harm. Yes, Eddie received some degree of protection in the more neutral arenas. He was fed and changed. He was dressed and kept warm and clean. He was maintained in a nice house and protected from the routine dangers of the household—sharp objects, a hot stove, falling down the stairs, and so forth. On the other hand, the more important arena of protection was in the domain of maternal abuse itself. Eddie was woefully unprotected. His mother, who ought to have been his very source of protection, turned out to be the perpetrator from whom he needed protection. The absence of protection played a significant role in his experience.

Over the course of the next three years, operating from his theater, Eddie fielded and digested his maternal/family experience into his cortex. In concert with this, the incredible morphogenesis of his limbic cortex continued until it reached a high enough level of order to create his fully formed representational cortical top-down play.

Eddie's representational self was the fifth morphogenic incarnation of Eddie. First was zygote-Eddie, a unicelled organism floating free in a fallopian sea with no attachment to his environment. Then he implanted and became embryo-fetal Eddie, held in his mother's womb and attached to her via body membranes. At birth, we had newborn Eddie, out in the world, connected to his maternal environment by detachable physical membranes and autonomic brain operations. Then we had the creation of consciousness as Authentic-Being Eddie related by feeling to the Loving Other. He related to the world as his Authentic-Being, the original form of his self.

Eddie's transformation from a formless feeling of a being to the fully representational Eddie self would take place exclusively in the domain of consciousness. From now on, his survival-maternal experience was processed by the established limbic-cortical mappings that formed his self/other, no longer as organism-Eddie fielding direct experience. In other words, consciousness was the organization of the brain for the cortical top-down processing of the dramas of life. As a result, Eddie now related to the world as a synthetic brain creation, his self.

Consciousness is purely biological. Eddie's limbic-cortical personas are brain creations, not computer-created digital figures. They come from extremely high levels of order of webs of constellations of constellations of constellations of neurons, from perceptions, impulses, appetites, cravings, images, emotions, ideas, and memory. The textured depth and seeming aliveness of his personas flow from the brain-body itself. The limbic cortex is body and is connected to his living body, neurologically and hormonally. Likewise, we will see that Eddie's transformation into the fully representational "Eddie" in the theater of consciousness will follow similar biological pathways as his earlier incarnations.

As Eddie began the three-year morphogenesis into his fully dimensional play and characterological self, he continued to map his survival environment through his limbic system into his cortex. As we have seen, in addition to loving responsiveness, two other aspects of his maternal experience now came into play—abuse and protection. These three elements of his maternal environment are not theoretical or arbitrary categories but literally encompass and define Eddie's survival environment.

As a result of abuse, two additional personas materialized in Eddie's play of self and other—the Abused and the Abuser—who relate together by sadistic aggression. Their mappings are infused by the limbic system with the serotonin/adrenaline fight-or-flight response. These personas are formless like the Authentic-Being and the Loving Other. Under the best of circumstances, there can be no such thing as perfect maternal responsiveness. There can only be good-enough loving for all of us. There is always some element of abuse and deprivation in ordinary life. Mothering can range from minimally problematic all the way to seriously destructive. The prominence of Eddie's mapping of the Abuser/Abused scenario would reflect the degree of abusive experience, over time, that he received.

Likewise, active protection is a natural function of maternal provision. Biological life always has to contend with survival. There is no such thing as a free, safe life. Mother literally keeps her child alive by feeding and protection. She protects her vulnerable child from harm. Consequently, this function is mapped by an additional pair of invisible personas derived from protection—the Protector and the Protectee, who relate together by protective maternal aggression. Protection experience is limbically mapped by good aggression, which is to be differentiated from sadistic aggression. Protective aggression is not directed at the child by the mother. It is in his behalf. The Protectee is connected to the aggression of the Protector through the limbic system in safety, reliability, and trust. The prominence of Eddie's mapping of the Protector/Protectee scenario would reflect the actuality of his experience of protection.

Beginning in the first months of life, Eddie's self in consciousness was composed of three invisible personas: the Authentic-Being, the Abused, and the Protectee. Likewise, his other was composed of the Loving Other, the Abuser, and the Protector. Eddie's self and other related together by feeling. The prominence of each of the formless personas in Eddie's early theater reflected the actuality of responsiveness, abuse, and protection he received.

And so over the next three years, Eddie's maternal nurture was mapped. If Eddie had received good-enough loving, the mapping of his experience of self would have been an elaboration of responsive loving for his Authentic-Being. The circle would have been unbroken. As it was, the absence of love was reflected in minimal mappings for Eddie's Authentic-Being. His maturing self was minimally infused by his Authentic-Being. Likewise, his maturing other was minimally infused by the Loving Other. There was certainly a lot of activity in the Abuser/Abused domain, which resulted in significant mappings. Consequently, the major personas in his forming play were the Abuser and the Abused, with their sadomasochistic bond. There was a minimal presence of the Protector is his forming other, while the Protectee in distress was a factor in his developing self.

However, the final form of Eddie's representational play was not just a direct rendering of the actual experience of Eddie and his mother. His developing image of self and his play, were digested and reconfigured by his temperament. Temperament is the nature that fields maternal nurture. Temperament is composed of a set of four genetically determined pairs of elements that order and organize the formation of the play in consciousness. The four elements of temperament are *Internalizing/Externalizing*, *Introversion/Extroversion*, *Active/Passive*, and *Participant/Observer*. Each element operates on a different aspect of play formation. All four temperamental pairs worked in concert to write the final form of Eddie's play.

The formation of Eddie's play in the theater of consciousness followed the same biological principles that we saw with the ameba as it introjected its environment, digested it, and synthesized new products. It retained some inside and projected others back across its boundary. Eddie's temperament operated in like fashion as he took in information about his salient maternal environment—love, abuse, and protection—and processed them into his developing three-dimensional theater. Each operation of Eddie's temperament ordered a different aspect of this information into the top-down units of self and other, and determined how his personas and their relatedness were aligned and formed into representational consciousness.

Eddie's play was principally composed of the formless Abuser persona attacking the Abused in the context of the Protectee in distress. His specific temperament then digested, reconstructed, and synthesized a new scenario. Some elements of his personas and their relationships were retained and realigned inside, and other elements were projected. Likewise there were various reconfigurations and identifications in regard to self and other that gave form to his unique characterological play as a whole. Here is how the elements of temperament operate.

Internalizer/Externalizer

The personas of Mother—the Loving Other, Protector, and Abuser—are introjected inside the limbic-cortical theater. Internalizers and externalizers handle the personas of other in opposite ways. Externalizers re-project the other personas back outside onto the projection screen of real people. As a result, externalizers locate and experience the feeling of other as coming from other people. For example, if the predominant persona is the Loving Other, an externalizer will be oriented to feel and seek love from others. Internalizers, on the other hand, do not re-project the personas of other back onto a projection screen of other people outside the theater. They retain the personas inside the theater. Consequently, they remain invisible, a formless presence inside the theater. An internalizer with a predominantly Loving Other persona will experience the source of love, the feeling of relatedness, as coming from inside. He would carry the feeling and assumption inside that he is loved.

Eddie was an internalizer. How did this element of his temperament inform the writing of his play? When Eddie introjected the Abuser persona attacking the Abused into his theater, as an internalizer he retained the Abuser on the inside, with no actual form. Consequently, the scenario of Eddie's play was that the Abuser on the inside attacked the Abused self, who was also on the inside. This means that the location of the attacks between the Abuser and the Abused in the sadomasochistic play took place internally. Since Eddie located the source of attack as coming from inside him, he experienced the attacks as a kind of unheard voice inside. It was manifest as self-hate: "I'm bad; I'm inadequate, I'm stupid, I'm ugly." In the context of shaming abuse, Eddie, as an internalizer, felt *ashamed*. Eddie' s play was composed of a steady state of internal attack between the Abuser and the Abused. This defines the depressive position of the sadomasochistic play.

This ongoing internal war was feeding on Eddie's serotonin system and would eventually overwhelm it. His routine self-attack and self-hatred would then flower into a fuller so-called depression. Since an internalizer views himself as the problem, Eddie was oriented to seek a solution by changing himself rather than blaming others. Consequently, his internalizer orientation made him a seeker and led him later to try to fix himself in therapy.

If Eddie had been an externalizer, the same sadomasochistic play would have generated a very different scenario. Since an externalizer projects the Abuser onto other people, he is predisposed and oriented to feel attacked or criticized by others. He locates the source of attack, hatred, or criticism as coming from a person outside of him. For example, from a legacy of shaming abuse, an externalizer experiences being "shamed" by a person outside him, not *ashamed*." His orientation is as a paranoid blamer. As such, he would be inclined to blame and fight with others. Psychiatric symptoms for externalizers are paranoia (believing other people are out to get them), blaming, and fighting.

Introversion/Extroversion

Introversion means that the scenario of the play is oriented from the point of view of oneself, while an extrovert operates from the point of view of other people. Introversion literally means to turn inward. The primary reference of an introvert is his own self, not other people. He is self-oriented. In the context of good-enough loving, the introvert will be naturally oriented to his own internal endeavors and creative imagination, which come out of his self. The literal meaning of extroversion is to turn outwards. An extrovert's primary reference is with the self of the other person, not his own self. The extrovert is other-oriented. He is naturally tuned into what is going on inside the other person. In the context of good-enough loving, the extrovert's primary orientation naturally generates responsiveness, thoughtfulness, and consideration toward other people. (I am not using these terms in the conventional sense, where extroversion means outgoing, and introversion means shy.)

An introvert who has been subject to abuse tends toward narcissism. As such, his "me" orientation focuses on himself as the injured party. He is furious and outraged at slights and injuries directed at him from others. He leads with an exposed nerve and indignantly feels, "How dare you treat me this way?" An extrovert, in the context of abuse, tends toward echoism. (In the Narcissus-Echo myth, Echo is a nymph who longs for Narcissus's love and attention. Unfortunately for her, he is completely self-absorbed, admiring his reflection in a pool of water. Echo desperately hopes and yearns for Narcissus to love her but to no avail. In his pure self-involvement, he doesn't notice her at all. Eventually, as she waits and waits and pines for him, she loses all form. She remains only as an echo, an echo of other people, reflecting their voices back to them.) When blamed and attacked, an echoist will be located over there, at one with the other person's view of him. An echoist's default frame of reference is the attacker's view of him, rather than inhabiting his own view of himself. He agrees with the injured narcissist and understands that he deserves to be attacked. He takes in the other person's projection of him as lacking and defective, and identifies with it. The echoist tends toward pleasing behavior to ward off and ameliorate attacks.

To illuminate these two opposite orientations, I'll give an example of a byplay between an extrovert, Mrs. Carter, and an introvert-narcissist, Mr. Miller. When Mr. and Mrs. Carter made airplane reservations, they reserved two seats together on the same row in order to sit next to each other. Mr. Miller tried to do the same thing, but he made his reservation too late, and there weren't any contiguous seats left for his wife and him. The best he could do was to have his wife sit in one row (which happened to be next to Mrs. Carter) while he was to sit in the row in front of his wife.

When the Carters boarded the plane, Mr. Miller was sitting in Mrs. Carter's seat. Mrs. Carter said, "Excuse me, but I believe you are sitting in my seat, 22B."

Mr. Miller replied, "I have seat 21B in the row in front of me. But

I want to sit next to my wife. So I'll sit here, and you take that one. It's the same center seat."

Mrs. Carter's inclination was to give him her seat without reference to herself, her own wishes, or her legitimacy. She felt his pain at not being able to sit next to his wife and would have felt guilty if she'd deprived him of his wishes. Her extroverted position was to inhabit Mr. Miller's frame of reference, not her own. She wasn't even thinking about not sitting next to her own husband.

Mr. Miller, on the other hand, operated purely from the introverted "me" position. He wanted to sit next to his wife. Mrs. Carter didn't figure into his frame of reference at all. There simply was no consideration for her. What we have here is that the introverted Mr. Miller was located in Mr. Miller, while the extroverted Mrs. Carter also was located in Mr. Miller. Neither one of them was inhabiting Mrs. Carter.

On this occasion, however, Mrs. Carter went against her extroverted grain. She didn't like the fact that he hadn't even asked her and had been so pushy. "No, actually, this is my seat," she explained. "I'm sitting here next my husband."

Since Mrs. Carter had the gall to actually think of herself, Mr. Miller became furious. Despite the fact that he was 100 percent in the wrong, he viewed himself as the injured, aggrieved party. In his view, he was the victim of selfish Mrs. Carter. He demanded more vociferously to sit next to his wife. He raised his voice and argued with her all the more. As far as he was concerned, she deserved his attacks. Mrs. Carter held her ground and called for the flight attendant, who told Mr. Miller to get out of Mrs. Carter's seat and go to his own. He got up, visibly angry and indignant at the injustice.

We can see here the opposite orientations of extroversion and introversion. It was hard for Mrs. Carter to hold her ground because, as an extrovert, she "understood" Mr. Miller's wish to sit next to his wife. By not capitulating to his demands, she felt bad, as if she were hurting him. When he attacked her, she felt guilty, as if it was deserved for being so cruel to him. And she felt hurt that Mr. Miller didn't like her.

Eddie was extroverted-echoistic. As such, he was oriented and grounded in his mother's self as his base of operations, not his own. Consequently, he saw his mother's attacks from her point of view— that they were properly directed at him. She saw Eddie as bad. As an extrovert, he joined his mother's view of him as "bad," echoed it and identified with it, and operated as if it were so. He was in agreement with her that he was to blame for her attacks. He had no inclination to blame her. Both Eddie and his mother blamed Eddie. Operationally, he experienced that he deserved to be the recipient of attacks. It was his fault. He was the source of badness, and he deserved to be punished. His default position was one of guilt. This contributed to Eddie's masochistic orientation.

Active/Passive

An individual with an active temperament naturally operates as the possessor of aggression and primarily identifies with the protective persona. An individual with a passive temperament does not operate as the possessor of aggression and primarily identifies as the Protectee persona.

One can readily tell whether a child is active or passive. Active children sit and walk and climb early in childhood. They take off at the beach. The active child is naturally physical, physically expressive, and action-oriented. He is oriented to active, muscular, good aggression. In the context of good-enough loving, the active child, identifying with his active strength, operates as a take-charge doer. The passive child is not oriented by muscular, good aggression. In basic orientation, he is more absorbed elsewhere. He tends to be off daydreaming. He locates the Protector strength and capacity outside of himself. The passive child depends more on someone else to provide shelter from the storm. He identifies as the recipient of action rather than as a doer.

Eddie had a passive temperament. He did not identify as possessing and dishing out aggression. Aggression was located in the other person. How did Eddie's passive temperament operate in the context of his mother's abuse? Eddie did not identify as the possessor of aggression, but as the helpless one who was the object of aggression. The Protector in Eddie's play was too minimal to protect him from the steady state of sadistic attacks, which were too powerful and overwhelming anyway. Since he didn't identify as the failed Protector, this left him in the position of the distressed and exposed Protectee, anticipating external attacks, with no possibility of protection. As the recipient of attacks, in this context, he was inclined toward masochism—or more specifically, maso-sadism.

In addition, Eddie's passive temperament, in the context of his sadomasochistic play, defined the circumstances that generate anxiety. Anxiety results from the anticipation of, and the experience of, ongoing attacks without the ability to protect oneself in the context of a passive temperament. It derives from sadistic attack directed by the Abuser toward the Abused-Protectee, with insufficient and failed protection. And not surprisingly, Eddie was no stranger to considerable anxiety as a teenager and into adulthood. Anxiety was the inevitable expression of the sadomasochistic attacks of his play via his passive temperamental orientation.

If Eddie had been active rather than passive in the context of his sadomasochistic play, he would have generated an opposite scenario. He would have identified with the active position of dishing it out, with the potential for sadism. He would have been predisposed to become a bully, and make someone else anxious, as well as the unprotected object of attack.

Participant/Observer

The temperamental position of participant and observer addresses how one relates to the play scenario as a whole. A participant is naturally oriented to be immersed in and emotionally involved in the play scenario. He easily and naturally engages through feeling. The natural orientation of an observer, on the other hand, is to process at a distance, rather than be immersed in the feeling relatedness of the scenario of the play. An observer tends toward thinking, caution, circumspection, reticence, and figuring things out.

For example, let's say a participant type is diagnosed with lung cancer. From his emotional orientation, he plunges into pain and fear, sadness, despair, and anger. He wells up with tears, cries, and screams that his life is over. An observer type, in the same situation, removes himself to "understand." He distances himself and analyzes the situation. He discusses the implications. On what is the diagnosis based? What are the survival rates? What are the treatment options? What are the protocols, and what are the side effects of the drugs? "Understand" literally means to "stand under" and evaluate rather than to be immersed in and feel the scenario. In that sense, he stands outside of the scenario. Nonetheless, the observer is still a part of the play and subject to its plot. He is in the same situation as a participant, but he is removed and doesn't feel it.

In the context of abuse, a participant tends toward over emotionalism, loss of control, and boundary blurring with others. An extreme participant might do well to be more like an observer and pull back and have some perspective. Whereas an observer, in the context of abuse, tends toward distancing himself, removal, emotional withdrawal, and obsessing. In fact, in the extreme, when he separates himself from feeling his anger, he is literally *beside himself* (with anger). He might do well to be more like a participant and be more engaged and reactive. We are all participant/observers of our plays. Our primary orientation is just a matter of where on the participant/observer axis we fall.

Eddie was an observer. As such, his natural inclination was to distance himself from feeling the pain of his sadomasochistic drama. Eddie's observer strategy was to flee off the stage of engagement (i.e., flight, not fight). He withdrew and removed himself from emotional absence, rejection, and abuse, as well as from physical abuse. This did not, of course, remove him from the sadism. In fact, it had the unintended consequence of subjecting him to even more abuse than should have been bearable. We have seen how this worked when he was beaten. His observer response was to withdraw from feeling the sensation of being hit, to numb himself during the beatings. Since Mother's goal was to elicit a participatory response from him, to make him cry and beg for mercy, the unintended consequence of his observer withdrawal was to increase the attacks and S&M engagement. His observer temperament contributed to his masochistic position in his play.

Emotional absence and rejection was the most important aspect of Mother's sadism. Eddie's response to the pain of Mother's absence and rejection was to remove himself emotionally. Eddie's Authentic-Being protected itself from this inhospitable environment by taking flight off the stage to protect himself from pain. He protected his unloved self by a hibernation from the maternal nuclear winter, a withdrawal from the inhospitable theater of consciousness. His Authentic-Being did not die: it remained inaccessible, timelessly removed in an coma. Eddie became withdrawn and inaccessible. As Simon and Garfunkel put it, "I am a rock. I am an island." He became cold and removed, like his mother.

Not only do each of us have a unique constellation of temperament, but every person has a specific balance for each temperamental dynamic. Each element of temperament is really on an axis, on which there is a predominant, prevailing position. For example, internalizers have some degree of externalization, and vice versa. Thus, an externalizer is really predominantly an externalizer. He will have some degree of an internal location of attack. And likewise, an internalizer will do some externalizing and project onto real people to some degree. In other words, one may be an extreme 90/10 internalizer/externalizer or a 60/40 internalizer/externalizer or even a 50/50. This is true for all four elements of the temperamental pairs. Not only that, but one or another of the four temperamental elements may be more pronounced and powerful than the other ones. This would make that specific element of temperament more influential in the formation of one's personality.

Since all of us have both aspects of each temperamental pair, the full range of the human drama lies within the consciousness of all of us. We have within us, and within our image-inations, all of the features of all character worlds. In fact, we dip into aspects of many of them in our daily lives. We all have the potential for love, caring, and creativity, as well as selfishness, cruelty, abandonment, emotional isolation, projective blaming, rage, egotism, fears, anxiety, so-called depression, flight from unwanted moments, fraudulence, emptiness, helplessness, and hopelessness in our routine living. This is the stuff of human drama. Each of us settles on our particular character drama as our major life solution.

I want to emphasize that, by temperament, we are talking about inborn temperamental styles not pathology. It is the degree of abuse that is digested into our plays that generates suffering. The individual array of our temperamental aspects when digesting parental responsiveness create the varied and wonderful scope of human personality. Our cortical image-ination, oriented by our temperament, writes a specific and nuanced character world in each of us, which is as unique as our fingerprints.

As with the list of personas, this temperamental grouping might seem to be arbitrary and idiosyncratic. Nonetheless, I propose that these four dynamics truly represent how the brain actually operates as it constructs our plays in consciousness and that they encompass and determine the full range of human character.

In the beginning, Eddie's Authentic-Being was nurtured by responsive loving and mapped through his limbic system via the oxytocin avenues. As his play was elaborated, his experience shifted from good-enough loving to being subject to his mother's abuse and neglect. Consequently, the cortical mappings of responsive loving ceased being the operational center of his experience. The mappings of his Authentic-Being and responsive love remained, but they did not extend into the mappings of Eddie's new experience. Consequently, his evolving representational self was not significantly infused by the presence of his Authentic-Being.

Trauma at such an early stage of play formation had enormous consequences and controlled the writing of Eddie's play. His limbic activations shifted to the fight-or-flight avenues of serotonin/adrenaline. As this was mapped, the evolving representational image of Eddie's *self* did not extend the mappings of his Authentic-Being. From his extensive experience of maternal abuse and deprivation, he took the Abuser/Abused relationship inside his theater. These two personas, connected by the sadomasochistic bond of anger, along with the helpless Protectee, became the basic unit of his internal drama.

Eddie's play was written through the digestion of his nurture by his nature. We have seen how his temperament fielded his personas to write his cortical top-down play. His temperament—internalizer, extrovert, passive, and observer—through his image-ination wrote

111

and cast his specific characterological self, as well as his unique character play, with which we are familiar.

Once formed, Eddie's play was to be the stuff of his dreaming and waking trances. Eddie's dream plight in his ogre dream perfectly embodied his internal play. In his REM trance, Eddie's self and other cast as three-dimensional, feeling, alive-seeming figures projected into a synthetically created hologram of the world. Eddie and the ogre depicted the pure scenario of his play. When awake, the holograms of Eddie's self and other were invisible, rocks-under-water, synthetic representational images that were projected onto sensory images of real people as its projection screen. The *drama of Eddie and his mother* was simply experienced as real, whether dreaming or awake.

How would this established play inform Eddie's future? From now on, he would experience the world through his invisible top-down cortical play. It would serve as a prism and filter for digesting his ongoing experience, which continued to be damaging and problematic. Here's a taste of what would follow: Eddie was chosen as mother's specific target for a number of reasons. First and foremost, it was because his temperament was a perfect complement to hers. His physical resemblance was mostly Mother. He looked a lot like her. Eddie always felt that he was very similar to her. This made him the perfect projection screen for her externalized self-hatred, hence, the chosen one for attack.

Wasn't Margie subject to the same mother? Why didn't she turn out the same as Eddie? Because Margie was the first child, Mother wasn't as drained as she was with her third child. She wasn't as angry toward females as she was toward males. And most importantly, Margie had a very different temperament from Eddie and Mother. She was an introvert (narcissist), active, participant, and externalizer, in that order—very much like Father. She soon emerged as the special and admired child. This made her immune from being an object of overt attack. With Eddie's internalizer (low self-esteem) and echoistic propensity, he too participated in the admiration for Margie.

The substance of Margie's favored status was, in fact, illusory. She was as damaged as Eddie, and the real deprivation and coldness in her world came home to roost later in her own life. As an adult, Margie became bulimic, alcoholic, sexually inappropriate, and deluded. By then, Eddie had become disappointed and bewildered when he discovered she was not as special as he had imagined. But this realization came too late to alter the internal image of Margie that he carried in his play. That remained in force. He had long since internalized Margie's contribution to his internal Abuser persona. The admired "inner Margie" played a role in his later choice of a girlfriend.

Eddie's younger brother, Larry, was a different story. He too was spared from being Mother's central object of sadism. Larry was a rather homely and dull child. Mother was, in fact, embarrassed by Larry's apparent deficiencies. She countered her embarrassment about Larry and compensated for her narcissistic injury by project-ing special qualities onto him. Eddie could never figure out what she saw in Larry. He didn't know that Mother's apparent fondness for Larry was not as it appeared.

Eddie was filled with jealousy that Larry seemed to be the object of Mother's loving and protective attentions. In response to this, Ed-die was cruel toward Larry early in their childhood. He felt distain for Larry as an ugly, stupid little runt. He didn't even like to see Larry standing. He felt that being down on the floor was Larry's rightful place, and he was more than willing to knock him over. And he did so often. Larry had a very different temperament from Eddie. He was an externalizer, passive, introvert, and observer, in that order.

Mother protected Larry from "bad" Eddie's anger. This com-pounded the story. It made Eddie angrier. It prompted him to act out against Larry even more, which, in turn, generated increased protec-tion of Larry. This resulted in more beatings for Eddie and amplified the judgment that he was a bad boy. Eddie's attacks against Larry were very similar to his mother's attacks toward him. Mother, in the social world, was not at all actively aggressive. She was shy and pas-sive-aggressive, In public, she was deferential and admiring toward her husband, although she would sneak in subtle put-downs. It was only in private and in secret that she unleashed her active sadism, physically and emotionally, toward Eddie. Eddie did the same with Larry. Eddie was shy, quiet, and reserved in public. He only acted overtly sadistic to Larry in private. Although Eddie's primary tendency was masochistic, with power over a younger, weaker brother, he acted out his opposite tendency. Remember, masochism is really maso-sadism. When he was older, Eddie felt guilty about his mistreatment of Larry, and he went to great lengths to make it up to him. Larry's preferred and protected status didn't do him much good. As with Margie, it lacked real substance. He grew up to become an entitled, blaming, irresponsible, grandiose, and ineffectual character.

Eddie's second sister, Clara, was a positive and benign presence. Temperamentally, she was an externalizer, extrovert, passive, and participant. As such, she was a sweet person and the only warm presence in Eddie's life. Unfortunately, she was insufficient as an antidote to the rest of his family, and she was not significantly consequential in the construction of his world. As an adult, she married a devaluing and bullying man and led a life of quiet, masochistic torment.

Eddie's play was a dark drama, which generated a dark character world. The absence of the infused presence of the Authentic-Being left Eddie with a sense of emptiness, fraudulence, and hopelessness. In addition, his other was not infused by the presence of the Loving Other persona. It is by the presence of the Loving Other that one carries a sense of being loved. Its absence left Eddie with a hopeless aloneness. This resulted in a world where respect and love did not exist at all. To fill that aloneness and emptiness, he was prefigured to seek engagement through the substitute relatedness of sadomasochistic relationships that were consonant with his inner world. His self was the projection screen for the Abused/Protectee, and his identity was that he was bad and inadequate.

Both Eddie's Authentic-Being and the later representational image of his self were synthetic illusions, created by his brain. Once his fully developed play had formed, Eddie lived its scenarios from the top-down cortical illusions of his brain theater, unawares. The rest of his childhood, through the prism of his cortical theater, extended and nuanced his basic play.

Prior to three years old, Eddie did not have a developed representational consciousness. It didn't exist before this time. The transformation from his rudimentary consciousness to the illusory three-dimensional plays of self and other took place during this specific time period. Eddie's cortical play was the expression of his brain-created world of consciousness. It was not the world. It was art-ifice. It was brain art, the organized replication of reality by the brain, in the brain.

I want to downplay a familiar and major neuroscientific question about the art-ifice of consciousness: "We cannot account for the leap from the neurochemical, electrical, hormonal activity of the brain into human consciousness." How consciousness springs into existence is a fun and mysterious question. Our inability to characterize the mechanism of this leap suggests to many people, even serious scientists, that the self is some kind of exception to biology, and is therefore a spiritual presence. They conclude that somehow the self is not a biological production created by our genes and its programmed morphogenesis.

In fact, the synthetic creation of representational illusion is a prosaic and common manifestation of brain-body. All of our senses routinely take this same leap. Vision is ubiquitous throughout the animal kingdom. With our eyes, we see. Vision is a brain-created synthetic illusion that is believed to be real. And despite the fact that we cannot account for the leap from neurochemical activity into "seeing," nobody believes that vision is somehow spiritual and not genetic/biological. If Eddie suffered a brain lesion in the visual areas of his cortex, his vision would be destroyed and gone. Similarly, if he were to suffer a significant brain damage that disrupted the cortical circuits of his play, that synthetic illusion too would disappear and be no more. As far as Eddie would know, it never was. Alzheimer's disease is a tragic brain disease that causes precisely this damage. It destroys the self, personality, and the play of consciousness in exactly this fashion.

We have seen that Eddie's character and his ongoing play was shaped by the damaging consequences of deprivation and abuse. Eddie's self was not sufficiently infused by his Authentic-Being. As a result it warped his internal dramas in such a way as to remove him from his own authenticity and capacity to love. The ongoing plot of his play was sadomasochistic aggression in play all the time. This continuous and steady state of fight-or-flight would eventually put an unsustainable strain on his supply of neurotransmitters. As Eddie's outer life played out his established inner drama, it was only a question of *when* not *if* his play would break down. He did, years later, reach a breaking point that generated the considerable suffering that brought him to psychotherapy.

Sadly, estrangement from one's Authentic-Being by virtue of neglect and abuse is not an unusual story. It happens to many of us. Eddie's particular version was, of course, unique to him and his circumstances. Although his play reflects the unique consummation of the interplay of his nurture with his nature, Eddie's story is the story of all of us. The varieties of responsive and abusive provision, digested by the differences in our temperaments, write the unique character plays for every one of us. They create the seven billion individual character worlds that populate the earth.

9

THE AUTHENTIC-BEING AS PLAYED BY SLEEPING BEAUTY

WE HAVE SEEN IN EDDIE'S cortical play how abuse and deprivation damaged his Authentic-Being and his capacity to love. Although the style, the degree, and the specifics of abuse differ in all of us, as do our temperaments, the story of the cortical play is universal. It is the central issue of human character in every culture and every civilization throughout history. The underlying story of damage and recovery of the Authentic-Being is the human drama.

Fairy tales have been told to children for centuries. They depict the central themes of the cortical play, the damaging impacts of the Abuser, the fate of the Authentic-Being, and the processes of recovery flowing from the Loving Other. Let us explore the universal cortical play in *Sleeping Beauty*, which stars the personas of the theater of consciousness. Then we will address the lesser-known second half of the fairy tale, which illuminates the play with even greater clarity and depth. Let's begin with the cast of characters:

Dramatis Personae

Authentic-Being—Sleeping Beauty
Loving Other—The Fairies, Prince Charming
Abuser—Thirteenth Fairy
Abused—Sleeping Beauty

Protector—Twelfth Fairy, King/Father
Protectee—Sleeping Beauty

The king and queen held a great celebration for the birth of their much-wanted daughter. High on their guest list were the twelve fairies who lived in the kingdom. During the festivities, each of the fairies gave the baby princess a gift. They conferred onto her all the wonderful human gifts—beauty, intelligence, and virtue. They gave her the wit of an angel, grace in all her pursuits, and the abilities to be a perfect dancer, to sing like a nightingale, and to play music to perfection. The fairies represented the Loving Other, whose legacy is for the child to thrive and flourish. The beauty and perfection of the innocent princess is the symbol of the Authentic-Being in all of us.

Now, there was a problem with having invited these twelve fairies. There were actually thirteen fairies in the kingdom. Because there were only twelve golden plates suitable for fairies, one had to be left out—the thirteenth fairy, but she hadn't been seen for quite a while anyway. (She was, of course, old and ugly.) Big mistake. She found out about the snub, and her twisted nose was out of joint. Sure enough, she showed up—and was she mad! (Read: narcissistic injury, for the slight of not being invited or receiving riches.) She represented the bad mother, aka the Abuser. She cursed the princess: *"Because you did not invite me, I tell you that in her fifteenth year, your daughter will prick herself on a spindle and fall over dead."* Age fifteen is when a girl becomes a woman. The witch did not want the innocent princess to thrive and flourish, to grow up into a fulfilled woman. She wanted her dead. Spinning is the symbol of womanly pursuits. From this very pursuit, she would prick herself with the needle and die. The needle itself is the symbol of violation and penetration, the agency of the bad mother's murderous sadism.

The twelfth fairy, the symbol of the Protector, had not bequeathed her gift yet. Hers was to protect Sleeping Beauty from the evil fairy, even though she was too weak to reverse the curse. She, however, was able to save Sleeping Beauty's life by substituting a hundred-year sleep for death. This would allow Sleeping Beauty to survive but not to live. The king, Sleeping Beauty's father, also a Protector, tried to circumvent the evil fairy's curse, by banning all spindles from the kingdom. Unfortunately, protection in the external world cannot block the legacy of the Abuser, which comes from the internal world. The influence and power of the internalized bad mother is inexorable.

Sure enough, when the princess grew up, the inescapable scenario of the evil fairy's cruelty would be played out. As a young woman on her own, without the protection of her parents, the witch's malevolence would come home to roost. It is built into maturation that the princess will become a woman. Her fulfillment and thriving as a woman is precisely what the Abuser sought to destroy. Sleeping Beauty followed her own curiosity and discovered the very pursuit from which she was protected all her life—spinning at the spinning wheel. When exploring, off by herself, she discovered an old spinning wheel in a dusty old room in the far reaches of the castle. She pricked her finger on the needle, and she fell into a deep sleep. The legacy of the Abuser's hatred is destiny. The inner scenario is destiny. Character is destiny.

The story now illuminates the fate of the Authentic-Being when damaged by the Abuser. Sleeping Beauty fell into a coma. In her state of hibernation, she was withdrawn behind the impenetrable wall of the castle and a giant hedge of thorns. She remained in a timeless state of removal, inaccessible to living. In her removal off the stage of life, she was protected by the wall as her shield and the thorns as her sword. Over the years, many princes tried to penetrate the wall of the hidden castle. Just as she had been attacked and killed, so were they. They were pricked by the thorns and died. The thorns of her protective wall allude to the internalized bad mother's sadistic needle. Needle and thorn are the same instrument of violation and penetration.

It wasn't just Sleeping Beauty, however, who went to sleep. All the regular scenarios of castle life were put to sleep as well. It is consistent with our understanding of consciousness that it is organized as scenarios. The scenarios of castle life were frozen in time. This represents that the withdrawn Authentic-Being plays no role in the living of a life. In its absence, we have only the endless sadomasochistic war between the Abuser and the Abused, walls and thorns. The hundred years of sleep is a symbol that the legacy of the Abuser is timelessly enacted.

The antidote to the wicked fairy's curse is love. In adulthood, we have a second chance for good-enough loving, a life mate. This would be the prince. When the prince approached the castle, he did not try to penetrate Sleeping Beauty's thorny wall. All who tried were killed. Sleeping Beauty let him in. The thorns were transformed into flowers and a path was opened for him. The instruments of war were transformed into flowers, which are a symbol of beauty—a symbol of Sleeping Beauty. The path was opened to her heart. After the prince gained access to the castle, the flowers turned back into thorns. Once again, she was protected from danger and harm, protected from false love.

The prince entered into the castle, which was frozen in time—a mausoleum, no life. The Authentic-Being princess had been withdrawn and was non-participatory in living. The redemptive kiss is the symbol of love. The prince brought the presence of the Loving Other to counteract the Abuser-Other. This was an innocent and authentic love. The prince told her that *he loved her better than he did himself* (i.e., it wasn't narcissistic). The participatory feeling of love is one of tenderness and sweet sadness. It cannot be encompassed by language. *They wept more than they talked. There was little eloquence and a great deal of love.*

Thus, we see the universal story of the cortical play. It is a story of damage, retreat, and recovery. The Authentic-Being withdraws from life due to the malevolence of the Abuser. What remains is the ongoing torture of the Abused by the Abuser. The trade-off is that despite the fact that the Authentic-Being won't get killed, there will be no participation in life. It is out of reach. Recovery comes with the presence of the Loving Other. We now have a newly written play where the Authentic-Being will re-emerge back into life to love and flourish. Sleeping Beauty will marry and have children. This stands in contrast to the original scenario of malevolence, sadism, destruction, and death.

Just in case you think I am squeezing this fairy tale into my own box, let's look at the lesser-known second half of the story. Like the second chapter of a dream, Part II of *Sleeping Beauty* illuminates and

120

spells out with deeper clarity the issues of the cortical play depicted in Part I. Let's start with the dramatis personae of Part II:

Dramatis Personae
Authentic-Being—Sleeping Beauty, Morning, Day
Loving Other—The Prince, Sleeping Beauty, the Cook's Wife
Abuser—Prince's Mother
Abused—Sleeping Beauty, Morning, Day
Protector—The Cook, the Prince
Protectee—Sleeping Beauty, Morning, Day

Nota bene: As in a dream, characters may play multiple roles.

The prince and Sleeping Beauty married and had two children: a daughter, Morning, and a son, Day. This refers to a new chapter in the life cycle. They all lived together at Sleeping Beauty's liberated castle three or four nights a week, and then the prince returned to his parents' castle. However, the prince kept all knowledge of Sleeping Beauty and his new family a secret from his parents. He lied and said he was going hunting. The purpose of his lie was to protect Sleeping Beauty and the kids from his mother, who, as it turns out, was from the race of ogres. Here's the problem: ogres eat children. The prince knew of her ogre-ish inclinations. Despite the fact that he didn't trust her, the prince still loved her as his mother. His attachment to her underlines that the child is attached to his parents, whether they are loving or abusive.

Meanwhile, the queen became suspicious of her son. He was away for too long and too often on these hunting trips. She was angry that his attentions went elsewhere and she suspected that he was lying to her (read: narcissistic injury). Obviously, the queen mother now represents the Abuser. The ogre thing is not terribly subtle. Eating one's young is not exactly the same thing as provision and responsiveness. The prince kept Sleeping Beauty and the kids out of harm's way by keeping them, once again, hidden behind the protective walls of Sleeping Beauty's castle, as well as by the thorns of his lie.

After two years passed, the king died. The prince stepped up to be king and took his place in the world. He then brought his family out of the hidden castle to live in the palace. This meant that Sleeping Beauty and the kids were no longer protected from the ogress. To make matters worse, a couple of years later, as king, Sleeping Beauty's husband went off to war. He left his ogre mother in charge to take care of the government and his family. This represents that the Abuser was in charge, as she is, timelessly, in the cortical play. She would take care of them, all right.

The ogre queen, unfettered, now acted on her true colors, playing out the sadomasochistic drama in pure form. She ordered the cook to kill Morning and prepare her with a sauce Robert, so that the queen could eat her. The cook drew his knife ... but couldn't do it. Instead, he deceived the ogre queen and substituted a lamb for the meal. The ogress had great delight—with no misgivings—in devouring what she thought was her granddaughter. Meanwhile, the cook hid Morning away in his cottage, to be taken care of by his own wife.

Then we repeat the same story, this time with Day. The cook hid the boy in the cabin; then he substituted a goat for the child and served it with sauce Robert to the delighted ogress. The repeated story represents the timeless sadomasochistic scenario—the Abuser kills and eats the Abused, over and over. The ogre mother delighted in her evil, with no misgivings about her cruelty to her grandchildren (read: children).

Just in case the storyline is too subtle, the ogre queen decided to eat Sleeping Beauty as well. At this point, the cook was too terrified of the queen to dare to trick her again. He resolved to kill Sleeping Beauty. But still, he couldn't bring himself do it. When he confessed his mission to Sleeping Beauty—that he was supposed to kill her—she begged him to go through with it. Still believing her children were dead, she wanted to be with them. Her motives portray the love of the Loving Other mother. In contrast to the Abuser, her children meant more to her than life itself. He then told her they were alive and well and were secretly living in his cottage. She joined them there. Once again, the Protector removed the Authentic-Being into a safe house, walled off from the Abuser and from participating in life.

And the story repeated, with his substituting a deer and serving with it sauce Robert, to the queen's delight.

But soon enough, the jig was up. The ogre queen figured out the ruse when she overheard and recognized the voice of Sleeping Beauty as she disciplined Day for being naughty and Morning's arguing to protect him. This is a scene of a good-enough mother maintaining boundaries with her children. This isn't an idealized version of an idyllic life. It is real life, real love. The aggression of Sleeping Beauty's disciplining Day is good aggression, very much at variance with the sadistic aggression of the ogre queen. Child rearing is composed of boundaries and love. This is the stuff of living. This scene echoed a similar scene in Part I of the story. When the whole castle was put to sleep, the cook was frozen in the act of disciplining his young assistant. When awakened, he resumed, boxing the assistant's ears.

When the ogre queen realized her sadistic will had been thwarted, she was furious. She then went all out to kill everybody—Sleeping Beauty, the kids, the cook, his wife, and throw in the maid for good measure. The mechanism of her sadistic frenzy was to throw them into a tub filled with toads, vipers, snakes, and serpents—all symbols of the ugliness of her murderous rage, of the Abuser herself.

Once again, as in chapter one, the Loving Other/Protector king returned in the nick of time to thwart his mother. In her fury, the ogress self-immolated. She jumped into the tub herself, where she was killed and eaten by the ugly, evil, sadistic symbols of herself.

The king still felt bad about the death of his mother. He retained that attachment to her, despite the fact that she was evil. She was his mother. This emphasizes that the child is always attached to his mother, whether through love or sadomasochism. He was upset at her death. He had to mourn his negative attachment to her in order to be free to participate once again in his life with Sleeping Beauty and his children.

Sleeping Beauty gives form to the universal human drama—the play of consciousness. The figures of the story are representations of the internal personas in their timeless scenario. The ogre queen represents the fully developed Abuser as an unloving, evil, narcissistic sadist who wishes to destroy and devour the Authentic-Being. The

123

failed Protector keeps her from being killed by removing her from danger, placing her in a cocoon where she can survive but not live. What remains is endless sadomasochistic war between the Abuser and the Abused. Redemption happens when the Loving Other dismantles the power of the Abuser. The sadomasochistic attachment must be mourned and abandoned before the Authentic-Being is free to re-emerge to live and love.

This ends our bedtime story. It's time to return to the evolution of consciousness and personality. We will now get back to Eddie and explore the play of consciousness in four-year-olds, for whom the world is still a magical fairy tale.

10

DO YOU BELIEVE IN SANTA CLAUS?
Enculturation in Four-Year-Olds

ONE DAY MY FOUR-YEAR-OLD SON, Gabe, sat me down in the library and said, "Daddy, George Washington is the oldest man in the world, right?"

"Yes, he is."

"And he lives to be a hundred years old, and then he dies, right?"

"Yes, that's right."

"So when you get to be a hundred years old, you will die. And then you will become my baby, and I will take care of you the way you take care of me."

My daughter Lily, at four, had a group of imaginary friends—the girls, Emma and Sarah; Brady, the bad boy; and Vic, the parrot. Whenever she was discovered to have done something wrong, she'd say, "Brady did it!" When driving her to school, she always insisted on sitting in the back seat with her "friends." When we arrived at school, her teacher would open the back door of the car. She would let Lily out and then Emma, Sarah, Brady, and Vic. "Is everybody out, dear?" she would ask.

"No!" Lily would say with alarm. "Vic is still in the car!"

"Is he out yet? Good. Okay, I'll shut the door now." We all knew them.

Okay, what is going on here? Did Gabe believe in reincarnation? And what was with Lily? Was she crazy and hallucinating? The answers are no and no. They were both four-year-olds. Gabe was living in four-year-old consciousness world, which was seamlessly magical. He had taken in the persona George Washington from the culture around him. George Washington was recreated by Gabe's persona image-ination and got incorporated as a resident persona in his theater. To Gabe, George Washington was an old, wise man—a loving, father persona. In Gabe's theater and image-ination, his George Washington was a real person. Gabe didn't know about the American Revolution or its great leader, general, and then first president of the United States. He didn't know what a president was—or what the United States was, for that matter.

Simply put, Gabe was telling his father that he loved him. He recognized the imbalance in the caretaking of our relationship. He came up with a scenario by which he returned the love through a story of caretaking. This was Gabe's point, communicated from his unique four-year-old image-ination.

If I (and our culture) believed that reincarnation was real, this belief would have been validated and encouraged. If I had psychologizing beliefs, then I might have incorrectly interpreted Gabe's story as one of fear of my death and loss. I would have missed the actual communication. I received the meaning of his George Washington story for what it was, because I was touched by the feeling of his communication. It was about love and appreciation and giving.

Gabe was talking from his four-year-old magical theater of image-ination. His characterological self was infused with his Authentic-Being. He was talking to my Authentic-Being. The source of love always and only comes from the Authentic-Being. The resonance between our two Authentic-Beings was felt by both of us—a tender moment. If Gabe and I had lived in a different culture, with a different language, in a different time and place, he wouldn't have used George Washington. He would have used a persona image from that culture. The real communication—the resonance of love—would have been given and received.

What about Lily's imaginary friends? She walked around all day accompanied by these figures. These creations of her image-ination were living entities. Her unique consciousness gave form to her persona world in active fantasy, with tangible personas and their stories. Most of us do not do this. Lily's particular image-ination provides us with a window into the organization of consciousness. Her imaginary friends illuminate that consciousness is organized as personas and their stories. Consciousness in all of us is organized in exactly the same way. We just don't give quasi-representational form to them. They remain invisible. Vic was to Lily as George Washington was to Gabe. Despite the fact that Lily was deeply involved with her imaginary friends, she never really confused her image-ination with reality. It was clear that she actually knew the difference between Brady and Emma and her actual brothers and parents.

Now, I confess I colluded with their four-year-old magical world and enjoyed it. When my children were young, I would pull coins from their ears. They looked a bit wide-eyed but took it as a matter of course. I not only pulled out coins but pencils, M&M's, and toy cars. My coup de grace was nailing an entire blankie out of Lily's ear. One day, I was reading, and Gabe came over to me and said, "Can I have a Snickers bar?" At first I didn't know what he was talking about. What was I? A vending machine? Then I noticed he was inclining his head in an odd way, with his ear sticking out. I realized what was going on. He *really* thought I could pull Snickers out of his ear. He believed in the magic of my illusion. He just wanted some candy. I knew I was in trouble. Fortunately, I escaped suspicion by telling him I'd look and see if there were any Snickers in there. So I looked in his ear, fiddled around, and pulled my hand out several times with anguished effort. I told him, "I can't find any in there. You must be out of 'em. Your head is empty." He was disappointed, but my explanation appeared to satisfy him.

The four-year-old cortex is maturing still at an astronomical rate. Now that sufficient symbolic order for the drama of consciousness has been established, the brain is busy building depth and texture into the plays of the internal theater. The major cortical development at four is to enrich the internal theater. The four-year-old brain now takes in information from the outside world in the form of stories and personas. It incorporates stories from the culture. That is to say, a four-year-old can be told a story from the culture around him, and he will feed it into his receptive image-ination. Consequently, personas and scenarios from the outside enrich and give texture to the internal plays. The inner theater is filled with stories.

The four-year-old's theater now encompasses the stories out there in his cultural environment. His limbic-cortex takes in family and cultural myths through the agency of language and all the art forms—stories, pictures, music, dance, plays, puppets, cartoons. The plays of his theater are broadened and amplified with richness and depth. His consciousness is at one with this magical theater.

So, what about the Santa question? A roly-poly old man dressed in a red cloak with white fur rides a sleigh through the sky, pulled by flying reindeer. The lead reindeer has a red headlight for a nose. Santa magically comes down the chimney, which is too narrow for him to actually fit through. He leaves wrapped gifts for each child and knows what each child in the world wants. The one qualifier is the child has to be good. Then he magically flies back up the chimney by putting his finger up to his nose. He makes his entrance and exit with equal aplomb, even in the absence of a chimney and fireplace. He gets to every home in the known world in one night after kids have gone to sleep, and he gets his list of toys all right.

How did the story of Santa, along with the whole scenario of wonder, giving, fear of badness, magic, and bounty, get inside our children? On Christmas Eve, we hung the stockings with care. We lit Christmas candles and read *The Night Before Christmas*, which they knew by heart anyway. The children put out a plate of Christmas cookies and milk for Santa and carrots for the reindeer. Then they went to bed. Each of my three children, at age four, informed me that he or she heard sleigh bells on the roof. We had to wait hours before they finally fell asleep. We filled the stockings, took the too-many presents out of their hiding places, and strew them under the tree in front of the fireplace. Then we ate Santa's snacks and left well-placed crumbs and carrot tops on the plate. Santa did write them a thank-you note.

My wife and I planted this story in our children's theater with a little help from Clement Moore and others. Once upon a time, I too was four. The Santa story was planted in my image-ination. I remember sneaking down the stairs at 5:00 AM for a peek, with excitement and dread, to see if Santa had come, and then being thrilled and relieved by the scene of all the presents. Yes, my consciousness did mature. I learned about reality. I was crestfallen and a little humiliated to learn there was no Santa, although I seemed to forget that when Christmas rolled around the next year—at age five, six, seven, etc., the magic repeated itself.

Years later, I became Santa. My wife and I bought the presents; wrapped them; strew them around the hearth; ate the cookies; and retired to bed, exhausted. And when I watched our children, wide-eyed, exalt in the magic of Christmas morning when I came down the stairs myself and saw the presents that I had strewn under the tree, I still believed in Santa!

The historical context of the Santa character and myth goes back to AD 300. It began with a Christian monk in Turkey named Nicholas. He was a generous, wealthy man who gave gifts to children, especially poor children, and often threw the gifts through their windows. The story morphed in Holland, where Sinter Nikolass wore red bishop's robes with white fur. His name was shortened to Sinter Klaas. He left gifts for children in shoes and stockings. As the story morphed again in German culture, a man dressed as a roly-poly St. Nikolaus went from house to house, giving gifts at Christmas. Since German culture has a darker cast to it, the myth expanded to include a dark figure, St. Nikolaus's evil twin, Knecht Ruprecht. He was the devil-like scrawny character, dressed in rags, who carried a whip for the bad children. During the Middle Ages, Ruprecht was the more pronounced figure. Interestingly, there were times when they switched roles, and Ruprecht became the good one and gave the gifts. The tradition morphed into leaving shoes (stockings) by the window, where St. Nikolaus filled them with gifts. There also was a tradition of wish lists for the children and trees brought inside the house. By the time the myth morphed for American children, Santa no longer had a whipping double. All that remained of the Germanic judgment was that gift giving was only for the good child. The Santa myth was forged out of a distant historical figure of our ancestors. Santa became cast in resonant symbolic form. The story and figure is passed from parent to child to fill our inner drama, as a morality play of love.

The symbolic imagery of Santa is universal. He is a warm and generous father image. His physical form, the roly-poly physique, resonates inside us as a symbolic fecund man/woman, an image of loving softness. This can be contrasted with the Ruprecht image of scrawniness. His symbolic image is similar to that of Cassius in Julius Caesar. Shakespeare describes him with a lean and hungry look. He is a wolf, a predator.

There is a figure in Asian culture who is similar to Santa—the Laughing Buddha. The Laughing Buddha is obese and full of laughter, a loving and friendly figure. He carries a never-emptying sack filled with precious things, rice plants, and candy for children. Sometimes the woes of the world are in the sack, and sometimes children (an image of precious value) are in the sack. Often, there are children at his feet and robes. Sometimes the Laughing Buddha carries a wish-giving fan. The historical origin of the Laughing Buddha came from a Chinese monk named Hotei who, in approximately AD 1000, wandered around China removing sadness from the world.

I'll not belabor the processes by which I transmitted the Santa persona into my children's theaters. In short, Santa was a resident persona in my theater. He had achieved persona status when I was four, my brain having mapped this persona image and story into its symbolic form through the feeling directives of my limbic system. The story is one of a loving father who judges his children to be good and gives them their heart's desire. I employed my expressive symbolic language code to my children. They receptively translated my vocal phonemic symbols through their image-ination to create the Santa story in their theater. All the other art codes were in play, enriching the story—Clement Moore, illustrations, TV, movies, etc. Remember, language itself is an art form. Then we enacted the illusion with a theatrical performance of Christmas morning. As this story becomes part of a child's inner drama world, it links to the basic, actual story of father-love inside each child.

During this period, the brain has matured to the point where the child blends his own internal plays with the stories he is fed by his cultural environment. The four-year-old continues to live in a magic world. His blended stories crystallize to become the warp of his unique consciousness. It is important to recognize that stories that come into the inner theater through the culture do not alter or rewrite the basic internal drama of consciousness. They are, however, filtered through the primary play and taken in through that prism. The essential primary dramas were written from the early formative experiences. Only actual personal experiences throughout the formative first three years always create the basic internal dramas. The brain mappings for these essential dramas, as we have seen, loop through the brain nuclei, the limbic system, memory, the early brain, hormones, and the body itself. Information that now comes in as story and myth, purely on the symbolic level, do not have the depth to create a primary internal play.

Each individual child has his own texture and coloration of the persona of the good—or not-so-good—father, as well as of the good or not-so-good self. Whether in a fatherless home, a loveless home, a home with a stingy and cruel father, or a home with a good and giving father, the child infuses his creation of the Santa persona and story with his own colorations from his own internal world. And this infuses the drama of Christmas morning with his own private meanings. So my Santa story is not the same as any of my children's or the same as yours.

Let's go back to Eddie. We have seen that his father story was written from his actual experience. It was of an absent and narcissistic father who did not protect him from his mother, never mind the deeper story of his ungiving and cruel mother. This comprised his basic parental-love story. When the Santa story came into his theater, it did not rewrite his father story. His Santa story was, in fact, filtered through the prism of his already existent internal story. Cultural myths that Eddie was fed inhabited his theater in profound ways, but they did not alter his basic story. They certainly took their place in his ongoing belief world, which flowed from his enriched inner theater. For Eddie, the Santa story stood in contrast to his father story. The issue of badness and fear of no presents played a large role for him. The receipt of presents that were disappointing contributed to his sense of being undeserving. For him, the Santa story took its place as an unfulfilled wish that held forth the torture of false hope and private pain. Later in life, this led to a cynicism and bitterness about Christmas and his having a Scrooge-like attitude.

The major enterprise in the development of consciousness for four-year-old Eddie was to write and consolidate the enriched basic stories of his internal world. The myths of his culture became incorporated into these internal plays. His internal dramas were amplified by the stories and characters that were taken inside from the culture—through stories, myths, books, media, parents, teachers, religious teachings, art, theater, music, movies, television, and authorities. All of these forces fed his image-ination. His brain had morphed to this high level of symbolic order to receive and receptively create worlds inside.

His cultural environment enriched and gave texture to the plays. By the time he was five, Eddie encompassed the full scope of his enriched internal plays. This fusion of his basic plays with their cultural trappings comprised his unique theater—his timeless theater—for the rest of his life. They comprised his invisible dramas during the day and his dreams at night. They wrote his ogre dream. They constituted the timeless scenarios of his consciousness. From then on, he experienced reality through the prism of these plays. They informed the way in which he processed the rest of his future experience. (We will see later that the exception to this lies when one is subject to major trauma. It is major trauma that has the power to rewrite the basic scenarios.)

At this wonderful age, the internal magical theater of personas and their dramas continue to be alive and well and center stage. Four-year-old consciousness is primarily at one with the aliveness of the internal plays. It remains in ascendancy and is inhabited as real. While the magical theater is being fulfilled, morphogenesis is also inexorably marching on. By five, from sufficient maturation, the focus of growth begins to shift and cross over to a more predominantly reality orientation. This is built in. The evolution of human consciousness is in the service of living a life, not just to remain in dream and magic land. It operates in the service of survival and functioning, thriving, loving, and procreating as an adult. As this takes place, the enriched theater of plays now begins to recede from active visible consciousness.

By five, Eddie's brain had matured to the point where reality functions overrode the internal plays. He was no longer aware of them, and he no longer inhabited magic land. They became invisible, as he became lost in reality. Of course, this was gradual, and the theater world still was easily accessible. All it took was turning off the lights for Captain Hook to appear, or the telling of a compelling story, or watching a cartoon. Over time, this discrepancy became more so, and the surface of reality prevailed. However, even in adulthood, like me on Christmas morning, the magic is still there, underlying reality.

Eddie's primary identity consolidated as his characterological self. His sense of his Authentic-Being and the internal plays were lost in the mists. The inherent split between his Authentic-Being and his characterological self happened. His underlying character plays were fully established and in place. Over the next fifteen years, Eddie transformed, through morphogenesis, into his adult self. The central locus of his brain-body development now took place in relation to the reality sphere, always invisibly filtered through his internal play. His full character as an adult would be an extension of and an elaboration of his characterological self that crystallized at age five.

We will now trace the morphogenesis of brain and body in Eddie's dance of self and other from age five to adulthood.

11

EDDIE LEARNS TO SWIM
The Juvenile Play Solidifies

FIVE-YEAR-OLD EDDIE'S FULL CHARACTER PLAYS were written. He was anchored as his characterological self, embedded in his fully representational plays. We have seen that they were created by his image-ination through the impacts of his formative nurture on his nature and enriched by the stories from his cultural environment. From now on Eddie would know himself as his representational self. The dissonance between Eddie's Authentic-Being and his character-ological self was inevitable. It was built into his maturation, as it is for us all. His Authentic-Being continued to be mapped and present, but was no longer directly operative in Eddie's conscious experience. It would occasionally shine through as a sense of deeper authenticity, as well as the source of his conscience. Eddie was fully differentiated from his parents and the outside world. He was a separate self, living in his own theater. He was still a very long way from being autono-mous, never mind independent.

The massive manufacture, ordering, and mapping of brain cells that created his theater slowed way down. The time for formation of his basic internal play was over. Morphogenesis now shifted to a different locus—to the cortical mapping that reflected Eddie's learn-ing the various skills, values, beliefs, and socialization of his culture. Over the next eight years of his childhood, this would coalesce as an expanded foundation for his theater, which would continue to de-velop, deepen, and broaden his already crystallized plays.

Eddie was now ready to undertake learning in the broader world around him. His ongoing dance of self and other continued. His growth and development would take place within the safe circle of his family and community. This holding environment is the heir to the womb. It is a metaphoric womb in differentiated form, out of which Eddie will emerge to be on his own in adolescence.

When Eddie was six years old, he went to an overnight summer camp for eight weeks, where he learned to swim. Eddie stood on the sandy shallows of the lake and walked with his counselor into the water. His counselor held on to him and encouraged him to put his head underwater. Eddie was afraid and refused. With encouragement, he finally dared to submerge his face. He panicked. His counselor lifted Eddie out. He didn't die. He was afraid. With more encouragement and reassurance, he tried it again. This was repeated over and over. Finally, Eddie was thrilled that he could put his head underwater for a count of four and lift his head out to breathe again.

Then it was time for the next step. Eddie was excited and afraid. His counselor held Eddie in his arms and walked out to the deeper water. Eddie held onto him. He encouraged Eddie to let go, but Eddie balked and refused. Finally he did, and slid under the water. His counselor fished him out. Eddie was terrified. With more encouragement, he tried it again. Same thing. Eventually, he floated by himself in the water. His counselor was right there by his side. Eddie was free to grab on to him. He let go again and trusted the water by himself. Eddie was safe. It wasn't long before he went off on his own, a swimmer. Eddie's experience with his counselor is paradigmatic of the holding environment. The counselor maintained a safe boundary around Eddie, within which Eddie took on new experience.

How did swimming relate to Eddie's internal play? As it happened, Eddie had a problem. He couldn't stop water from pouring into his nose and sinuses. This was painful and uncomfortable. It didn't occur to him to tell his counselors, never mind his parents, so he could have gotten nose clips. It didn't occur to him that anyone would be responsive to his needs. He just lived with this and compensated by holding his head above water while swimming. Consequently, he swam awkwardly and tensely. Swimming with his head up was very tiring, so that he couldn't swim very far. As a result, Eddie never really enjoyed swimming. He was always more afraid than playful in the water. Swimming was not fun, just something he had to do at swim time. Eddie watched the other kids splash around without a care, having a good time. He felt alone. We can see that swimming was filtered through his play. The water was the projection screen of danger. He expected no responsiveness. He felt bad about himself that he wasn't a good swimmer. And he hung back from playing with his friends.

We see that these new circuits of experiential memory weren't just plink, plank, plunk—stand-alone things. They were incorporated into Eddie's internal scenarios and filtered through his cast of characters, relationships, and plots. They were incorporated into the structure of consciousness in the context of the already formed stories. The experience of swimming extended his play, his sense of himself, and his relatedness to others. To talk himself into diving into the water, Eddie took to counting to four. Sometimes, he counted two or three times before he would take the leap. This was the beginning of what would become a regular practice. No one knew what was going on in his mind, and he wasn't about to tell anybody.

In childhood, parents, family, teachers, and friends maintain an unbroken boundary around the child. Learning to swim is a metaphor for all of Eddie's immersions into the age-appropriate new facets of life—in school with academic learning, on the playground with sports, and in Sunday school, as well as music and art and dancing and biking and games. New experience is mastered and digested within the holding of this external boundary. Within it, Eddie was able to risk the leaps into the new and unknown in bite-sized, manageable pieces. From his mastery and internalization of life skills, he would be able to be on his own later. It does take a village to raise a child. Childhood learning takes place within the safe harbor of parents and village—the unbroken circle of childhood.

Eddie, at seven, was back at camp. The day of races and competitions approached. He had won the races the previous year, but this year there was a new kid, Peter, who was faster than Eddie. The day before the races, Eddie and a friend were off by themselves, throwing some construction debris over a stone wall. At some point Eddie heard a commotion on the other side of the wall. An ambulance came and took an injured kid away to the hospital. It was said that a square piece of wood had sailed over the wall and had hit a kid in the temple. The kid was Peter.

Eddie had flung this piece of wood. He had no idea anyone was on the other side of the wall, never mind that it was Peter. He was scared he'd killed or permanently damaged Peter, and he was so afraid he'd get in trouble that he didn't tell anyone. The word got around at dinner that Peter was okay, but he wouldn't be able to race the next day. Eddie was relieved but still very distraught.

The next day at the races, Eddie felt sick to his stomach. He refused to run. He wandered away from the track and across the road to a field of wildflowers. He spent the rest of the morning there by himself. He noticed that the clover was covered by tons of butterflies and dragonflies. He stood there, totally still, and studied them. He figured out how to bring his hand quickly from behind a butterfly and with a light touch, press its closed wings between his thumb and forefinger. He would catch a butterfly, examine it, and then release it; same with the dragonflies; same with the needle flies, the thin neon-blue ones. He wouldn't hurt them.

Eddie didn't play much baseball the rest of that summer. He'd wander back over to the field to catch butterflies. He never joined any of the formal nature activities. He had seen a collection of butterflies in the nature cabin that had been killed and preserved. He wasn't going to do that. He just went off by himself.

This event crossed the threshold of trauma—that is to say it had the power to rewrite his internal drama. In this case, Eddie became conflicted about his competitive aggression. He, in fact, loved sports. But now he carried a plotline of guilt, as if going full out was murderous aggression. Eddie had almost killed Peter. This blurred with Eddie's wish to defeat Peter in the first place, as well as his frustration that he couldn't. He knew Peter would have defeated him in the race. Although hitting Peter in the head was purely accidental, it contaminated the competitive aggression of Eddie's inner world. It was also linked to his inner confusion between good aggression and sadistic aggression. This confirmed that all was sadistic aggression and dangerous. Later, in an intensely competitive situation, an element of guilt surfaced, and Eddie tended to hold back.

This trauma was consonant with Eddie's belief that he was bad in the first place. It colored his natural good aggression with a darker hue, even darker than it was already. Ironically, the outcome of this trauma wasn't all negative. Fortuitously, it spurred Eddie's lifelong interest in and sense of intrigue with nature. Eddie began a current of authentic investigations that served him well when he got older, as a naturalist and biologist. This also highlights that the plays of consciousness are creative, living stories. They are rich and complex, not narrowly reductionistic.

It was visiting day in Eddie's third summer at camp. He was eager to see his parents. In the realm of emotional holding, Eddie had very low expectations. He wasn't aware of this. It was just the way it was. Nonetheless, at camp, he was homesick every year. It wasn't that he missed his parents. He didn't. Yet he often walked around with an amorphous dread, a nameless discomfort, with nowhere to turn. Remember, it's easier to leave the dinner table when you've eaten your fill than when there hasn't been enough food.

Cars pulled up, and happy campers jumped into their parents' arms. Eddie waited. Would the next car pulling up be the familiar Plymouth? Eddie kept his eyes on the bend in the road and waited ... and waited and waited. Eddie had a sinking feeling in his stomach. All the other parents had arrived. Where were his? He couldn't stand it. Finally, an hour later, they arrived. Eddie burst into tears. His parents were disgusted. "Stop acting like a baby. No one else is crying. We're here now." Besides, his father had cut short his golf game to make the trip.

Eddie was pitching in the afternoon baseball game, and he wanted them to see him in action. In the middle of his no-hitter, they left. There was no good-bye. They had to get back to something important at home. When on deck to hit, Eddie looked into the stands, and they weren't there. Tears of bewilderment filled his eyes. He took his turn at bat. Eddie knocked the first pitch as far as one had ever been hit on this field. His homer was written up in the camp newspaper.

Eddie felt the power in his muscles when he hit that ball with all his might. Eddie felt nothing. Where were they?

Life at home continued on. As Eddie got bigger, the physical abuse lessened. And he quietly went about his activities. He wouldn't have said that he was unhappy. This was just the way life was. At the dinner table, Father pontificated, and Mother was cold and silent. Eddie wouldn't say that he was angry either. His obsessional-compulsive symptoms—counting and tapping—were secret. He would give the finger under the tablecloth and maybe snap a pea off his plate at his brother when no one was looking. In the privacy of his room, he dreamed he'd be discovered as a great singer and be famous. He won academic and music awards in school, as was expected. He didn't think much of them. Eddie didn't count. Margie got all of the special acclaim. She was the chosen one. Clara was quiet and didn't disturb anyone. Life went on. Since the family had a good reputation, no one knew the real circumstances. Eddie participated in the social myth that he was from this special family, which coexisted with his private knowledge of coldness and brutality.

Eddie went to Sunday school and Bible study at his father's church. He was fascinated by the Bible stories. Not surprisingly, he had a significant fear of a punishing God, and he became somewhat overly scrupulous to be good. He was vaguely aware of the fact that his parents didn't seem to act very Christian at home, but he didn't think about it much. "Honor thy father and thy mother." Religion gave Eddie a framework of meaning. Christianity gave him an avenue to redeem his sense of badness. Childhood is a period of indoctrination. To "indoctrinate" means that an adult places a doctrine inside of the child. It is the natural task of childhood to take in the teachings of parental and societal authority. This happens in all societies. It is natural for children to learn the skills, beliefs, values, relationships, conventions, and cultural stories of their tribe. Childhood in humans, like with other mammals, is a playtime of learning as preparation for survival as an adult.

We still operate tribally. But in contemporary America, we don't all participate in a single, unified, cultural, tribal world. Instead, each family carves out a world of beliefs, values, skills, and teachings from disparate sources. You practice one religion. Your neighbor practices another. Some have the teachings of our public schools. Other kids go to private schools, with different approaches and different values. Books contain information from so many different vantage points and values. Then there's the information learned from media—TV, radio, video games, and the Internet. Each family raises its children with its own unique value on learning, on skills, on the arts, on athletics, on religion, on the military, etc.

Eddie was busy—at school, at home, and on the playground— mastering the skills he'd use later in adult life. In fact, Eddie had considerable native talents. He was very intelligent, and academic learning came easily to him. He was a very accomplished pianist and studied with a world-famous teacher. He was one notch below a prodigy. Nonetheless, he didn't really enjoy the piano, and he didn't like to practice. But he went through the motions enough to get by on his talent. Likewise, he was a very good athlete. Despite his secret removal, Eddie built a rich body of skills and knowledge in the course of his childhood education.

The fact that he excelled in childhood learning was, however, insufficient to alter his sense of himself as bad and inadequate. He was shy at school. His teachers were concerned about his inwardness. He was actually well liked, but he didn't particularly notice that others liked him. He was uncomfortable socially and didn't "play in many reindeer games." Although he always had a best friend, he felt inferior and grateful for the friendship.

In review, we see that Eddie was contained inside the holding bubble of childhood. Within this circle, he learned mastery over the valued practices of his culture. Eddie's childhood was filled with adventures, skills, thrills, security, love, loneliness, fear, boredom, loss, pain, victories, defeats, triumphs, learning, belonging, and rejections. These elaborated his internal dramas throughout his childhood. Eddie fulfilled his individual potential and built his cultural foundation within the holding of his village, in preparation for the next great transition—adolescence.

At the same time, his experience was filtered through the prism of his internal plays, as it refined those plays. In addition, he continued to be subject to the same problematic home environment that was influential in creating his plays in the first place. In childhood, we do not have the creation of new plays. They are already formed. They become extended, modified, and deepened through childhood experience

By age twelve, Eddie had mastered the teachings of childhood. He had his elaborated theater—a set of mastered skills, a body of cultural values, and a set of cultural beliefs. He had taken in the myths of his family, as well as the myths of his culture. Eddie's experiences in childhood, in the context of his unique theater, further developed and nuanced his plays, writing them into living memory. Eddie was a complex kid, a good kid, who never got into any trouble. Yet he felt profoundly bad about himself. His considerable talents did not alter his already established bad-self persona. His inner plays ruled his experience of himself and the world around him.

What would happen to Eddie, with the advent of adolescence, when he took leave of the intact circle of childhood and moved toward becoming a man in the world?

12

ADOLESCENCE
Eddie Embodies the Inner Drama as His Own

ONE DAY, THIRTEEN-YEAR-OLD EDDIE WAS walking down the street, or maybe he was on his bike, or watching a movie, or doing homework, or playing ball. He could have been doing anything. His morphogenic time clock kicked in and turned on his testosterone pump. It wasn't noticeable at first blush. But soon he was sleeping more. He got grumpy. He finally started growing and put on some height. His genitals grew and became active, with a mind of their own. Hair appeared over his lip, on his face, under his arms, and around his genitals. His voice began cracking. Whereas he used to have two eyebrows, now they seemed to have joined into one.

Humans blossom into sexual maturity for the same reason as the rest of nature—to propagate the species. Human consciousness leads us to assume that somehow we are outside the flow of biological nature. This is pure hubris. It is arrogant to think we are anything but biological creatures, like all biological creatures. We live out our capacities for survival and our trajectory of propagating the species through our unique rhythm of human morphogenesis and human consciousness. We are no different from dogwoods and orchids and dandelions and ferns and caterpillars/butterflies and lions and weasels and rats and wolves and orangutans. We, as mammals, seek the most suitable mate to create our offspring. We master the skills to survive, feed, shelter, protect, and provide for ourselves, our mate, and our offspring. In our unique human consciousness, we live it out through social relatedness with family and tribe. We fulfill and transmit the culture, the values, and the art of living to our progeny.

Eddie's testosterone pump was the egg tooth that burst the amniotic bubble of childhood. Unlike birth, which takes maybe a day, his emergence from childhood to adulthood had a time frame of eight years. This is adolescence. We have seen that the central and most important species-specific aspect of the human animal is human consciousness, through which we live our lives. Consequently, the transformations in the play of consciousness are at the center of human adolescence and will be our focus.

Eddie left the protective womb of childhood and would emerge by the end of adolescence, a man. Eddie's theater of operations now shifted to direct experience, where the internal cast of characters, self and other, collided with life, unmediated by the parental world. The major processes of adolescence would transpire through the collision of his childhood self with experience.

The etymology of "experience" is from the Latin *experiential*—act of trying (*ex* + *periri*—akin to *periculum*, or attempt). The definition is "direct observation of or participation in events as a basis of knowledge." So experience means testing oneself in reality. This is the adolescent's task. It is of interest that "fear" comes from the same Latin root, "periculum," meaning peril in the attempt. Fear impedes the fulfillment of experience. It causes the individual to hold back from attempting. Fear too plays a role in the evolution of the adult self.

Likewise, Eddie would move toward adult relatedness, with another actual adult, unmediated by his relations with family and friends of childhood. The adult fulfillment of relationship is intimacy. The etymology of "intimacy" is from the Latin *intimatus, intimare*—to put in—and *intimus* (innermost) and *interus* (inward). Intimacy is two self-contained people putting their innermost self into the insides of each other.

During adolescence, Eddie took leave of the protection and care of childhood and stepped out on his own. He undertook the wherewithal for provision and protection by himself. Metaphorically, he learned to hunt for his own food, rather than being provided for by his parents. He became a man. Likewise, he left home and ceased to relate in a primary way as a son and friend. He would establish his own autonomous relationship with a mate for love, sex, and children. He was impelled from within to stake his own claim in the world. Morphogenic biology was unfolding.

The ruptured boundary of childhood doesn't just dry up and disappear like the amniotic sac. It is an eight-year process. During this time, Eddie tested the limits of reality, experience, and himself. He emerged from the intact circle of his parents, tribe, and culture, and threw off the mantle of the rules of the parental world. His collision with experience was a long, slow journey. Parents and the tribe were still there. They surrounded adolescent-Eddie now with a circle of broken lines. Eddie went out through the spaces of the broken circle to venture into new and direct experience. He had to bump into the consequences of experience for himself in order to find his own way. When he went too far, he retreated back to the security of the boundaries provided by his parents and society—like a child who cuts his knee, he turns to his mother to be held and quieted, and then, once again, goes back out to take on the world on his own.

In adolescence, children need their parents more than ever. This is a time when parents must be there to provide the holding and care as the partial circle. Adolescents don't make this easy. But being a parent isn't easy. Like transition in childbirth, they break you, and then you regather yourself to be there for them. The most difficult and necessary part of the job description is to hang in there. This is what they need. And there will be many times when their teenager goes out through the broken lines, and like at birth, the parents hold their breath, wondering if their adolescent will make it. Then they breathe easy again. It's probably a good thing that parents don't witness everything their children are doing.

It is natural for children, like other juvenile animals, to submit to unquestioned adult authority. And Eddie had taken in the skills, values, and beliefs of society obediently. The internal dramas of childhood are morality plays, forged in concert with the imposed rules and beliefs of adult society. Adolescence was not a time when Eddie created new dramas and personas. It was the time when his already established inner plays would collide with experience. Eddie's plays would be on the front lines of adolescent experience. As Eddie plunged into new experience, he said no to the rules and constrictions imposed in childhood. He would try out everything for himself. Possibilities were limitless. Eddie tested the boundaries of reality and the boundaries of himself. He steered his way through experience to find out and fulfill who he was.

Societal authority plays very important roles in the adolescent's journey, as it forges the values and character of its people. The character of a culture impacts both the closed circle of childhood and the partial circle of adolescence. All cultures are not the same. Some embody respect, responsiveness, freedom, and responsibility. Others have darker traditions of cruelty, dominance, humiliation, and violence. Societies may err in the absence of a sufficient provision of the holding boundary, the hyphenated circle, for their kids. This promotes its adolescents to spin out of control, creating adults unprepared to manage their impulses and lead responsible lives. Or, societies may err in the direction of overcontrol and repression. This leads to stultified lives full of secret, suppressed impulses. These will either smolder in the dark or generate repressive, zealous paranoid attacks on other freer and responsible people. Life is difficult, and the living of an easy life is not an entitled privilege that is conferred upon an individual. An intact and good-enough culture needs to embrace and foster constructive values for the exigencies necessary for the sometimes harsh difficulties of adulthood.

Society's attitude toward adolescence is the final form of holding. A constructive society must let go of control and understand and respect the importance of an adolescent's need to try out life on his own terms. Likewise, the adolescent must be able to rely on the provision of wise boundaries and be able to refer back to and hold onto these boundaries in his quest. In order to choose a constructive adult life, every teenager must grapple with life's temptations, and recover when he inevitably strays too far. As the adolescent digests experience, he comes to choose his own authentic values as an adult.

Some of these may be the same as his discarded parental values, and some may be new and different. They will now be his own. Finally, to become a full adult, adolescents must do a walkabout to test their self-reliant capacities.

It is illuminating that an intensely constrictive and rule-driven culture like the Amish understands that an adolescent must try things out for himself. They allow their teenagers a period of *Rumschpringe*. This is a rite of passage where the kids are encouraged to break all the rules—dress in contemporary clothing, wear makeup, use machines, and try tobacco, alcohol, and marijuana. They understand that for a teenager to choose the Amish way of life, he must do so authentically. Consequently, Amish culture gives them the latitude to break the rules and experiment for themselves. It is then the choice of the adolescent to renounce these experiments and sign on to the adult strictures of the Amish, or to leave and go to the contemporary world. If they authentically choose the Amish way of life, they sign on through an adult Amish baptism. The transgressions committed during *Rumschpringe* are then dismissed and are of no consequence.

As Eddie emerged out of childhood, it was natural for him to be self-involved and take himself very seriously. The two main components of this natural self-involvement center around survival self-importance and sexual self-importance. An individual is self-involved to achieve the wherewithal for his own survival in the world. Likewise, each man and woman is self-involved in furthering his or her own sexual, propagation, and relationship aims. This self-involvement is egoism, which is not to be confused with egotism. Each individual is impelled from the inside to utilize his good aggression toward these ends. Ultimately, it is in the service of the competition to pass on one's own genes with the best genes of a possible mate. With his egoistic self-importance, Eddie would plunge into direct experience on his own.

When each of us goes through adolescence, we think we are unique in the world. In terms of the specifics of our experience and our internal play, that is true. On the other hand, we all go through the same thing. Adolescence is written into the human genome. Morphogenesis was not limited just to embryonic-Eddie, fetal-Eddie, and infant Eddie. As the unfolding of his genome, it was ongoing. Eddie's childhood had been a relatively slow period of morphogenesis—a time to build skills and values, a time to solidify and enrich the internal play in consciousness. Morphogenesis was quietly operative to consolidate a foundation of self in the cortex.

At puberty, morphogenesis exploded anew. It was a period of major and turbulent change. Its rapidity and scope was second only to the growth and transformations of embryonic-Eddie. The morphogenic processes of Eddie's adolescence allowed his childhood plays to become authentically his own. Eddie was the manifestation of the expression of his genome all the way through life. His genome expressed itself in an ordered and sequential way. At all times, the new and alive unfoldings adapted to their specific environment, and built on the actuality of previous adaptations.

The hormonal eruptions and all the body changes are not the central locus of adolescent morphogenesis, although they are very important. The major transformations are cortical, the elaboration of the plays of consciousness into adult form. The plays are the highest order of brain organization. It is important not to divide Eddie into a body, a mind, a soul, a social creature, etc. He is one organism. His physical tissues, his organs, his brain, his hormones, his synaptic mappings, and his plays of consciousness are all the expression of genomic morphogenesis.

His childhood self was a symbolic representation of Eddie, reflecting the incredibly high level of cortical order sufficient for top-down cortical processing. It gave him a functional identity. It would hardly be efficient for the organism, Eddie, to pull together some idea of Eddie from scratch each time he had to decide whether or not to brush his teeth. His brain activated this default mapping, by which Eddie knew himself as Eddie on an ongoing basis. New and extended mappings of the collision of his body/self with experience would now be at the center of adolescence.

Direct experience results in a massive new cortical mapping, filtered through the limbic system, where child-Eddie self gets elaborated into his adult self. Hence, the following were mapped: feelings, impulses, body sensations, sexual impulses, stimulations, fantasy, actions, and plots; sadomasochistic sensations of the body and plots; drink and drugs; physical and sensational actions of the body-self; the deeply powerful feelings of adolescence—the pain of rejection, the agony of defeat, the ecstasy of triumphs; and all of the newly opened plots of the internal drama played out on the projection screen of reality.

We must remember that Eddie was unaware that his internal scenarios and personas were invisibly guiding him through experience. (Behind the scenes, they are the key players.) His choices and temptations were filtered through those internal personas and scenarios. As Eddie mapped his new and direct adolescent experience, he fulfilled and extended those scenarios into the adult form of his play. Over time, Eddie formed judgments from his own experience and the consequences of his behaviors for himself. This is how he authentically embodied his adult self as his own.

In fact, Eddie's judgment was not yet fully developed. As mentioned earlier, myelin sheath development follows a morphogenic timetable built into the genome. The neurons of the prefrontal lobes are not scheduled to myelinate until late adolescence. This area of the cortex houses intention, planning, and judgment. Consequently, the large-scale frontal lobe synaptic mapping, in concert with the myelinization of the prefrontal lobes, are at one with the consolidation of adult judgment at the end of adolescence. Prior to this, the younger adolescent operates without fully evolved frontal lobes. Developmentally, the younger adolescent operates as if he has had a prefrontal lobotomy. You may have noticed that teenage judgment is not of the highest order. It coalesces from adolescent experience.

The holding circle of provision, protection, values, and attachment would now shift to Eddie's internal theater, replacing the previous external bubble of childhood. These attributes were no longer outside of Eddie. The legacy of holding moved inside. This was the final chapter of the dance of self and other. Eddie would operate from his adult personal capacities—his own internal, authentic, independent wherewithal. This would constitute his adult character.

Every teenager comes into collision with the smorgasbord of life's temptations. The list of temptations is not long—sex, drugs, drink, gambling, eating (from gluttony to anorexia), reckless action and sensation-seeking, stealing and cheating, egotism, and sadomasochistic attachment and anger. Why do some kids experiment with and then stop self-destructive behavior, while other kids go deeper into the dark side of life? The teenager who has had good-enough loving in childhood retains the presence of his Authentic-Being as the core of his self. The Authentic-Being is the rudder by which one navigates through the smorgasbord of experience and life's temptations. When this adolescent strays too far in a self-destructive avenue, as all kids do, there is a quiet voice inside him that says, "What am I doing? I've got to stop this."

The Authentic-Being is the most important possession of an adolescent. It is his foundation. It is what allows him to pull back and relinquish a problematic temptation. It is a kind of gyroscope that rights him, from the inside, to find his way to a character of solid and constructive values. And why does one kid select one of the problematic temptations and reject the other ones? We will see that the actual constellation of the inner play, reflecting the unique array of temperament, deprivation, and abuse leaves one susceptible to different temptations.

How did this play out for Eddie? In childhood, he had taken in the values and preparatory skills of his society. He exercised discipline in school; he practiced the piano; he embraced his Christian values; and he was obedient in his social world. His internal play in childhood was sufficiently intact for him to function quite well. He appeared, on the surface, to be a boy of great promise. We know he lacked a sufficient foundation of Authentic-Being. We know that his inner play had the dark cast of sadomasochism. We know he was not surrounded by a caring, holding, partial parental circle. We know that Eddie lacked a good-enough internal foundation and that the external holding of adolescence would be insufficient. This did not portend well for Eddie's adolescence. And so as Eddie began puberty, his internal play collided with experience.

Like all teenagers, Eddie threw off the imposed rules of childhood. No longer saying yes to those values, he now said no. Eddie completed his Bible study and confirmation. As expected, he won special commendation. When it was time for his confirmation speech, when he was to thank his family and the like, Eddie couldn't think of anything to say. He felt empty and lacking, as if there was something wrong with him. To come up with something, he plagiarized from Margie's speech two years earlier. It was well received, and no one figured it out. He felt shame about this secret, but it worked. Eddie never looked back. He quit the church and refused to attend any of the teenage activities. Suddenly, he was drawn to Holden Caulfield in *The Catcher in the Rye*. He grew his hair.

Eddie became quietly rebellious and defiant. He quickly developed contempt for prevailing conventional ideas and proudly saw himself as a nonconformist. Since his temperament was passive, and he bordered on being phobic, Eddie was never an actively aggressive behavior problem. He didn't get into fights. He didn't study much in school, but still managed to get all *A*s. He knew he wasn't learning anything in depth, but he didn't much care. He was able to stay under the radar. He continued his science, which was easy for him, but he was more and more drawn toward the artistic kids. He gradually drifted away from his old friends and fancied himself as "deep." He lost interest in organized sports, seeing them as meaningless and superficial. He wouldn't be a stupid jock. He began to devalue and diminish those who were not like him. We see from this that he was consolidating an egotistical surface, by which he was compensating for feeling inferior, lacking, and empty.

Eddie had been a classical pianist, but at fourteen, he quit studying classical piano altogether. His teacher cried, but Eddie was not to be dissuaded. His parents haughtily disapproved of all music except classical. He rejected classical music because it felt imposed, borrowed, and inauthentic. He wanted to be free. Never having played off the notated musical page, he wanted to play by ear and improvise for himself. He switched to jazz. People thought he was pretty good, but he felt earthbound. He never got comfortable playing by ear. He felt his improvisations were studied, uninspired, and obvious. By the time he got to college, he hated his music. Once again, Eddie felt even his jazz playing was empty and copied. He quit the piano altogether.

The underlying issue in Eddie's musical quest was the inaccessibility of his Authentic-Being. Music was a vehicle for his quest for authenticity. By virtue of his emptiness, he endeavored to create something out of nothing. He couldn't do it. He felt inauthentic. He felt like a fraud. He hated himself for his inadequacy. This did not reflect an absence of talent. His musical failure confirmed that there was something missing in him. The self-fulfilled prophecy of his emptiness played true.

Now to the smorgasbord of temptations: Eddie experimented with alcohol but wasn't much interested. He played some poker with his friends and was good at it, due to his math abilities. But he shied away from stakes that were higher than nickel or dime. Likewise, he participated in some car racing and chasing and pranks but always as a follower. He was uncomfortable in the context of recklessness and danger. He often felt scared but pushed himself to participate, feeling ashamed of his reticence. When his friends went parachute jumping or lit fires in the woods, Eddie would have no part of it. But his hesitancy wasn't a balanced and mature moral decision. He was afraid, and he feared getting into trouble. His secret phobic hesitations kept him in check. He actually felt inferior and inadequate that he wasn't more of a "bad" boy. He was ashamed of being a "good" boy. The wrong reasons kept him out of trouble.

One night, at age fifteen, he and his friends got jumped by some college football players. They were walking home at midnight after a prank where Eddie had tagged along. Some of his friends got seriously beaten up. Some ran. Eddie held his ground, despite his fear. Miraculously, he didn't get punched. As a result of this event, Eddie was terrified to walk the streets at night for years, He felt a paralyzing apprehension in his chest. This anxiety was a secret shame, which he never mentioned to anyone. This phobic state, in fact, was generated in resonance with the violent anger he carried from the beatings by Mommy Dearest.

Stealing was a minor issue for Eddie. At thirteen and fourteen, he repeatedly shoplifted candy at the corner drugstore, where he was well known as a good kid. This left a guilt legacy. For years after whenever he walked out of a store without buying anything, he was certain that the cashier thought he was stealing something.

Eddie did not seem to have any eating issues, but this wasn't accurate. From earliest childhood, he always ate a lot to fill his emptiness. However, by virtue of being constitutionally thin, this never showed. So an eating substitute for love was present but masked.

Eddie was deeply private about his sexual awakening. He was quite prudish about his first sexual stirrings. Eddie's image-ination created, gave form to, two internal images of rejecting, unloving females. One was of a beautiful, unattainable blonde goddess. The other was of a dark-haired, cold, evil, exciting temptress. These became his masturbation fantasy images. Sex felt forbidden and desirable before masturbation. It was always followed by a sense of shame and self-loathing.

Adding to his secrecy was some frequent masturbatory activity with his neighbor Marie, from ages thirteen through fifteen. Both of them kept their clandestine meetings top secret and never divulged them to anyone. They were in different social circles at school and barely acknowledged each other publicly. He did not have love feelings for her. He had sexual feelings for Marie and for her servicing him. He was not interested in her for an above-board relationship.

Even though Marie took the lead in their sexual play, his own desire made him feel and know he was responsible. When Marie had problems of an ill-defined nature later in high school, Eddie blamed it on himself. His secret sex with Marie was compartmentalized. Co-existing with their secret practice, Eddie longed for a girlfriend and felt despondent about his lack of success socially. He went through the motions but was shy and uncomfortable. He felt inept. He shied away from girl talk and sex talk, because he felt too ashamed. We see that his early adolescent sexuality—masturbation, and Marie—were clearly informed by his inner play. It was infused with shame, badness, and guilt. This early adolescent sexual experience was mapped accordingly. Sexuality would soon play a pivotal role in the all-important arena of relationships (i.e., attachment experience).

The three remaining temptations—sadomasochistic attachment, egotism, and drugs—comprised the perfect storm, where Eddie lost his way. The presence of his dark play and the absence of the Authentic-Being reference inside fostered a destructive path from which he could not recover. The most important and destructive temptation, which soon was his undoing, was in the realm of attachment, where the projections from his inner world were played out in experience.

As a junior in high school, Eddie met Cathy, who was then a sophomore. He was completely smitten. (Notice the etymology of *smitten*: to defile, to kill or severely injure by smiting; to attack or afflict suddenly and injuriously.) He was totally infatuated. He had a crush; he was bowled over. She was a poet, pretty, light-haired, and edgy. He felt unworthy and was shocked that she would even look at him. To his surprise, she was interested.

They kissed. Eddie felt an incredible high. Nothing ever tasted any better than this. The beautiful golden girl chose him. She wanted him. Eddie was hooked. This was it for him. Cathy was everything. Nothing else mattered. They did become boyfriend and girlfriend and continued to be so for the next three years. His thoughts, twenty-four hours a day, were about Cathy. He was consumed by her.

Remember, we already know that Eddie had given up and closed off from his need for love by the time he was three years old. Any need for love was hopeless and would be forever unrequited. His solution was to have no needs. He had withdrawn his Authentic-Being and the need for love behind a castle wall of thorns to protect himself. But in adolescence, this all got reopened. By the kiss, Sleeping Eddie awakened and opened himself up anew to the need for love. This was the most powerful moment of Eddie's life. Eddie was judged to be wanted and "want-able."

Not surprisingly, the golden moment didn't last long. Tragically, Cathy was not Princess Charming. She looked like her. She was, unfortunately, perfect for the replay of the substitute for love that Eddie was primed for—sadomasochistic attachment. This, of course, corresponded to the central scenario of his play. It was to be his temptation of choice.

Eddie's internal attachment scenario invisibly projected itself onto the Eddie/Cathy relationship, where it would play itself out in experience. She was a perfect fit as the projection screen for the image of this female persona. Her physical appearance corresponded to his sexual fantasy—the unattainable, rejecting, attractive, blonde female. Cathy was a self-involved narcissist. She possessed the attributes that he admired—her writing and superior creative intellect. Eddie didn't notice her narcissism, as he was as Cathy-involved as she was, his own temperament being echoistic. Her self-involvement, beauty, special worth, talents, and narcissism, her rejecting and judgmental coldness worked beautifully. She became enthroned as the self-fulfilled prophecy of the judge who had the power to affirm him as want-able, or to reject him. Cathy was a dream come true. Unfortunately, he didn't realize what kind of dream this was. He didn't know it was to be the ogre dream.

No matter what, Eddie always felt unworthy and never trusted Cathy's commitment to him. He never believed that she truly accepted, loved, or even liked him. He was always reading Cathy for signs of disinterest in him. The torture of rejection was played out over and over. This was his context of maso-sadistic attachment. Eddie had to prove himself worthy (i.e., disprove that he was unworthy) with the narcissistic surface as its projection screen. He was always jealous and filled with insecurity that she'd choose somebody better. Since Eddie carried no reference in him that loving was for one another's Authentic-Being, he lived out the available substitute. Relatedness was needle on thorn.

And so it went. Eddie quickly sank back into his regular feelings of deficiency and unworthiness, his default position. We know that in his play, he was unloved and hated. He carried that he was rejectible on the basis that he was bad and unworthy. With Cathy as its projection screen, Eddie's image-ination had long since created the internal figure of his female persona from a combination of his mother and Margie. The primary sadistic female figure derived, of course, from Mommy Dearest. The narcissism and special worth derived from Eddie's internal image of Margie.

Sex became the special courtroom where Eddie's worth was on trial. He constantly read Cathy's responsiveness to him as her verdict. Any slight hesitation, never mind disinterest, was a rejection, confirming his unworthiness, sending him into desperation. A positive response was an affirmation that he qualified and was worthy. At its best, however, a positive response never really affirmed his value. It temporarily disproved that he was rejectible. This lasted only as long as the flavor lasted. It never undid the underlying conviction that he was bad and unwant-able.

People often assume that sex is just sex. But we can see that the meaning of Eddie's sexuality derived from its incorporation into a relationship of sadomasochistic attachment. This scenario was one of torment and rejection. Sex with Cathy was inseparable from that context. This was built on top of the badness and shame about sex, which was already established and mapped. His sexuality with Cathy was embedded in a scenario of torment, judgment, and rejection, played out over and over, with full body and emotional intensity. It coalesced as his sexuality.

We are not talking about intimacy between two whole people here. The very attributes that Eddie admired in Cathy were the attributes he felt lacking in himself. Eddie envied Cathy's gifts. He wanted to possess her special attributes for himself. He wanted to complete himself so that he would qualify as admirable, and hence, be "want-able." Consequently, sex wasn't an act of intimacy and love between self-contained individuals. It was actually a fantasy of merger, where he would be validated by her as worthy, based on possessing her attributes.

Eddie, who had never needed anyone, was now in desperation most of the time. The need was not really for love. He thought it was. It was this substitute avenue to complete himself and to undo rejectibility. Eddie was enormously dependent on Cathy's validation. She had total power over him. He kept all of this hidden, and no one would have suspected. Eddie had gotten used to putting on a mask for the world. But he was really living out this consuming torture. No one knew or saw, but this was the actuality. This is what was mapped.

Eddie didn't have any hint of an "Uh-oh. Hold it here ... what am I doing?" from a grounding in his Authentic-Being. There was no one in his life—parent, family, or friend—who could have said, "Hold on a minute here, Eddie. She's bad news. What are you thinking?" It isn't clear that he would have listened anyway. Despite his torment—or because of it—Eddie's enthusiasm for deepening this self-destructive relationship was like a freight train.

When he left home to attend an Ivy League school, he missed Cathy terribly. He feared she would find someone new and better. Her absence was a torture. Eddie was not able to concentrate on his schoolwork. He felt like he was in a fog. And for the first time, he didn't do so well in his courses. And then it happened. That summer after his freshman year, Cathy broke up with him. Eddie was devastated. His worst nightmare had come true. She did find someone new. She had found somebody better.

The crowning blow of maso-sadistic attachment was rejection. The enactment of his play was complete. It was what he had protected himself from in the first place, when he first withdrew into his fortress. The rejection fully confirmed him as bad and unwant-able. He was shattered. He cried uncontrollably for weeks, having never shed a tear in his life. He couldn't go on without her. He was distraught for the entire summer.

Finally, Eddie withdrew back inside a protective shell. He hardened and closed off emotionally, and resolved never to let anyone hurt him. He would not let anyone in again. His fortress would now be impenetrable. He would become the rejector, not the rejectee. He would never give again.

Eddie now deepened his immersion into egotism. His echoism had been a perfect fit with narcissistic Cathy. After the rejection, he switched teams over to the narcissistic side to prove himself special. He identified now with the aggressor by doing to others what Cathy had done to him. He turned the tables and became as critical of others as he had been of himself. He attacked others with his own sadistic judgments toward their shortcomings. He relished his sharp tongue and cynical attitude. It became his preferred mode of relating. He was no longer the nice guy, and he liked that. His mantra became "I don't care."

He went through lots of girls. The pattern was always the same. There was an initial attraction. And then what followed was seduce, conquer, lose interest, reject, and drift away, over and over. As Eddie deepened his narcissistic solution, there was no Authentic-Being to call him back, no quiet voice that said to him, "Get over yourself." Nor was there a parent or friend who could take him down a notch or three.

Eddie's denouement came through the final temptation: drugs. Eddie turned to drugs to fortify himself, to fill his emptiness and loneliness, and to inflate his ego. Cigarettes worked up to a point. Always a smoker, Eddie increased his smoking to over a pack a day. The process of smoking, filling the lungs, coincides with the physical location in the body for the feeling of emptiness. It is felt in the chest. Eddie filled his emptiness with a drug. Nicotine also has the drug effect of constricting the arterioles all over the body. This physical shutdown at every capillary mimicked a physical holding, which fortified and fed his emotional shutdown.

Marijuana worked even better—a psychotropic, also inhaled. His lungs, full of THC smoke, was a full-filling experience. He felt that it stimulated his creativity. He believed it made him a deeper and creative thinker, the very attributes he felt were missing in himself. Marijuana fostered his specialness, which had already become the criteria for his value as a person. And he quickly became dependent on it to inflate his burgeoning and false sense of superiority. Marijuana also amplified his sensations, which gave him a false feeling of participation and engagement in life. He often smoked before social situations to undo being exposed as lacking and worthless, and to diminish his social anxiety.

Eddie had no access to an inner voice saying, "Wait a minute—what am I doing?" He went the other way: "This stuff is great." He was actively seeking a drug to enhance his sense of specialness. Marijuana fortified his decision to harden himself emotionally, by numbing himself from human feeling. *I feel good. I feel great. I don't need anybody. I'm superior.*

Finally, the use of psychedelics—LSD, mescaline, and psilocybin—took it to the next level. This was to be the last straw. Eddie was hooked on filling his emptiness with artificial enhancements in order to be special, deep, spiritual, and creative—egotism, amplified through chemistry. He believed they gave him special insight, as he climbed the artificial, drug-induced tower of specialness. He was ready to crash.

After the breakup and the summer of hell, his brain fog lifted. His narcissistic and drug solution seemed to work for the rest of college. He was able to resume academic success and managed to accumulate an A grade-point average. On the surface, he lived a successful college life. Eddie was due to graduate with honors and was accepted into a prestigious PhD program in biology. All the while, he felt alone and dead inside. No one really knew him.

He met another very attractive girl, but it happened again. It always did. He succeeded in his conquest. Immediately, he felt the nausea and lost all interest. *Here I am. I should feel good, but I feel totally alone. I just want to get out of here.* He knew something was wrong. This was soon to be followed by a frightening LSD experience, which broke him. It all came tumbling down.

The self-fulfilled prophecy came true. Eddie was destroyed. He was frightened, anxious, and empty. He felt lonely and fraudulent. Drugs were the final avenue. But as we have seen, it was much more than that. The invisible power of his dark play had fulfilled itself. The inner story always plays true. Our Eddie was in trouble.

We have seen how adolescence put flesh on the bones of Eddie's internal play. The damage to his well-being, which happened early in life, played itself out. Eddie did not enter adulthood solid, whole, and prepared to take on life. He was not capable of building an independent life for himself. He was nowhere near a readiness for intimacy with a solid woman. Eddie was an empty narcissistic surface. Instead of the ability to love and have intimacy with another whole person, Eddie's mode of relating was via emotional hurting and being hurt.

This has been the story of Eddie. We have traced his evolution from Eddie the zygote to Eddie the adult. The focus has been on his adaptations to his salient environment throughout his development. We have seen Eddie's formless Authentic-Being coalesce. We saw it evolve into Eddie's self and the writing of his internal play. Then we saw its enculturation in childhood. And via adolescence, we have just seen his play morph into its final form where it was embodied as his own.

We know that Eddie's internal play was written from the impacts of extreme deprivation and abuse on his native temperament. Although he was a child with many gifts—intelligence, talents, and athleticism—this could not override the internal sadomasochistic play with a self, ungrounded in his Authentic-Being. It played itself out in adolescence to forge his adult character. Underlying his cultivated narcissistic surface, Eddie remained fundamentally a masochistic echoist. He related on the basis of sadomasochistic anger. He was prone to fears and self-attack. His identity was established as bad, undeserving, and rejectible. He felt empty and fraudulent. And from the consequence of drug use, he was shattered.

We have seen the evolution of Eddie's adult character. His play, all the way through his development, was the prism that informed his world. It invisibly determined the qualities of his experience. At the same time, as morphogenesis unfolded, the actual particulars of his life had not been predictable. The specific qualities of Eddie's parents, his brother, his sisters, aunts, uncles, teachers, friends, girl-friends, the culture, and the happenstance of the moment-to-moment experience of his life were all unpredictably alive and unique. His adult character was created out of all of these forces.

And so it is with nature and nurture for all of us. Our temperaments differ; our salient environments differ; our parents, our culture, and the happenstances of our lives differ. Consequently, each of our adult characters is absolutely unique. No two snowflakes are alike, but we are all snowflakes. And we all form the same way. The story of Eddie is the story of all of us.

When we began with the ogre dream, we saw it as a one night's creation of consciousness, triggered by an event of the day. It was, in fact, an enactment of the inner drama of Eddie's consciousness. It was the story of his life. Eddie now inhabited his adult character. He came by it honestly. The self-fulfilled prophecy of damage had materialized. The question is, do we have Humpty-Dumpty on our hands? Can Eddie be repaired to fulfill himself in a solid way as an adult? Can Eddie recover his Authentic-Being and the capacity to be, to live, and to love and flourish?

Our subject now shifts to psychotherapy, which, as we will see, specifically addresses the recovery of the Authentic-Being from damage done to the character by the forces of deprivation and abuse.

PSYCHOTHERAPY

13

THEATER, MASKS, AND DESTINY

As we go about the business of living a life, a major life decision for all of us is the choice of a suitable occupation. Most people, as a matter of course, tend to maximize the pleasure and satisfactions of life and minimize the pain. Pain is certainly the aspect of living that people with any common sense tend to avoid—or at least keep to a minimum. However, among the various roles of human endeavor, there is one walk of life in every culture that goes against the grain. This is the doctor/priest/shaman, who deals with human pain in the service of alleviation of suffering. He delves into the mysteries of life to serve the well-being, thriving, and healing of others in his society or tribe.

Psychiatry serves that function in our society. Toward this end, the therapist evolves a working relationship with the pains and suffering of human existence. The traditions of healing for the doctor/ priest/shaman throughout all cultures in history operate within the belief systems of their culture. We, too, operate within our own circumscribed belief systems. In order to grapple with human suffering and the human condition as fully and effectively as possible, it is incumbent upon us to ensure that our paradigm of human nature is as accurate as possible.

For an understanding of human nature to be valid, it has to conform to the actual brain-body in its development and organization. It cannot be a pastiche of ideas that fits somebody's theory but does not correspond to the actualities of the human genome as it orchestrates morphogenesis into the mature adult brain-body. Likewise, in order for an understanding of the operations of the brain-body to be meaningful, it has to be consonant with actualities of human life. We have seen, through the story of Eddie, that the characterological play in the theater of consciousness is precisely this organized creation of the human genome. It is through the internal drama that we live our lives. The play, within the theater of consciousness, encompasses human character, human struggle, dreams, myths, art, religion, and beliefs in general.

In order for psychiatry to be meaningful, it has to be consonant with the development and operations of the play of consciousness. We saw in the story of Eddie that his internal play was created as the impacts of love, respect, deprivation, and abuse were digested by his temperament all the way through his development. With good-enough loving, our adult selves are sufficiently infused by the Authentic-Being, which fosters authenticity and the capacity to love. When our character is too damaged, the Authentic-Being is diminished or absent as a presence in our adult selves. Our character plays then traffic in the currency of anger in the context of sadomasochism, as it did with Eddie. This is the source of human suffering, the subject of psychiatry.

The proper focus of psychiatry is to grapple with the powerful hold our problematic internal plays have over us. Psychotherapy will be shown to be that avenue, consonant with the workings and processes of the theater of consciousness, to foster recovery from the damage done to our characters. We are prisoners of a drama we can't even see. Psychotherapy is a kind of living theater that gives form to and access to our invisible internal play. In the context of genuine emotional holding, it allows for the mourning of our problematic plays and recovery from suffering. Psychotherapy has many features in common with the art form of regular theater. In order to appreciate the unique attributes of the living theater of therapy, let us first look at the operations of its first cousin, regular theater and its plays.

Let's go now into the theater and take our seats. The lights dim as the play is to begin. The curtain rises. One first sees a set design, which initially may seem artificial. It may be a literal rendering of a Victorian drawing room, or a minimalist suggestion of a setting, or even no staging, as with *The Syringa Tree*, where one's brain invents the entire implied landscape. Likewise, when the actors first appear, they may seem stiff. Their costumes may seem artificial. The language might feel stilted. You, in the audience, may be conscious of sitting in an uncomfortable seat with not enough leg room, and maybe you are subject to an offending cologne.

Relatively quickly, if the play is well written, well directed, and well acted, you join the art trance. You take leave of your regular self and are transported into the play reality via your image-ination. Within the art-ifice of the art form and within the boundaries of the theatrical production, the drama becomes alive. It comes to feel real. It can make you laugh or cry. It can make you be afraid. Since art is a partial trance, you aren't completely absorbed, as in the full trance of a dream. In the partial trance, one foot is inside the trance and the other foot is outside it. You, sitting in the audience, are both absorbed in the play and remain separate, reflecting on it. You are a participant-observer of the play.

What does it mean to be a participant? Inside the boundaries of the art form, you enter the trance state of the play reality. You enter the drama and feel what a character feels. Feelings aren't stand-alone things. They always take place within a scenario of personas. If you witness a character suffering from unrequited love, you may resonate with the forlorn character who is rejected. You may identify as the character who rejects but may not want to hurt the rejected one. You may resonate with one or the other or both of these characters, depending on your predilection. You may resonate with a character and any potential feeling he has towards an antagonist—love, hate, repulsion, etc. Or you may identify with a hero, or a villain, or a victim; you may identify with a quest for courage or with any of the various characters and plots that make up the whole spectrum of comedy and tragedy.

As a participant, you enter the play reality and are swept away in it. You do so from your human image-ination, which, as we have seen, is organized in the cortex as personas, feeling relatedness, and their plots. By dint of our image-inations, we are capable of experiencing the entire scope of human experience. It is not necessary to have had the same experience as the characters to vicariously live their feeling and their plot scenarios. While watching a play, you may come through hope and despair and disappointment and consummation and victory and defeat and pain and loneliness and loss and treachery and fear and cruelty and sexuality and humor and love.

As an observer, you remain outside the trance where you assess and analyze the goings-on. You watch what unfolds on stage, emotionally distanced from the drama and removed from the feeling and involvements of the characters. From this distance, you think about the play.

Each of us in the audience, according to our temperament, lies somewhere on the spectrum of the participant/observer axis. Some people may be on the far observer end of the axis. A few people of this persuasion may become theater critics. These people would do well to come the other way and join in the world of feeling.

Others may be on the far end of the participant side. They get overly involved with the dramas and don't retain sufficient observer separateness. These people will be prone to a boundary blur. They would do well to get some distance and a clarity of boundaries. The presence of a clear boundary keeps the audience member in his seat, silent and not jumping onto the stage. When I went to a production of *The Wiz*, there was an adorable six-year-old girl in the audience. At the moment the very scary-looking and powerful Wizard of Oz swung open a door and made his dramatic entrance on stage, she stood right up, pointed at him, and bravely said in a loud voice, "You go back in there!" This broke up the entire theater—both the audience and the cast. The Wiz himself came out of character and couldn't stop laughing. Similarly, during a production of *A Raisin in the Sun*, an elderly black woman in the audience so identified with the pain that she began crying and moaning uncontrollably, and had to be led out of the theater. It is commonplace for many of us in the audience to cry in the presence of deep pain while watching a play.

Art communication is geared to affect our internal theaters through participation-observer experience. Our image-inations take in the figures of the theatrical art-ifice and feed them into our cortex as feeling persona experience. When applauding at the end of a performance, it is not unusual for most people to trip over the blur between art reality and reality. Are we applauding for the actors' performance? Are we applauding for the characters they are playing? Or are we applauding for the excellence of the play itself?

Let's say you go to a cast party after the play and meet an actor who played an important character. It's hard to separate his character from the role he was playing. Sometimes it's even disappointing that he seems so different from a beloved or heroic character. If he played a scary character, he may continue to creep you out. The power of art is that it crosses the boundary into our internal theaters and joins our internal plays.

The personas, the relationships, and the plot adventures of a good play continue to live on inside us very powerfully. We may be deeply affected and changed by the experience. It may even rise to the level of being permanently transformative. This is actually the value and function of the art-ifice of theater. And it operates through participant-observer, limbic-cortical illusion.

To understand the operations of theater more fully, we need to plunge more deeply into the origins of Western theater—fifth-century Greek theater. It was convention in Greek theater for the actors to wear masks made of linen, wood, or leather that covered their entire heads. The mask was a two-dimensional representation of the character, a kind of caricature of the character being enacted. It helped the actor vanish into character and enhance his transformation into his part.

The actor behind the mask spoke his lines through a mouth hole in the mask. The etymology of the word "person" itself comes from the sound of an actor's voice coming though the hole in his mask. In Latin, *per* means through, and *son* means sound. A "person" is the being behind the mask. In fact, the use of masks in Greek theater itself derived from even older shamanistic rites of the Dionysian cult. The ancient shamanistic practices themselves were founded on the intrinsic duality between the inner being and the surface self.

It was standard in classical Greek theater to have a chorus. The chorus consisted of twelve men all wearing identical masks speaking in unison, who expressed hidden knowledge of the fate of the characters. Through the chorus, the Greek plays addressed the hidden source of the morality play. Thus, a character inexorably played out his destiny, which was known by the chorus but not by the character himself. He was oblivious that he was enacting a destiny that was built into his character. And he was likewise oblivious as to where it came from.

Destiny, and the story behind the story, are very much the subject of Greek theater. This is beautifully illuminated in the myth of *Oedipus*, as rendered by Sophocles, Aeschylus, and even Homer. Do not confuse the actual Oedipus story with Freud's projective misunderstanding of the meaning of this play. More on that momentarily. The actual story is illuminating.

It all started with Oedipus's father, Laius. As a young man, Laius's life was in danger in his native Thebes because of a revolution. He was rescued, taken in, and protected by a neighboring king, Pelops. Years later, King Pelops entrusted his son Chrysippus to Laius, who was appointed to be his mentor. A mentor is like a father and as such it is a sacred responsibility. Laius rewarded King Pelops's friendship and trust by abducting and raping Chrysippus. In addition to the betrayal of Pelops, the rape of a mentee is the analogue of incest, and even murder. Laius's crime was the source of all the trouble to follow. It angered the queen goddess Hera, who cursed Laius. This morality play of sadistic violation and its consequence was written in the context of the belief system of the ancient Greeks with their gods and goddesses.

Years later, after Laius captured the throne and became king of Thebes, he consulted the Oracle of Delphi to learn about his fate. We are all familiar with what he heard. As punishment for his crime, he was told not to have a child; if he did, his son would grow up and kill him and marry his wife, Jocasta. Hera would mete out justice for Laius's crime.

Laius, of course, ever the sexual profligate, carried on, got drunk, and impregnated his wife anyway. Jocasta gave birth to their son, Oedipus. To protect himself from his fate, Laius bound and impaled baby Oedipus's ankles together with a spear. He ordered Jocasta to kill her baby, but she couldn't do it. Instead, Jocasta gave baby Oedipus to a shepherd and instructed him to leave the baby on a mountain to die from exposure. The shepherd couldn't kill the baby either, so he took him home. But he couldn't raise baby Oedipus because he was too poor. He had heard that the king and queen of Corinth couldn't have children and were desperate for a baby. So the shepherd gave Oedipus to them. The king and queen of Corinth loved and raised Oedipus as their own son.

This is a common myth story. It is the same as the story of Moses. An astrologer had told the Pharaoh that the liberator of the Israelites would be born on a certain day, which was of course Moses' birthday. So he ordered all babies born on that day to be killed. At first, Moses' mother hid him away, but it became too dangerous, so she placed baby Moses in a basket and hid him in the rushes of the Nile. Pharaoh's daughter found him and raised him as her own. Neither the Pharaoh nor Moses himself knew who he really was. And sure enough he grew up and fulfilled the prophecy and defeated the Pharaoh. We saw the same story in *Sleeping Beauty*, when the cook defied the ogre queen's orders to kill the children, Day and Morning, and raised them himself.

Oedipus grew up and knew himself simply as the well-loved prince of Corinth. As a young man in quest of the truth of his past, he consulted the Oracle of Delphi. In this comedy of errors—actually, tragedy of errors—he was told not to go home; otherwise, he would kill his father and marry his mother. This was upsetting to Oedipus, as he loved his parents, the king and queen of Corinth. Consequently, to protect them, he resolved not to go home to Corinth ever again. Instead, he headed off to Thebes, unbeknownst to him, the home of his biological parents. Sure enough, he met Laius on the road. Laius imperiously demanded that Oedipus step aside and let him pass. Oedipus refused, and Laius struck him. Oedipus retaliated and killed him. Oedipus did not know who this man was or that he was the king of Thebes, never mind that he was Oedipus's father. The murder of his father was totally innocent and unintentional on Oedipus's part.

Meanwhile, Thebes had been under a curse by the Sphinx (a supernatural creature who felt wrath about something or another), which created hardships for the citizens. It was told that he who solved the riddle of the Sphinx would end the curse and become king of Thebes. *"What is the creature that walks on four legs in the morning, two legs at noon, and three in the evening?"* Sure enough, Oedipus solved it: *"Man, who crawls on all fours as a baby, walks on two legs as an adult, and adds a walking stick as an old man."* Thebes was freed from the curse. This upset the Sphinx, who promptly killed himself. Oedipus became king of Thebes, and was given Jocasta's hand in marriage.

In chapter two of Oedipus, the tragedy of errors continues. Thebes was once again beset by plagues. You know, the gods were still mad. Oedipus consulted the oracle again to try to fix things. He was told that the gods were angry again and the plagues were the result of the unsolved murder of the previous king, Laius. Oedipus was determined to save Thebes and find and punish the killer. He had no idea that it was actually he who had killed Laius or that Laius was his father. In his quest to find the killer, Oedipus consulted the blind seer Tiresias.

Tiresias, of course, knew the guilty party was Oedipus himself. He tried to protect Oedipus and discouraged his quest for knowledge. He wouldn't answer his questions. Oedipus was furious and threatened Tiresias. Tiresias then told him: *"The murderer is father and brother to his own children and husband and son to his own mother."* It didn't occur to Oedipus that he was the guilty party, since as far as he knew, his father and mother were the king and queen of Corinth. After a few more rounds of confusion, Oedipus got to the bottom of the story and discovered the truth. Jocasta then killed herself, and Oedipus blinded himself with pins taken from his dead wife/mother's clothing.

Here is the meaning of the myth: The sins of the father are visited upon the sons. Keep in mind that crime of violation was committed by Laius against his symbolic son. It had nothing to do with Oedipus. Oedipus was just a pawn in this game. The mask figure of Oedipus represents his characterological self, with a fate that was created by the abusive violations of his father. Oedipus was innocent. He was the Authentic-Being, the person behind the mask. The chorus, with dramatic irony, knew the truth of the mask. The oracle knew the truth of the mask. Within the play, the blind seer knew the truth behind the surface. It is common that the seer in Greek myths is blind. Cassandra, another seer, was blind. Homer himself was blind. They were blind to the surface reality. Instead, they saw the inner truth behind the mask. They saw the invisible underlying characterological play and its grounding in sadism and violation. The blind seer is the shaman-priest-doctor figure. His lot is to see the story beyond the masked persona. To cast them as blind captures that they see below the surface reality, and don't focus on the literal surface.

When Oedipus discovered the truth, he put out his own eyes. This has many levels of meaning. Blinding oneself is an image of shame—"*Out, vile jelly.*" When he saw the truth behind the mask, the surface reality ceased to be pertinent. He joined the blind ones focused on the truth behind the surface of things. The underlying prophecy had invisibly played itself out. When Oedipus finally saw the truth behind the mask, it was too late. His regular life had been spent seeing only the surface reality, while he fulfilled the invisible prophecy of the mask. Despite the fact that he was innocent, he did actually enact patricide and incest. His adult conduct was not erasable. So functionally, he was guilty as charged.

Oedipus played out the prophecy. The inevitability of his fate derived not from his conduct but from his father's transgressions. The gods were personifications, who caused to happen the built-in retribution for Laius's crime. He was caught in the crossfire. The play illuminates that the sins of the father are visited upon the son. And it probably goes back seven generations. We'll also modernize this to the sins of the mothers and fathers are visited upon the children. The son suffers from the consequences of the transgressions and violations of his parents. Oedipus played out a destiny that had nothing to do with him. Oedipus was an innocent being. He killed his father and committed incest with his mother in complete ignorance, with no intentionality. He bore no responsibility for what he had done. He had, in fact, taken extreme measures to protect his parents, who he believed were the king and queen of Corinth. He loved his Corinthian parents, and they loved him. Oedipus suffered from the legacy of Laius's violations. The legacy of this abuse was put onto Oedipus. His fate was to inexorably play out its consequences.

Let's interject a few words about Freud's misconstruction of this myth. His interpretation—that the meaning of the myth is that all sons want to kill their father and have sex with their mother—has come into our culture as psychoanalytic dogma. This is not the meaning of the myth. Freud, unfortunately, used the surface of the myth as a projection screen for what were, in fact, his own personal wishes. Have you ever met anyone who wanted to kill his father and marry his mother? I haven't. This imposed theory does not correspond to human nature. We know, in fact, that Freud was angry (murderously angry?) at his father when he discovered his father had a secret life, with a previously undisclosed first marriage. And we know that Freud committed the analogue of incest himself in two ways—an ongoing affair with his wife's sister, and his secret conduct of a psychoanalysis with his own daughter, Anna. The wish to kill his father and commit incest were, no doubt, part of Freud's own personal internal play. He then narcissistically projected his personal conflicts into a false idea of a universal truth, which he successfully imposed on others. It then got passed on to his disciples who believed in this imposed idea, and foisted it on their patients.

Nothing could be more clear from the actual myth of Oedipus, as told by Homer, Aeschylus, and Sophocles, than that there was no wish on Oedipus's part to kill his father and have sex with his mother. He was horrified and shamed by his horrendous enactments. They derived from the cruel legacy of Laius's treachery, which had predetermined the fate of the Oedipus persona. His Authentic-Being, behind the mask, was innocent.

We have seen that Oedipus's fate was inexorably predetermined by the seeds of something that were sown before, and not in his control. His father's violations had nothing to do with him. Does this sound anything like the story of our modern Eddie? Wouldn't his character, forged by his parents' violations, become his destiny? Eddie became a mask figure in a play that evolved as a result of the deprivation and abuse of his parents. His inner play became his destiny. Character is destiny. "The sins of the father ..."

The Oedipus myth, and Greek theater in general, grapple with the riddle of the Sphinx—the mystery whose answer is man. And so it is that psychiatry, in contemporary form, grapples with the same human mystery. In the theater of consciousness, "all the world's a stage," where, as our mask figures, we enact our invisible plays, which influence and determine our destiny. In all of us, there is a disjunction between the role of the adult self, the mask figure played upon the stage, and the *person* behind the mask, the Authentic-Being. We live out and enact our invisible internal play—all of us.

Now, here's the important question: is the destiny of the internal play and the "adult self" mask immutable? Is Eddie, like Oedipus, destined to play out his fate? Or can we intervene and thwart the gods? This brings us to the living theater of therapy.

14

BOUNDARIES AND THE RESONANCE OF FEELING
The Art of Psychotherapy

ONE DAY, AS A FIRST-YEAR psychiatric resident, I was assigned to take a shift to guard the door of a patient, Sandy, who was extremely manic. When she was out on the ward, personal contact with others had overstimulated her. As a result, she got even higher and increasingly out of control. Her treatment plan was revised to counter this by keeping her in her room. While sitting outside her door as a guard, I was fed a constant stream of objections about her confinement. "Why am I here? The sheriff is keeping me a prisoner! I haven't committed any crime. I have no rights? I'm a slave. This is cruel and unusual punishment!" And on and on for hours—eloquent, articulate, and heart-wrenching.

I felt incredibly guilty, as if I was the worst person an earth. My inclination was, *I'll open the door. I'll let you out. I'll set you free!* Nonetheless, I sat there doing my job, feeling bad for her and for me. Several days later, I had guard duty again, which I approached with considerable apprehension. But this time, something had changed. The diatribe was over. Sandy was calm, and no longer complaining, no longer eloquent about her lost freedoms. She was down from her mania. The strategy had worked.

Sandy was ready to leave her room and reenter ward life. As she walked out onto the ward, she turned to me and said, "I want to

174

thank you and the rest of the staff for keeping me in there. I was way out of control, and I now feel much, much better." I was startled. This was the last thing I expected to hear her say. She was expressing gratitude that we didn't listen to her humanitarian pleas. I was certainly glad that I hadn't honored my actual response to her. And it taught me one of the many lessons that led to this book.

My internal responses to her had certainly been real and inescapable. How could they have been so off? They had obviously and quite naturally resonated with her plight. She had been compelling in her soliloquy. In her play, my assigned role was as the bad sheriff. And it had worked. My internal response was at variance from my proscribed job instructions. I had wanted to rescue her from her victimization, from her pain and confinement. And in addition, didn't the wish to free her mean that I was a good person rather than a slave master? Nonetheless, in relation to her actual well-being, my response could not have been more upside down and backwards.

At that time, I was just a novice, and mania was still relatively new to me. I had no foundation and lacked any real knowledge. Sandy told me later how horrible the manic pressure and high actually was. The early phases of mania are misleading, because they can be filled with contagious humor, fun, and excitement. In fact, mania is a dire, angry, and out-of-control frightening psychotic state.

My responses certainly informed me about something, but it wasn't what I had thought. I was resonating with the contagion of her mood and the content of ideas. I hadn't understood that the presence of her manic play generated a powerful guilt pressure in me. I hadn't understood that my inclination to free her was itself the signal that she wasn't ready to leave her room. And conversely, it was the absence of that guilt pressure that indicated the manic process had subsided. That turned out to be the signal that she was ready to join the ward. Because my job had been to guard her door, the only thing I could do was listen to her soliloquy, have my emotional responses, and sit with them, while taking no action. Of course, my responses weren't really wrong. I just didn't understand them. She taught me that my resonant responses had important meaning, but I shouldn't assume I knew what that meaning was. By paying attention and being patient, it would eventually become clear as to what was actually cooking. Later, I learned to sit with all my resonant internal responses, pay attention to them, not act on them, not assume I knew what they meant, and allow them to become my guide into the unknown worlds of my patients.

Another lesson took place in a session with David. He was a young man who was an advanced practitioner and teacher of yoga. He sat in meditation several hours a day. He was an obsessional thinker who never showed any signs of emotion. When sitting with David I didn't feel any emotional engagement. Occasionally, he would take passive-aggressive jabs at me. On one ninety-five-degree day, he told me that my air conditioner was destroying the ozone layer, and hence the world. I should be more like him and forgo air-conditioning. These attacks were in the service of the "good," very defensible, always with coherent logical reasons. He never used an angry tone or an angry facial expression. I noticed and stored it.

Some time later, the following exchange took place: David and I were sitting in my office. There were two chairs with a metal plant stand, holding three flowering plants between them, slightly set back toward the wall. The session was silent, albeit a tense silence. I was aware of a feeling of tension in the muscles of my arms and legs and an uneasy feeling in my chest, which I couldn't account for. Most important, I began to have a very strong feeling that he was going to explode in a rage and smash the plant stand and the plants. Now, he had never done anything like that. Nonetheless, this uneasy fear persisted. There was, however, some precedent for my intuition. Several times in previous sessions, he had let out a piercing scream that jarred me to the core of my being. On each occasion, he yelled at the very moment when my attention had briefly wandered, catching me unaware. Exploration of these jarring yells hadn't led anyplace.

My fantasy that David wanted to smash my plant stand was very strong. And it felt imminent. I decided to take the leap and address it. But I was hesitant, fearing he'd think I was judgmental, uncaring, unprofessional, or crazy. So, I blurted, "I know that you would never do anything like this, and if you want to do it would be okay, but I have the fear that you're going to smash my plant stand." As you can see, I was so uncomfortable with my assertion that I tried to soften it. And it wasn't honest—I didn't want my plants smashed. I didn't want to accuse him of gratuitous violence, so I postured that for his sake, for the sake of the therapy, it would be okay. He responded, "What are you talking about? I would never do anything like that. What kind of person do you think I am?"

Chagrined, I apologized for being off base, yet I continued to have this powerful fantasy. So I tried again, but still I softened it by adding, "If you want to smash the plants, and if that would be constructive for you, then I wouldn't object, because they are just plants. But I don't really think it would be very constructive." I was still misrepresenting myself in a falsely therapeutic manner. He responded the same way: "What kind of person do you think I am? I would never do anything like that."

Once again I was embarrassed and worried that he'd think I was crazy. But I couldn't shake my fantasy and the tension. When I ventured forth for the third time, I decided to drop the pseudo-therapeutic posture. I hadn't been protecting him but myself. This time I said, "Look, I don't want you to smash my plants because I love them." To my surprise, he quietly responded, "Yes, I know. That's why I want to smash them."

This opened the door to his inner world. I learned about his angry impulse life that he had been so busy controlling. His mother had survived Auschwitz. The cruelties suffered there were never talked about. The Holocaust understandably was the sacrosanct, central moral issue of the family's life. Any complaint he might have had paled in comparison. The Holocaust understandably functioned to keep Mother as the supreme and unassailable victim, who could never be accused of any wrongdoing herself.

As it turned out, from early in his childhood, David's mother used to go into abusive rages, during which she'd explode and scream vilifications at him. She'd pinch him hard, bruising him all over his body. She always caught him off guard. He never knew when it was coming. It was always unpredictable, not linked to anything going on. Her attacks just seemed to come out of the blue. When these episodes were over, it was like they had never happened, and there was no acknowledgment or remorse. As a child of the Holocaust, he felt too guilty to ever accuse his mother of any cruelty, even in the privacy of his own mind.

David was filled with unacceptable sadistic impulses, masked by moral righteousness and moral superiority. This ongoing aggression, in general, was turned against himself in rigid self-attack and overscrupulousness. Under ordinary conditions, he identified with the masochistic David position. He attempted to control his sadistic impulses (the internal mother persona) through his practice of meditation. Consequently, he had led a life of flatness, removal, deadness, isolation, loneliness, and so-called depression.

From the plant stand episode, David's secret internal scenario of maternal abuse, with its personas and sadomasochistic relatedness, opened up. He had kept it at bay. On this occasion, David had identified with his mother's persona, while I had resonated with the complementary masochistic David figure, the recipient of the attacks. The characters of his drama were on stage and projected onto David and me. The key to unlocking the door of this taboo scenario was through my resonant responses to his projected drama. As the therapy unfolded, he began to peel the projections off of both of us and to face and mourn his actual internal scenario where it belonged.

I learned several things from this episode. First, trust myself. Second, never posture with a pseudo-therapeutic manner, no matter how well motivated. This is always boundary blurring and disrespectful. Third, don't take a reckless leap like this again. I was lucky on this occasion that my responsive intuition was consonant with his impulse. It might not have been. I hadn't learned yet to recognize that my inner response, although resonant with his characterological drama, was not necessarily specifically accurate about the content of his scenario. Sometimes it was, and sometimes it wasn't.

I hadn't understood that my fantasy scenario, generated by my feeling resonance, took form through my image-ination. In this case, it happened to coincide with his fantasy. The literal accuracy of my intuitive fantasy was not mindreading. Remember, the content of thoughts never crosses the boundary between people. Feelings resonate. No thoughts actually passed from his brain to mine. My intuitive fantasy had important meaning, but in general, the actuality and import of that meaning isn't known or immediately knowable. It was, however, the important vehicle that opened the door to access his invisible internal drama.

And finally, it opened me up to pay attention to the full range of my own inner responses, most of which are far more subtle than this particular intuitive one. I learned to sit with them, be patient, not assume, not act on them, and judiciously address them. My internal resonant responses would become my central guide to finding the way to my patients' salient and always hidden characterological drama. This is the Tiresias factor—the key to the story behind the mask, the destiny of the mask.

I learned to fully embrace the centrality of the feeling resonance to the invisible internal play of my patients when treating Mike. Mike had been hospitalized for paranoia and oddly threatening behavior with his family. Mike's speech was very flat and objectified, with no available feeling. During our sessions, I found myself constantly doodling on a piece of paper, which I never did in general or with any other patient. I took stock of my doodling activity and concluded I was busying myself to ward off sitting with an unknown discomfort. So I forced myself to put the paper and pen down.

Without this activity, I became very sleepy. Literally, I had a hard time staying awake. By doodling I was dipping into my own imagination and self-stimulating to stay awake. My state of heaviness and sleepiness was very uncomfortable. It bothered me that I was bored. It didn't seem professional. What kind of therapist must I be to not be interested in my patient? How could I not care about my patient?

Without my doodling I had to force myself to pay attention. The more I tried, the heavier my head felt. The more I forced myself to be a good, attentive professional, the more difficult it became to stay awake. The heaviness felt oppressive. I felt mortified at the possibility that I might actually doze off. What was I going to do? Maybe I should start doodling again!

I made a decision. I leaned back in my chair and let myself just float, leaving my consciousness free to follow its own paths. To my relief, the oppressive heaviness disappeared. Since the sessions contained a lot of silence, I contented myself with paying attention to my own images and daydreams, all the while keeping the remaining corner of my consciousness open to Mike. There were even times when the heaviness was sufficiently intense that I let myself shut my eyes, fearing I would nod off. Sometimes, I went to the border of sleep, but despite my apprehension, I never crossed it. Even in this state, one corner of my consciousness remained freely awake, alert, and available. It was a relief to me that I was now able to be free and genuinely available and responsive.

Once I got my own play out of the way, I could accept my responses, rather than be at odds with them. This then allowed me to attend to the meaning of my responses, which had been activated in the living theater of therapy. The deep heaviness and sleepiness was in resonance with his enormous emotional remove—the total absence of human engagement or feeling. It reflected the presence of a mechanical deadness. The distance between him and me was almost unimaginable. He commented that he felt like he was a piece of driftwood floating in deep outer space. He was truly that removed, and it accurately reflected what it was like to sit with him. There was no accessible genuine vitality of self. In response to his extreme emotional isolation, I was resonating with the vacancy of his absent and removed Authentic-Being. It was sealed off completely. Neither he nor I had any access to him. I was in resonance with Mike's internal play—an extreme schizoid one.

Mike felt completely empty, hollow, and mechanical. There was nothing real and alive for me to engage with. My sleepiness was the genuine and appropriate response to his actuality. Instead of being an impediment to the therapy, it became my guide to his world. It won't be surprising to know that Mike's work was to fix broken machines. He had an incredible ability with mechanical things. He was very attuned and accomplished with machines, but not so much with people.

As with regular theater, the feeling resonance may occur in different ways. With the scenario of a protagonist/antagonist and a feeling connection between them, you may resonate with one or the other or both personas through the feeling between them. With an alone character, you may resonate with him and his plight in the universe. You may resonate with a mask character; you may resonate with the Authentic-Being. All of this takes place through a resonance of feeling. Clearly, I resonated with Mike's character persona—a piece of wood drifting through the ether—rather than an alive person. My response was appropriate. My resonance was fundamentally with Mike's isolated self, not a complementary person in an invisible scenario with him. He didn't really have any scenarios of relatedness.

However, there was more. I also felt that unnamable oppression. The sleepiness was not just present. It was powerful and oppressive. Remember, I felt forced to be attentive. Likewise, I felt that I shouldn't feel bored. I should have been lively and interested in him. But I couldn't be. Initially, my responses seemed inappropriate. I felt defeated. I noticed that when I tried to override, to "do the right thing," I felt a resentment. This, in turn, distanced me from both myself and Mike. My own hidden resentment actually made me less available to him. This opened me up to the darker side of Mike's character. My resonance was with a persona who was being forced, oppressed, and defeated with humiliation and shame; someone who refused. This fierce control struggle felt quite amorphous but strong. Beyond this, I didn't know the particulars of his fierce sadomasochistic battle. But I knew it was there.

Once again, I had the opportunity to consider what this all was about. I didn't really know, but it certainly was some kind of powerful and fierce control struggle. I knew I would eventually get to the bottom of it. And finally, as I embraced the freedom to drift into my own daydreams, I accepted the absence of a real engagement with Mike. And I sat with the experience of inhabiting a very alone world of my own fantasy. What role did fantasy play, and where was it going to lead?

And finally, it was clear that regular therapy conversation was not to be the avenue of exploration. Mike did not initiate any authentic or real conversation. Talking was an avenue of going through the motions of what humans appeared to do, or it was a secret avenue of control struggle. It was dead. My living theater resonance took me to daydreams, to worlds of isolated, private fantasy. Even my initial doodling had been a form of private fantasy. We had here a state of extreme emotional removal, anger, and isolation. The question, then, was how I would reach Mike across the chasm of such enormous distance and make human contact.

During the silences in the our sessions, we sat together with parallel fantasies. As I allowed myself the freedom to drift with my own daydreams, I trusted that in some way, my fantasies were resonant with his, through the avenue of participatory feeling responsiveness that takes place in the theater. My fantasies were, of course, my own content, in my own personal language and context—my side of the inviolable boundary between the two of us.

It never occurred to Mike to expose anything authentic to anybody. Because he trusted no one, he didn't initiate any real discussion. I realized Mike could not expose his vulnerability. So I decided to take the onus off him. Rather than expect him to open up, which he couldn't do, I decided I would take the lead. Because Mike was not trusting enough to disclose his own fantasies, I decided to tell him mine. When I felt that it was a judicious time, I told him something of where I went in fantasy. The purpose of this was not to discuss my fantasies, which we never did. Mike was an introvert, and his responses were always about him, never about me. It simply allowed him to play off my fantasies and respond from his world. This is exactly what transpired. It gave him something to safely bounce off.

Mike used my fantasies as a projective surface. Consequently, they opened up a discussion of what was inside him, or they triggered germane memories, or he simply told me his own stuff that resonated with what I had brought up. This conversation became the avenue for an incipient albeit tenuous engagement.

As a result, Mike's story opened up. He was the youngest of three sons in an Irish Catholic family. Mother was very religious and moralistic. She was cold and severe and, not surprisingly, the source of his emotional deprivation. The substitute for her unavailability and uncaring were moral and religious judgmental attacks. There was nothing there. A much more active avenue of sadomasochist engagement came through the father and brothers. Father was physically brutal and abusive to all his sons. When his mother determined Mike was "bad," she handed him over to the father for a beating.

Mike always felt his mother was the power behind the throne, and his father was merely her lieutenant, carrying out her orders. Father then beat the guilty party until he broke him. The signal to end a beating was for his son to cry and beg him to stop. Mike refused to cry and beg for mercy. His technique was to defeat his father by never giving in. Consequently, because Mike wouldn't cry and beg, Father's beatings would go on endlessly. Finally, while trying to maintain his pride and defeat his father, Mike developed a strategy to outsmart him by pretending to cry. This way he tricked him to stop. It was never clear, however, if the fake cry was real and who was defeated. It was all about humiliation.

It's of interest that late in his life, Mike's father had Parkinson's and was rendered immobile, without the ability to talk. Mike spent a lot of time, in silence, in fantasy, sitting by his father's bed, believing that the two of them were communicating.

Mike lived out different forms of the fighting paradigm in many different ways. On school mornings, Mike pretended to be asleep, so he wouldn't have to get up and go to school. At his mother's behest, his older brothers set about waking him up in the family tradition. Normal shaking did nothing, as he was faking being asleep in the first place. So they beat on him. He refused to budge and maintained the pretense that he was asleep. No matter how considerable their beatings, which were considerable, he would never give in. Eventually, he'd open his eyes and stretch like he was waking up naturally, as if unaware of the beating he was receiving. His oldest brother became an FBI agent. His other brother became a career criminal.

Mike played out a form of this same scenario at marine boot camp. The recruits had to jump into a swimming pool in full gear and tread water until the sergeant told them they could grab onto the side of the pool. The point of this drill was to break the recruits' will and humiliate them. The sergeant would wait until they couldn't stay afloat any longer. He forced them to give up, fail, and grab onto the side of the pool. As you might anticipate, this was right up Mike's alley. He refused to give in and beg. He held out, preferring to go under and drown before he would ask out. Consequently, he defeated the drill instructor by forcing him to fish out a half-dead Mike.

His scenario was consistent. At school, Mike was the class bully always fighting. His MO was to smash his opponents' heads into the sidewalk, while begging them to "give up so I won't have to kill you." At confession, he developed the following strategy to defeat the priests. First, he would make up sins that were of sufficient gravity to satisfy the priest but minimize the severity of the penance. His punishment might be to say four Hail Marys to atone for his fake sins. However, instead of reciting the full "Hail Mary, full of grace ..." four times, he would repeat each word four times ("Hail, Hail, Hail, Hail ... Mary, Mary, Mary, Mary ... full, full, full, full ... of, of, of, of ... grace, grace, grace, grace ...")

Once, as a teenager, Mike stole a gun and ran away from home. He committed armed robberies all the way down the East Coast from New England to Florida. He didn't get caught, but the authorities eventually brought him home as a runaway. He never told anybody what he had actually done to survive. He had no friends or relationships and trusted no one.

Even though he was magical at his work, he worked only with great reluctance and resentment. All of his adult life, he refused to get out of bed and go to work, just like with school. When threatened with getting fired, he adopted different strategies. He'd stay up all night and refuse to give in to sleep. Then he'd go to work after twenty-four hours of sleep deprivation. His other alternative was to go on strike, refuse to get out of bed, and get fired. He didn't care.

During one intense session, Mike turned to the rug in my office, saying it reminded him of a rug in his living room as a child. He recounted sitting on this living room rug, playing Dvorak's *New World Symphony*, over and over, on the phonograph. He then burst out crying at top volume, with an odd booming voice. This shocked me, because I was so used to his showing no feeling. And further, I couldn't tell if the crying was real or fake. Usually, deep tears elicit a tenderness in me. These tears did not, although I felt they should. Was he giving me what he thought I wanted, as with his father? Or was his odd crying genuine, reflecting an unfamiliarity with human emotion,? I didn't know.

Mike feared emotional closeness as much as he needed it. As is always the case with an extreme schizoid solution, his emotional isolation was intolerable and unsustainable. It periodically led to paranoia. He had been hospitalized for paranoia a number of times before I met him. The advent of emotional closeness was equally frightening and disruptive and dangerous. It too led to paranoid symptoms. This is the need/fear dilemma—he couldn't tolerate too much isolation or too much closeness. So the therapy was to have a lot of back-and-forthing. When the therapy got too close or too distant, Mike got into major struggles at work or with his family. His mother was usually the focus of murderous wishes. His paranoia was always directed toward others, never toward me. I felt oddly safe with him in therapy, despite the violent content of many of his fantasies.

In the therapy, it was essential for Mike to face the emotional content of his story. In the course of this, he developed a tenuously trusting relationship with me. Mike had never had any closeness or trust with anyone in his life. He had never carried on a real authentic conversation with a living soul. Our engaged connection, something entirely new, fostered mourning of his pain, both of his isolation and of the abuse.

The journey together, of exploring the story behind Mike's mask, opened up the need for and the danger of simple human contact. It was human closeness, emotional engagement, emotional trust, and reliability of a respectful and caring person (me) that led us to the most important element of therapy—the awakening of his Authentic-Being in the context of safe, emotional holding. The central element of the therapy journey now turned on the need for, and the danger of, emotional closeness. Opening access to the very vulnerable feeling of his being was understandably very tenuous and dangerous. He had been badly burned.

Only Mike could take this leap of feeling, this leap of trust. Whenever I am in the neighborhood of this leap with a patient, I always respect that this is a choice my patient must make for himself. I cannot influence it. Remember, Mike inhabited his play of pure danger and absence of love. He did not see outside it—he couldn't. For him, to entrust the feeling of his being was like deciding to put his hand on a hot stove. Because he believed the stove was hot and would burn him, he wasn't about to put his hand on it. This central leap is never based on a leap of faith. No one can believe something he doesn't believe. I could not reassure him, "The stove isn't hot—trust me. Go ahead. Put your hand on it." The only way he could choose to do it, was despite his certainty that he would get burned. He could not believe in advance that it was safe. If he chose to take the risk, only afterward could he conclude for himself whether or not it was hot. Only after touching it could he know for himself that he didn't get burned.

Mike and Mike alone—in his own way, in his own time, and with his own responsibility—could take this risk. When a patient does so, it always very moving and elicits enormous respect in me. If a patient doesn't take this step, which sometimes happens, I accept this as well. There has to be complete respect for the autonomy of the patient who struggles with a problematic characterological play. A therapist doesn't have the power, by dint of his wonderful character, to convince a patient to trust. Such a false assumption would be pure self-aggrandizing therapist hubris.

As Mike approached closeness, the atmosphere of the sessions changed. The feeling of enormous distance diminished. I no longer had the sleepy and oppressed feeling. I no longer operated from my own world of fantasy. There was human engagement. Our discussions had the flow of regular conversation. A softer feeling was present—it felt like Mike was in the room with me. When Mike took the leap of feeling, my most important resonance came into play. This was not a resonance with the characters of his play. This was a resonance with his Authentic-Being itself. I felt it with my own Authentic-Being. It was a feeling of tenderness, sweetness, and sweet sadness. It was enormously touching. Yes, it is the same resonance as maternal love.

With Mike, this full engagement didn't have a simple happy ending. It was still too much for him. In the following session, I immediately sensed something was wrong. I felt a disturbing fear. The hairs on the back of my neck stood up. When I addressed this, Mike indicated that he was having threatening and violent thoughts, this time about me. He believed I was going to hurt him, and his murderous rage was pointed in my direction. Mike had pulled back into paranoia. He was back in his play, where there was only danger and harm. We retained enough of a connection that Mike agreed to be hospitalized, where it would be safer for both of us to get through this.

The hospitalization was brief. It provided boundaries of protection that allowed us to explore what had happened. As it turned out, Mike never approached the full authentic feeling state again. He settled on a more comfortable distance, and stayed in the neighborhood of closeness. This was vastly different from floating mechanically in outer space. Instead, from this safer emotional proximity, Mike built a more satisfactory life. He worked regularly and made some friendships. He was never frankly paranoid again and never needed another hospitalization. He did not find a deep intimacy, but he accepted that that wouldn't happen.

As a therapist, I do not have control over the therapy, nor do I have control over how far it will go. Control over the journey was in Mike's hands, not mine. This is as it should be. The pace of healing is built in and reflective of the nature and degree of the damage that created his problematic characterological drama in the first place. In my experience, most patients take the leap of feeling and trust. This is actually the transformative element of therapy. However, an extreme schizoid-paranoid character play, like Mike's, comes from very severe damage. He came as far as he could go, and it was good enough.

My resonances with Mike, in the living theater of psychotherapy, illuminated and allowed me to engage with his play and ultimately with his very being. My resonance of feeling was my guide. It led me to grasp his enormous remove and his sadomasochistic relatedness. It allowed us to bring his invisible internal play to light, and then to face and mourn the source of his play—the deprivation and abuse in his family. We saw that once his play was established, it was invisibly repeated over and over again in his various life contexts. The most important resonance in the therapy was to his Authentic-Being itself. In addition, it was resonance that informed me of the danger of his paranoia.

The stories of Sandy, David, and Mike were chosen to illuminate the importance of the resonance of feeling that takes place in psychotherapy. These therapies were formative for me as a young psychiatrist, where I began to learn about real therapy. Therapy is a special relationship of intimacy, where we explore the invisible internal play of the patient through resonance. There is nothing magical about the process. The resonance of feeling is a commonplace avenue of consciousness. It is really an extension of the same participant/observer experience that is in play with regular theater and movies and all the other art forms. We have seen that it is actually in operation in everyday life. The art of therapy is an unusual context, where ordinary feeling resonance is refined and attended to, in order to illuminate the hidden character play that is on the patient's internal stage.

Lest you think there is any hubris attached to this process, I can assure you this is not so. The course of a therapy is ever humbling. Mike's therapy shows that with really profound damage, one doesn't necessarily recover a full self, although his recovery was very rich and rewarding. The time required for mourning and healing has its own pace. Like the speed of sound and the speed of light, it's a constant. One can't speed it up. But, through egotism, and by trying to override the natural processes, a therapist can certainly slow it down.

Just in case I was prone to any self-importance, Mike taught me a very important lesson in humility. I regularly saw him as my last appointment of the day. One day, early on, during the time when we were sitting with considerable silence in parallel fantasy, I was coming down with a major case of the flu. It hit me very fast. I had begun not to feel well in my previous session. I felt rapidly worse between sessions and debated whether or not to cancel. But Mike was already in the waiting room, and I didn't want to disappoint him. I thought I could push through it.

As soon as the session began, I knew I was in trouble. I developed a total head and body ache and couldn't think or feel or concentrate at all. It was a moment-to-moment torture. As it turned out, I had a fever of 104. So I sat there, struggling, regretting my decision, and wondering how much longer I could take it. I was just holding on and counting the minutes, which seemed like an eternity. I made no contribution at all. Mike apparently didn't notice. For him, it was a typical session with significant silence. As the session drew to a close, I was feeling more relief than even guilt over my inability to contribute and be available. When I finally ended the session, Mike turned to me and said, "I want to thank you. This was one of the best sessions we ever had!"

We have seen with David and Mike that psychotherapy operated through participant/observer experience, with their inner character plays. It was through the resonance of feeling that I gained access to the invisible story of their internal plays, the hidden personas, and their feeling relatedness. And it is through resonance that I was touched by the feeling of their Authentic-Beings and participated in that essential holding. Keeping this in mind, we can ask, "How does therapy actually operate? And how does it specifically address the healing of human suffering?"

15

THE LIVING THEATER
OF THERAPY

WHY WOULD SOMEONE COME INTO my office to be a patient in psychotherapy? Why would he decide to subject himself to the inconvenience, the considerable expense, the uncertainties, and the discomfort of confiding in a stranger, while contending with stigma and shame?

A patient comes to a psychiatrist for relief from his suffering. The word patient itself comes from *patiens*—"enduring pain and suffering." Human suffering takes many forms. People may feel unhappy, lonely, angry, or sad. They may have symptoms—obsessive, compulsive, anxiety, so-called depression, panics, phobias, paranoia, or delusions. People have character behaviors that get them into trouble—drinking, drugs, gambling, eating (anorexia, bulimia, overeating, bingeing), sexual perversions, impulsivity, rages, emotional isolation, narcissism, echoism, sadism, masochism, low self-esteem, and psychotic and manic states. They may have crises in their lives—divorce, death, loss, illness, rejections, failures, disappointments, traumas of all kinds, and post-traumas.

As we have seen, suffering does not exist in a vacuum. It flows from our damaged plays of consciousness. Since there are built-in fault lines to every problematic play, the way we break down follows along those fault lines. The way a person breaks down reflects the way he is constructed. Suffering is the manifestation of something having gone wrong in one's characterological play.

To attend to a patient's suffering, we must explore his inner play. This exploration is the journey of psychotherapy. It proceeds through a responsive conversation between therapist and patient. What transpires is far more than the cognitive content of the words. It is the exploration of a patient's invisible, unique inner drama—his cast of characters, the feeling relatedness between them, and how they developed by virtue of his formative environment of deprivation and abuse. People often misunderstand the word explore. They take it to mean "figure out, analyze, find some answer, or come up with an explanation." Explore means to venture into new and unfamiliar territory, where there is no map. My patient has no map of his internal play, and neither do I. I do have experience with journeys into these unknown terrains, having been an explorer on many expeditions.

However, the transformative process in therapy, ultimately, does not turn on this exploration, per se. It follows from the responsive engagement between us. Emotional holding allows one to digest and mourn the internal play. And finally, it is responsiveness and holding with the patient's Authentic-Being that fosters the writing of a new play, grounded in authenticity and love.

Psychotherapy is a specialized communication. As we saw in chapter 4, all forms of communication are art forms—highly refined symbolic order through which feeling stories are expressed and received (language, writing, theater, paintings, music, novels, poetry, and dance). We will now add the living theater of therapy to the list. The specific function of psychotherapy is to address the patient's internal story and engage with his Authentic-Being. The exploration of the inner drama is through participant/observer experience as it is in regular theater. However, in the living theater of psychotherapy there is no stage, no costumes, and the actors and the actual plots are invisible. What does the therapist have to work with? Consciousness itself. The central thesis of this book is that consciousness—my consciousness, your consciousness, my patient's consciousness—is organized as a living drama with a cast of characters, the relations between them, and various plotlines. I relate to my patient's invisible play by resonant feeling. We each have human image-ination beyond our personal dramas. And of course—and most important—there is his Authentic-Being behind the mask. This is it.

Let us set the stage for our theater of operations. In my office, my patient and I sit in very comfortable stuffed leather chairs of the same design, each with a footstool. Both chairs can swivel 360 degrees and can recline with ease from a sitting position to a horizontal position. The chairs are not facing each other directly. Each chair is turned at a 45-degree angle. This way, both my patient and I are free to turn toward each other in engagement or turn away to be free to attend to fantasy and memory. My patient's inner play and his cast of characters is our focus and will be attended to. Over time, the invisible characters, dramas, and roles of my patient's play will descend upon him and me, and use us as its projection screen. There is, of course, the added complexity that my patient has no awareness that he is living the invisible projected images of a brain-constructed illusion, playing out its plots, over and over.

Let us first address the participation element. As presented in chapter 14, the key to access a patient's invisible drama is through a resonance of feeling. It is through feeling that the therapist engages with his patient's personas and their relatedness, as well as the plots of tragedy and comedy that are on stage. As I sit with my patient and listen, I am attuned to the full range of responses inside of me. I pay attention to my own emotional responses and whatever imagery appears in my mind. I notice the presence of certain feelings, images, body states, disconnected ideas, and fantasies. Resonance of feeling is the therapist's most important tool.

If my patient feels sad, I will feel touched by sadness and will feel sadness. If he is angry, I will resonate with an angry tension in my body. Or I may have an angry fantasy. Sexual provocativeness stimulates sexual responses. If he is manicky and ebullient, I will feel up. If he is down, I will feel down. If he feels tenderness, I will be touched by tender feeling. If he is emotionally withdrawn and is denying his need, I often feel a hunger in the pit of my stomach. If he is removed and distant, I may feel the sleepiness that I felt with Mike. I often don't know what my responses mean, but I know that they do mean something. Eventually it becomes clear. Sometimes, I simply notice and store them and wait. At other times, they inform my response. And most important of all, the eventual resonance with a patient's Authentic-Being, when present, will elicit a certain sweet and tender feeling.

Remember, we aren't talking about stand-alone feelings. Feelings come from the internal personas relating together. This is how consciousness is organized. My patient, although unaware of it, identifies with certain of the internal characters of his play, and is emotionally reactive to others. I resonate with his activated personas and their plotlines, which take form in me through my image-ination. What gets activated in me does not have to be in my experience. Human image-ination allows us to encompass the full range of human experience. If you watch a horror movie that depicts horrific occurrences that have never happened to you, you nonetheless respond in an appropriately terrified way.

Now, here's the tricky part. Sometimes an activated persona of my patient's play will activate a persona of my own internal play. I am no different from my patient in the sense that my various characterological personas also hover around, ready to be activated. I am potentially reactive with a complementary or similar persona from my own inner play. So what happens then?

For a therapist to be clear and genuinely available, he needs to have explored and digested his own characterological world. Having mourned his own play sufficiently, the therapist retains a grounding in his authentic self. This grounding is an anchor that allows him to notice the presence of internal responses from his own play without being reactive to them. As he is not imprisoned by his own play, he develops a working relationship with it. Instead of being controlled by his potential reactivity to his own pain, his own activated persona now orients him and becomes a major guide in the exploration of his patient's invisible drama.

For example, let's say a patient manifests emotional coldness, hardness, and blame. I may notice the muscles of my arms tightening. Or I might feel a masochistic temptation to pursue a warm connection from this person. Or I might want to distance myself from this person. I notice these inclinations. I reflect on the presence of my response, which derives from a significant internal persona of mine who was hurt by a cold, distant, and paranoid persona. But I don't act on it. I am then free to sit with, and provide the emotional holding for my patient to face, bear, and mourn his own pain about the cold and harsh person in his formative past, so that he is no longer ruled by that figure.

I want to underline that the particular response in me is reflective of my play, not my patient's. But it is resonant to an important something. Once I get out of my own way, my inner response points to the presence of an important persona in his drama. I am then able to address the issue. A different therapist might have a different resonance to coldness. Whatever his specific resonance might be would guide that therapist to the issue.

We all have the regular human struggle in our lives. Nobody— neither patient nor therapist—is spared his fair share of tragedy and suffering in life. Having sufficiently dealt with his own characterological world in no way means the therapist is better than his patients or a kind of superior being. It allows him, however, to have enough internal and external resources to deal with his own ongoing life issues, so they don't interfere with his clarity and genuine availability to his patients. Even if he does get temporarily reactive and lost in his own play, he can quickly recover.

As a young therapist I prided myself in my ability to understand my patients because I had a relatively broad base of experience, and I could identify with their plight through empathy and sensitivity. I got over this the hard way. One day when sitting with a patient, I learned that I was barking up the wrong tree. Here is what happened. Janice arrived on the inpatient ward and was assigned to me. She had overdosed when her brutal ex-husband had threatened her once again and was heading to her apartment for a confrontation. In fear and despair, she overdosed. She had no money, and her ex-husband was not paying the alimony or any child support. This was her story. I met with her in therapy for a couple of weeks. I felt for her as a victim. I was empathic for her plight. I understood. I felt like a good psychiatrist, sensitive to her needs and pain.

A couple of weeks later, we were meeting for our regular therapy session. She began the session. "Sorry about this, but Dr. X told me you would fill out the food stamps form. Okay? Here it is." She explained that early in her hospitalization, my chief resident had arranged to get her on food stamps to feed her three-year-old child. I hadn't known anything about it. When Janice approached him to renew the food stamps, he told her to finalize the application with me.

I responded that our relationship would just deal with therapy, and I wouldn't be involved in getting her or denying her money. If she wanted food stamps, she should go back to Dr. X. At first she got angry and accused me of not caring about her hungry baby. "It's not a big deal. Just sign the form!" Her aggressiveness began to ring funny to me. I continued to draw the line until, to my surprise she suddenly changed her tune. "Dr. X is a self-important fool! Here's the real story. My ex-husband was coming over for dinner ..."

"Huh? I thought he was a monster."

"Well, actually, he comes to dinner several nights a week."

"He does?"

"Um, we've been doing that for a while. He sees the baby and, you know, it's good for her to see her father ..."

"This isn't adding up right."

"Okay, here's the real truth. We got divorced to qualify for housing assistance. They wouldn't give us any money because we were married. My husband is a good man who works very hard and makes a good living. It's not fair that only single mothers get assistance. The divorce was just to get money. What's the difference? We're still together. In fact, we live together in our apartment full time. We had had a fight and he went to work. So I called him at work and told him that I had overdosed. Of course, I hadn't. I knew he would come to my rescue as he always did. The problem was that he would come home and realize I hadn't overdosed. He'd see that I had lied again, and he would really be fed up. So while he was on his way home, I had to force myself to swallow enough pills, and time it right that he would find me unconscious. Sure enough, it worked. He found me, called the medics, and here I am."

I certainly didn't see this coming. But it effectively taught me to listen, pay attention, and not assume I understood. Once I got myself out of the way, I was free to listen, pay attention, be open, and be responsive to Janice's actual play of character. Now the therapy could begin. It taught me that therapy is not about empathy but responsiveness. If it were the otherwise, I would only be able to treat people who were just like me. I couldn't treat a female, or a person of a different race, ethnic background, religion, or temperament. I would have to have the same sexuality or the same alcohol or drug history as a given patient. There was a whole world out there, most of which was outside my personal experience. It opened me to the whole gamut of human experience, As a therapist, I must be open to working with the full scope of all characterological plays, including all imaginable aspects of the dark side, the source of suffering.

The therapist has to be open to learning about his patient's characterological world, wherever it takes him. This means a willingness to be open to whatever is stirred up in himself—the full range of human experience, identities, and feelings. This ranges from the sublime and tender to the dark forces of horror, terror, depravity, and cruelty. The therapist must genuinely be willing to sit with aspects of all of these forces, anything stirred in him, in order to sit with his patients' characterological dramas and explore them.

A therapist is simply human like everyone else. The only way he differs from other people is through his role and capacity in psychotherapy. It is the Tiresias factor. No, this does not mean the therapist is a seer. He does not know in advance the inner play of his patient or the destiny of his mask figure. It means that he is attuned to the exploration, and he must be adept at pursuing the inner story below the surface. He is accustomed to peering into the darkness. He has a willingness to sit with "unacceptable" impulses, wishes, and feelings, both in himself and in his patient. And most important, he has learned to work with his own characterological play as his most important tool in therapy.

This goes against the natural human inclination to avoid discomfort. It means a therapist has to allow himself to sit with the full range of human darkness, as well as human splendor, in himself. Consequently, I know in myself the worst and the best of the whole range of human impulses. This is not always easy. People tend to want to see themselves as good and to see badness as located outside themselves. A therapist is willing to resonate with the full range of his patient's characterological dramas, while possessing the facility to retain his grounding in his own authentic self.

All humans are capable of the full range of human possibility. Our persona imagination encompasses the full scope and is resonant with even the greatest extremes. The range of personas runs the gamut from Gandhi to Jeffrey Dahmer. We all carve out our unique character plays from the collision of our temperament with our developmental experience. In this sense, we all come to our characterological positions honestly. If I felt a resonance with Jeffrey Dahmer, this does not mean I would cannibalize someone. But it is in my image-ination potential and in yours. No character personas are outside the great human drama. Being human encompasses them all. With a sufficient anchor in his authentic self, the therapist accepts that all potential persona identities and motives are in us but not of us.

Because a therapist may not have a particular sinister element in his own characterological world does not mean he is better or superior to his patient. He will need to allow himself to be stirred by resonances to the dark side. This does not make depravity acceptable. It isn't. When there is depravity, it is important that the therapist address and characterize it clearly. This can be done only if the therapist does not see himself as superior or better.

On the other hand, if a therapist secretly or overtly has a depravity similar to his patient's, he might then feel himself to be empathetic. Isn't that a good thing? Doesn't this mean he understands his patient because they are the same? He might assume his patient would find this trait sympathetic and nonjudgmental. He might believe this would facilitate closeness and trust. Nothing, however, could be further from the truth. Such a scenario blurs the observer boundary. A patient does not need a symbiotic sameness from his therapist. He needs differentiated boundaries, respect, and a holding responsiveness.

Patients always know, no matter what, that something is amiss in them. They are relieved by the boundary that depravity is disturbing, destructive, corrosive, and hurtful. Keep in mind that psychotherapy is an exploration of the patient's characterological world and the forces that brought it about. A depraved characterological identity does not encompass the Authentic-Being of the patient. The point of the therapy is recovery from a problematic character identification. The problematic character identification is in the patient, but it is not reflective of the patient's Authentic-Being or potential recovered self.

The therapist's observer function, in the living theater of therapy, allows for a safe exploration of the characterological world of the patient, and for a safe and trustworthy engagement. A balanced observer distance honors personal boundaries and the boundaries of psychotherapy. It provides the structure for a safe exploration for both therapist and patient. The boundaries are relatively straightforward and few. The session starts on time and ends on time. Bills are paid in a timely manner. There is no sex, no violence, and no exploitation. The sanctity of the therapy does not lend itself to exploitation of any kind. The list of exploitations isn't long—sexual, sadistic, power, financial, ego aggrandizement for the therapist, or having the patient serve the therapist's emotional needs. Both parties are sitting in their seats and do not engage in any action, impulsive or premeditated. All activity is properly on the screen of the living theater in the office. And finally, confidentiality is of the highest order.

Respect for the patient means respecting the boundaries. Exploitation means violating the boundaries. Violation of boundaries always leads to sadistic aggression and is the source of violence itself. The therapist's provision is much like that of a good parent—boundaries and good-enough loving. I reiterate "good enough" because as in child raising, there is no such thing as perfect responsiveness in therapy

Let us begin with the two major structural boundaries of psychotherapy—time and money. Each session has a fifty-minute time limit. (It obviously is not inherent that a session must be fifty minutes, but that is the convention with which I work.) It begins punctually and ends punctually. This sets the parameters for the patient's safe entry into, immersion in, and exit from the journey of each session. The fifty minutes impact each patient in a unique way, in concert with his characterological position. For example, obsessional people, who are emotionally removed, commonly dip into engaged feeling in the last five minutes of the session. This is safe for them, because they know they will be going soon. A beginning therapist might be tempted to extend the session from his enthusiasm that that his patient has finally engaged. This would be a mistake. Bending the boundary of time would remove the patient's security that the session is about to be over. In the long run, this decision would be counterproductive. In the next session, he won't trust that he can dip in and get out safely, so he will be more reticent about opening up at all.

Other patients may operate as if any attention given within the proscribed time allotment is false. They assume that attention is real only after the session has ended. They want extra time. All kinds of strategies may be employed to cross this boundary. At the end of a session, there might be a crisis of anger, or desperation, or crying, or panic, or a flirtation, or the allure of a revelation of a long-withheld secret. Explicitly or implicitly, they will seek to be "saved" or "helped" or "understood" or "cared for" by an extended session. Often, they are angry if they do not prevail.

It is actually reassuring for the patient to fail in his attempts to cross this boundary. In the patient's problematic characterological play, there is no such thing as trustworthiness or genuine caring and respect. It is a world in which the only available attention is exploitative attention, and this is taken for granted. If the therapist yields to his demand, the patient will actually conclude that the therapist gave extra time to exploit him for the therapist's own aggrandizement, his inflated self-importance, or to serve his own needs. Maintenance of the time boundary is always reassuring in the long run. It paves the way for the potential leap of real trust.

One could make a case that fifty minutes a week is not a lot of time. It doesn't compare favorably with the other 167 hours in a week, with six days and twenty-three hours of separation. In this case, appearances are deceiving. We aren't talking about real time. We're talking about drama time. Think of all that transpires in an hour episode of The Sopranos. Then it's over. And after a week's separation, you're right back in it. With the next episode, continuity from the previous episode is resumed, as if there hadn't been a whole week in between. The six days and twenty-three hours was but an intermission. Similarly, the drama of therapy lives in its own continuous time. There are intermissions, and then the aliveness of the drama is resumed. Thus, therapy reality is continuous, like *The Sopranos* series, with breaks between episodes. The beginning of a session serves as a transition back into therapy reality. The end of a session is a temporary transition back out to regular reality.

Two, three, or four sessions a week allows for considerably more intensive engagement time. Likewise, the separations between sessions are shorter. When there is more participatory time and less separation time, there is an enhanced continuity of engagement and emotional connectedness, and a greater possibility to challenge distrust. This affords a greater continuity, intensity, and time to grapple with the play and, ultimately, with trust and intimacy itself.

As a boundary, money is a biggie. Even though I make a good living from my profession, psychiatry is not money-centered. Psychotherapy is a profession, not a business or industry. The issue is only the work of therapy, in the service of the recovery of the well-being of the patient—period. Money is *not* the bottom line. This is reflected in the language. I do not employ the word "client." Client comes from *cliens, clientis*, which is a reference to a financial and power relationship between a vassal and a feudal lord or patron; the vassal is under the protection of the feudal lord. Therapy is a doctorly relationship with a patient, not a power, dependency, and financial relationship.

Money is the payment for the therapist's time and wherewithal in the therapy. He makes his living by his hourly fee. The psychotherapist had better be a professional and not an amateur. A patient signs up for one or more of the therapist's hours per week. This hour becomes the patient's therapy time. My personal practice is to charge a set fee as my hourly rate. My patient and I are on different sides of the boundary of the fee. I charge, and he pays. This is the same for everybody, whether wealthy, poor, or in between. I try to be fair about my rates. It is my patient's choice and responsibility for payment. I do not cross this boundary. There are many therapists with a sliding scale. This means that one has wealthier patients who subsidize poorer patients. I do not agree with this. The way my patients spend their money is their choice, not mine. Each person's charitable contributions are his own private decision. This might mean that a patient who is less well off may have to get an extra job to pay for his therapy. That is his choice. It is certainly the therapist's responsibility to be absolutely scrupulous about money. He cannot extend a therapy one extra session for his own gain.

Money itself is a very important projection screen. What are the common projective issues about money?

- The therapist is a prostitute who sells affection and pseudo-caring for money.
- The therapist is just in it for the money.
- The patient is paying for friendship.
- The patient is paying for support.
- The only reason a therapist would put up with such a miserable wretch is because he is getting paid.
- Because the therapist is exploiting the patient in the other ways—power, sexual, egotistical, sadistic, for his own emotional gratification—the humiliating coup de grace is to be doubly exploited; first, to be exploited and then have to pay money for the privilege.

For some patients, money is a vehicle for their own sense of entitlement. They've bought the therapist and own him.

- "Since I'm paying for this, I am entitled to violate you; it's my therapy."
- "This is my time, and you are my paid-for slave."
- "If I feel angry, I have the right to be true to my tantrum and take it out on you."
- "You have to take it, and you have to do what I say."
- Some patients feel their payments entitle them to play out private fantasy enactments, and they assume the therapist has to accept being a fantasy object.

To some, a fee means that all feeling and relationship is a lie. The only time there could be genuine feeling is if the therapy were for free. If the therapy were for free, then the patient could really be taken care of by the therapist. Some patients believe they shouldn't have to be responsible for their adult side of the therapy agreement. They are victims and besides, having to pay is victimizing them all the more.

Money is a trust issue. It's of interest that in this day and age, many people find it easier to divulge shameful sexual fantasies than disclose information about finances. Money, as a boundary and projection screen, illuminates much about the patient's characterological world. When money issues arise, as they always do, they need to be addressed and explored.

Therapy invites the patient to open up to his most sensitive emotional vulnerabilities. Likewise, as a therapist, I too sit with these same human vulnerabilities. The protections of the therapy boundaries make this safer for both of us than in regular life. It never feels safe, but we have a better shot at sitting with and exploring, rather than just being reactive.

Caring and real feeling can only be real. Caring is something that can happen genuinely only over time, when one gets to know someone. This is in contrast with a false position of caring at the outset of therapy or ever. False caring as a professional role is an act and a lie. A patient would do well not to trust it. The false therapeutic tone of caring is likewise something a patient ought to be suspicious of. This is not to say that a therapist shouldn't have a natural sympathy and receptivity to another person. That, of course, is a given and essential. Likewise, if a patient's problematic persona is in ascendancy, it isn't actually possible to have caring for such an off-putting persona. The presence of an unlovable problematic persona can then be properly dealt with as a therapeutic issue.

Confidentiality is the boundary that keeps a safe circle around the therapy. This means it is safe for the patient to say anything without reference to any consequences in the outside world. The only usage and value of what is talked about is in the service of the therapy itself. Confidentiality ensures that the content of the therapy will not be used for any advantage or disadvantage for either the patient or the therapist outside the therapy. This holds true even if a patient himself requests communication with the outside world, such as to a divorce court or to an agency for adoption or for money sources. If such a thing is germane, there is always an outside professional who will do some evaluation.

Therapy from the beginning to the end is a responsive engagement between my patient and me. A new patient comes to my office because he is suffering. I need to hear the nature of his suffering. I need to know something about his circumstances. And I need to get a preliminary sense of his characterological world and how it got to be the way it is. The first few sessions will be focused on this discovery. This is the evaluation. I am evaluating the nature of his situation in order to be in a position to address what would be involved in dealing with it. New patients often think when I use this word that I am evaluating them in relation to a judgment about their worth and value, or evaluating whether I would accept them into therapy or reject them. This is not the case. I am, in a preliminary way, getting to know them. Likewise, they are evaluating me based on their impression of me. They are, in a preliminary way, getting to know me. We are on equal footing, and all the processes that will ensue are purely human.

A new patient sees how I comport myself, how I dress, and my manner. Since my office is at home, he notices the house, the landscape, and the interior landscape of the office. Most important, he evaluates how I deal with him. We are two strangers, meeting. Am I someone he would be interested in working with?

A new patient gets a sense of who this stranger might be. This does not mean there is any focus on my personal life. Getting to know me does not mean knowing about me. I am not the center of the therapy. The subject of psychotherapy is not me or my internal play. It is the characterological world of my patient. Consequently, the "knowing about" will focus on the patient, not me. The subject of the exploration is, of course, him. In this regard, it differs from a social relationship, where the "knowing about" includes both parties. As we will see, my patient knows a lot about me anyway, just from my office and my manner. But more important, the real issue of knowing each other isn't "knowing about." It is about "being with," in feeling. My patients come to know me very well and very intimately, without knowing a lot of facts about me.

There are no formulas at the beginning of therapy or at any point during the therapy. As I open the door for the first time, I am open to the various impacts this new person makes on me: his appearance, his style of dress, the manner of his greeting, his response as I usher him to his chair. I do not study these things. I simply notice their impact on me. As I ask what brings him to my office, he tells me the specifics of his suffering. I listen to the content, and I feel the emotional impacts of his presence. I am responsive to whatever presents itself. I may continue the discussion of his "problem," or I may shift my response to the state of feeling that is present or the state of feeling that is conspicuously absent. If the person is reticent, I may be active in my engagement and actively responsive to what is presented. If the person floods the discussion, I may interrupt. If the person is tangential, I may refocus. If the person tells me his story, I may quietly listen. From the beginning, therapy is a responsive engagement.

The culmination of the evaluation usually results in the first connection between patient and therapist. Just to have someone hear the pain of the suffering without ridicule or diminishment is a form of emotional holding. This is amplified when there is shame involved. The initial symptom is always a veil for a deeper pain. When this is touched upon and addressed in the evaluation sessions, the patient is reached in his real pain. He feels understood and listened to.

All throughout the evaluation, I resonate with the emotional actuality of the patient, and address it responsively. It is only when the patient's real self is touched that he feels known and engaged. This takes many forms. Sometimes it means translating anxiety or so-called depression to the anger it actually is, and inviting unacceptable feelings to be felt. Sometimes, it means sitting with a painful sadness, and encouraging it to be felt rather than avoided. Sometimes it means addressing the hollowness, emptiness, or feelings that don't ring true, in order to reach the real person. In all the different forms, the therapist reaches and touches the real person with real emotional contact. Sometimes, this is the first time in a lifetime. This constitutes an important engagement and often brings some relief.

When a patient's suffering is linked to a preliminary understanding of the context of his inner world, he also feels understood. Connections are made to the salient issues of his family of origin. These deeper connections are made to his characterological position by which he has protected himself from intolerable emotional suffering. This links an understanding of his present pain to his internal world and how it got to be this way. It is ultimately his internal character, forged in relation to his early family, that determines the particular symptoms from which he suffers. I either give a running commentary of response or a session of feedback about all of these things to address what the therapy will be dealing with. This in itself usually makes the patient feel understood, known, and not so alone.

Even when some temporary relief takes place during the evaluation, as is often the case, this is not the treatment, and it is short-lived. This is the just the prelude. The evaluation isn't much different from the false intimacy of two people sitting next to each other on a long train ride. One may confide very private stuff to this stranger. The conversation feels very intimate, but it is an anonymous false intimacy, predicated on never seeing this person again.

The beginning of therapy is but an introduction to a stranger, making a first and an essential emotional contact. But we will see each other again. We will deepen our exploration. We will move toward a trusting closeness, which is not anonymous. Real trust always has to be earned. And as always happens, the patient's internal dramas and cast of characters will make their presence felt. In order to find our way, we always have to slog through the characterological dramas. They always come alive in the office. This is the hard part. In order to reach the patient's Authentic-Being, we have to grapple with this odyssey. It is only as this takes place that real trust can emerge.

I am not "healthy," and my patients are not "sick." They are not a DSM IV or V diagnosis of illness. They are human beings with a problematic character, which they came by honestly. To whatever degree, we all do. Everybody is responsible for the enactments of their character. Therapy is the patient's quest to grapple with his own character to recover his Authentic-Being.

To review, the therapist explores the patient's characterological world, no matter where this leads. He is open to the positive aspects of the characterological world and to the dark side. Likewise, he is predisposed to be available to care about the patient. It is in the emotional arms of the therapist that the patient mourns and digests his inner play and the damage done. There, it is safe for his patient's Authentic-Being to re-emerge, where he writes a new play that is consonant with his authenticity and capacity to love. These processes of psychotherapy deal with the way consciousness actually forms, operates, and heals. This is the human condition. And this is the therapy quest.

And now we turn back to Eddie and his psychotherapy.

16

EDDIE'S PSYCHOTHERAPY
Mourning and the Recovery of the Authentic-Being

I opened the door to the waiting room and greeted a thin, long-haired, casually dressed young man who appeared younger than a junior in college. He was clearly uncomfortable and distracted. I ushered him to his chair in my office. He sat down and lowered his head. I began, "What's going on that you've come to see me?"

"I had a bad acid trip."

"Yes, go on."

"I told my parents, and they sent me here."

Eddie spoke softly and didn't volunteer much information, so I began to lead the conversation. "Tell me what happened."

"I dropped the acid and was listening to music in my apartment."

"Yes, and then?"

"Then I had the bad trip."

"Tell me about it."

"I had this sense that I had a mission to fulfill in my life. I was supposed to be a kind of Moses figure, but I knew that I would be assassinated."

"Go on."

"I was supposed to be willing to be a martyr. But I was afraid. I saw someone like Jesus who was willing to die, but I was too afraid. I felt like a coward, a failure. My fear of being killed got worse."

"Tell me more."

"At that point I felt this terror. I tried to hide. I was even more afraid. I hated myself for feeling this way."

"So what did you do?"

"I didn't know what to do, but I couldn't stand it. I thought that when the acid wore off, it would go away. So I tried to just hold and roll to get through it. But it didn't go away."

"Go on."

"It lasted for hours ... I've been feeling this way ever since ... It's not quite as bad as it was."

"OK ... And then what?"

"So I went to my parents and told them."

"Uh-huh."

"I couldn't stop crying—I never cry."

"And?"

"They said I needed to talk to a psychiatrist. So here I am."

And so it began. From the outset I took it upon myself to keep the conversation going. Eddie seemed broken and conveyed a sense of considerable anxiety. I didn't know if he was always this withdrawn or if it was the result of his state of terror. Other than the palpable presence of this nameless dread, I didn't really get much of a sense of him.

Eddie came back for a second appointment a few days later. He told me that he'd had a dream the night following our first session:

"I had gone to bed early. *Suddenly, my body was paralyzed, and I couldn't move a muscle. I was awake. There was a long, dark tunnel that was like a vortex, with a brilliant light at the end of it. With a whoosh, I passed through the tunnel, and at the light, I passed into another place and time.*

"*I was sitting on top of a huge round boulder, twenty feet above the ground. I was chained at the wrists to an iron stake that was anchored deep in the boulder. The chains were held in place by an old rusted iron lock. In front of me was a long, well-manicured dirt road, lined on both sides by evenly spaced sycamore trees. You, Dr. Berezin, were walking toward me. You were tall and gaunt, dressed in black, wearing a pointed pilgrim hat. We were in the 1600s. You were coming toward me to set me free. As I sat there waiting for you, I realized that the lock was actually open. In fact, my hands were not actually bound to the stake at all. They only appeared to be.*

The chains were loose, and I was actually already free. But I had to pretend I was trapped in order to give you the opportunity, or the illusion, that you would free me. So I sat there, pretending and waiting. I was thinking, 'Why am I doing this? I'm already free. Why don't I just get down myself?' Yet I was too afraid. So I sat there and waited for this sham liberation. Then I woke up in my bed."

This was a hypnogogic state dream. A hypnogogic state dream takes place at an earlier level of sleep than REM sleep. In it one dreams he is awake, and one's body is paralyzed. But he is actually asleep. Remember, dreams are the enactments of our consciousness in sleep to digest what has been stirred during the day as it resonates with the issues of the inner play. This dream was about Eddie's anticipation of therapy and me. It gave us a window into his play and was a preview of coming attractions. This dream was so loaded and full of import that it popped right out as a hypnogogic state dream. It didn't even wait for the regular REM sleep stage of dreaming.

Eddie was cast as a kind of Promethean figure who, similarly chained, had his entrails eaten daily by a giant bird as punishment for giving knowledge of the gods to man in the form of fire. This myth encompassed the meaning of the dream. Knowledge that would liberate Eddie was forbidden knowledge. It was taboo. He was not supposed to recover and live. He was supposed to be an eternal prisoner in endless torture.

The image of me, gaunt and dressed in black, was as a pilgrim, a Puritan, a Calvinist. This depicts a cold, harsh, severe, and judgmental persona. It also set the tone for the general tenor of Eddie's play image of psychotherapy. Both therapy and I were a projection screen of Calvinism—dark and controlling, where all is predetermined and immutable and sin. This imagery for the liberation of Eddie was certainly not one that anticipated warmth and responsiveness.

The giant boulder represented his own private world, planet Eddie, that he inhabited alone. Even free of his chains, he couldn't get off because it was too high and dangerous. Eddie was trapped in his own world. The imagery was rock and iron and chains, hard and forbidding. The tree-lined path was cultivated and geometric. Nature doesn't have straight lines. This cultivated path was a symbol of unnatural imposed order, compulsive and rigid. His expectation was that he would be subject to rigid and imposed orthodox ideas, not a process that would be responsive to him. This dream landscape was a projection screen that accurately depicted Eddie's world.

The iron stake deeply embedded in stone symbolizes how deeply and firmly and hopelessly entrenched was Eddie's imprisonment. In the initial scene, his hands were chained. It was on a second take that they were not. This is a chapter two of the dream, illuminating chapter one. It revealed that Eddie would not be predisposed to trust me. It would be too unsafe. If liberation were to happen, the only person he could really count on was himself. He had only himself to turn to. In addition, he believed that he had to kowtow to my ego and let me think I was helping him. This suggests a submissive practice in relation to authority. Yet despite his apparent self-reliance, Eddie was too frightened to get off the rock on his own. This introduces that he was scared and anxious. He was not supposed to be self-sufficient or authentic, and it wasn't safe to trust. He had to play a meaningless and submissive game. Therapy was a sham.

Eddie's dream provided a snapshot of Eddie's underlying play and foretold what lay ahead in therapy. It revealed the tenor of his play, which was to be the prism through which he would experience the therapy and me. It was all there. Keep in mind that an understanding of the dream would play no role in short-circuiting what we were going to have to slog through in the therapy. This could only transpire in a real way as we did the work. The dream depicted the self-fulfilling prophecy of Eddie's invisible play of consciousness. My challenge in psychotherapy was to help him get to the bottom of it and work through it. It was to help him get free from those chains that bound him; to get out of his private dark world, inhabited by him alone; to help Eddie truly be free to be; to rely on himself; and to trust that another person—me—would be there for him.

After another two evaluation sessions, the therapy began. We started meeting twice a week and later increased the frequency. I asked Eddie to address whatever was meaningful in his life, and we would talk about it. In the early phases, I was very active on my end of the conversation and responsive to whatever was talked about. Otherwise, it was as if the conversation would just drop of a cliff.

Eddie told me that he routinely felt anxiety—at dusk, in social situations, if he ventured into unfamiliar places alone, if he drank a glass of wine. Under ordinary circumstances, he didn't tell anyone about his anxiety. He just lived with it. He said that he was so used to it that he didn't consider it noteworthy. In actuality, he was secretive about it because he was too ashamed to expose this "weakness" to anyone. He only discussed it with me because the intensity of his residual terror was so great.

In these sessions, I commonly felt a mild anxiety in my own chest. The anxiety didn't seem to be connected to anything that was being talked about. It was kind of free-floating and just there. When the session was over, my sensation would evaporate. I did not address this state but chose a course of watchful waiting. It provided a kind of barometer to his state of mind. Later in the therapy, when his anxiety lifted, my anxiety resonance disappeared along with it.

Eddie had been so frightened by the LSD trip that he decided on his own that this would be the last time he'd take any. In addition, despite the fact that he smoked marijuana a lot, he decided to stop using it as well. He had already recognized that he was using marijuana as a crutch to face people. It had ceased working anyway. Eddie said that for some time, smoking pot had made him "paranoid." This was actually a marijuana anxiety state. Even though it no longer worked and despite the amplification of anxiety, Eddie had kept right on smoking, trying to recapture his earlier positive experiences. Since he was such a veteran smoker, he also felt ashamed of the marijuana anxiety itself. His decision that drugs were over turned out to be very helpful for the therapy. I didn't have to deal with the often problematic decision to stop.

Marijuana has a characteristic effect on consciousness itself. It promotes a disjunction between thinking and feeling. It distanced Eddie from participation in his feelings, which he was wont to do in the first place. His thinking, ungrounded in feeling, was free to roam, untethered. In its early phases, this promoted a sense of creativity due to the unanchored ability of his mind to roam free. It also fostered obsessional and intellectualized "insights." Marijuana intellectualization was disconnected from feeling. And as we know, feeling is the anchor of the characterological play. This became an organizing feature of the neuronal loops of his experience and warped the workings of his consciousness. Through habitual usage, this "marijuana mind" was established in him, whether he was smoking or not.

Eddie took for granted that therapy was about intellectualized insights. (This is a common assumption, which is unfortunately all too frequently shared by many therapists.) This decidedly is not the case. Eddie's pride in his intellectualized insights was problematic for the therapy because it interfered with real engagement. Eddie valued his insights as special and impressive. His compensatory identity as superior was attached to being a user of not only marijuana but the other hallucinogens as well. And finally, marijuana served to heighten his senses. As a result, Eddie felt super-participatory in sensory experience. This was compensatory for Eddie's sense of removal as the observer/outsider he normally felt himself to be.

As is typical, in order for Eddie's brain to work right again, it took him a full year to recover from habitual marijuana usage. This was not about detoxing his system—that took place fairly quickly. Likewise, it was not a physiological dependence. The issue was marijuana's effects on his consciousness and a psychological dependence on this valued cast of mind, which I will call marijuana brain.

Psychotherapy is not a sequential process but rather multiple related pathways operating all at the same time. The two epicenters of the therapy are the same as those of the characterological play—Eddie's self and his relatedness with others. All the way through therapy, these would cross-pollinate. In terms of our relatedness, Eddie did not derive much comfort from my presence, as I was but the projection screen of the untrustworthy sadistic, abusing, and depriving ogre persona that I was in the midst of learning about. He was a long way from breaking through to trusting that I was sitting by his side so he could face the salient experience of his past and digest it. Nonetheless, just due to my ongoing reliable presence, our sessions were still somewhat salutary. As a result of Eddie having me to talk to, even in the absence of trust, he wasn't quite so alone. As a

212

consequence, his symptoms diminished somewhat and were more manageable. The terror dissipated.

During our discussions, Eddie told me facts and stories about himself, as if for my edification. He gave me intellectualized information that he thought I wanted to hear. It turned out that he was feeding me data in order for me to construct judgmental theories and insights to understand him. I had no interest in such an enterprise at all. However, he was absolutely certain that this was the talk of therapy, and I couldn't disabuse him of this notion. Due to his intelligence, his theorizing was, in fact, interesting. Consequently, I had to discipline myself to forgo the temptation to join him in those pursuits or to indulge in my own speculations. Ungrounded thinking serves to lead one away from real engagement.

During this time, I had no access to authentic Eddie, and, as such, there wasn't much to feel. Nonetheless, in concert with the surface content of our conversations, various feeling states arose in me that resonated with Eddie's mask persona. These would, in turn, guide me to his otherwise invisible play—invisible to him and to me. Learning about his play was the first phase of the therapy. I commonly felt a combination of sleepiness and a hunger in the pit of my stomach. The sleepiness wasn't nearly as intense as it had been with Mike but was certainly present. It taught me how removed Eddie was. The hunger could become quite pronounced. While sitting with him, I might find myself contemplating a honey-dipped doughnut. The intensity of my hunger reflected how significantly Eddie actually needed a safe and reliable connection. Need for relatedness is always a two-way street. My human need was open, but Eddie's need for connection was closed off. It was my unrequited need for engagement with him that actually generated my hunger response. This was something for me to notice and use as a signal to recognize what was going on under the surface. Immediately after a session ended, I would feel wide awake and have no hunger. There would be neither a nap nor a doughnut involved. And so I continued to learn about his play.

Eddie commonly assumed that I was criticizing him on every level—his conduct, his take on something, his grammar, his very choice of words. This wasn't a question, just a taken-for-granted certainty.

If I disputed this assumption, he didn't believe me. Instead, he took it as being told he was wrong, accompanied by an implicit judgment. The internal drama of a bad self being attacked by a criticizing judge came into focus.

At all times, Eddie denied feeling any anger about anything. No matter what we talked about, he took pride in the absence of any aggression, and a special pride in being a pacifist, with its attendant superiority. One day, well over a year into the therapy, we were discussing his relationship with Cathy. He always denied any anger toward her. He viewed her betrayal and rejection of him as deserved and inevitable. How could he be angry at someone he loved so much? He retained a loyalty to her and never said anything negative about her. The fault lay with him. He protected her against anything negative I might suggest. He always took her side and defended her against me.

One day, Eddie said, "Months after Cathy broke up with me, she called me out of the blue and said she had tickets to a Buckminster Fuller lecture. Did I want to go? She was up-front and said that this was not a date. We would go as friends. I was thrilled. While we were there, it felt like the old days, and I was very happy. But then when the lecture was over, she just left. And that was it. She was gone again. I felt just like I had when we first broke up."

"I think it was problematic for you to go."

"Why? I like Buckminster Fuller and wanted to hear him speak."

"Because it wasn't really about the lecture; it was about Cathy. 'Friends,' in this context, is always bogus. You knew that, and so did she."

"No, it's not her fault. She was up-front with me. I agreed to go on her terms, as 'friends.'"

"I don't even think she should have asked you. The pain that followed was 100 percent predictable."

"No, it was me. I messed it up. You're just taking my side because you're my therapist."

"That's not true. Obviously, you played a major role, but she is still responsible for hurting you. And besides, even though I don't know how exactly, I think it was manipulative on her part."

"You're just blaming her because you don't like her … Now you're real angry at me!" As he spoke, the little finger of his left hand visibly twitched.

At this point I felt a tension in my chest and my arms, my resonance with denied and suppressed anger. I said, as I usually did when he was mistakenly certain that I was angry, "No, I'm not angry."

Then he looked at me funny and said, "Maybe you're not … I'm the one who's angry! I'm really angry! I feel a rage!" The twitching stopped.

This may seem like a small event, but it was major. His normal persona designations had been that I was the projection screen as the angry attacker, while he was the projection screen as the recipient of the attack. Remember, his masochistic orientation was really maso-sadism, an inverted expression of his own anger, by which he was the designated object of attack from others. He had located his anger as mine rather than his. He had been uncomfortable sitting with these unacceptable feelings as his own. At this juncture, Eddie re-internalized his own projected anger. He literally retracted his projection off of me and located it inside himself, where it belonged. Eddie dared to own that the anger was his, not mine.

Eddie's wherewithal to own his anger was intrinsically related to a breakthrough of trust. This time he trusted me when I disavowed being angry. He trusted that it was safe for him to feel a heretofore unacceptable feeling and that I would accept him without condemnation or rejection. The tension melted away. I felt a soft feeling of connection with Eddie when he took this first leap of trust. Eddie had opened the door. The leap of trust was actually a leap of feeling. It was a courageous act that came from himself, from his own testing of experience. When Eddie took this leap for the first time, it generated in me a genuine feeling of him, as well as respect and admiration. I resonated for the first time with Eddie's being behind the mask. He had someone with him, wanting him to be, to know, and to feel. He wasn't alone.

This moment of trust was partial and temporary. A few moments of this was all he could tolerate. Then he went roaring back to his comfort zone—the maso-sadistic beliefs. But he did venture forth again. There was to be a lot of back-and-forthing, but our exploration now extended into new territory. The incipient safe harbor of trust in our relationship was entirely unlike anything Eddie had known.

Therapy turns on the real establishment of a trusting relationship. This is the central issue in all psychotherapies. A beginning trusting connection was something entirely new for Eddie. It was the first time in his life that he ventured outside the certainties of his play of sadism and abuse. It was well over a year before Eddie took this first leap of trust. Prior to this moment, it wasn't possible for Eddie to believe that I was not attacking him. As long as I was the projection screen of the sadistic, attacking Abuser of his play, how could he possibly trust me? The leap of trust came only after his own testing of his beliefs, on his own terms, in his own time. Only then could he draw a different conclusion for himself and know from his own experience that I was safe.

Through my resonance with his mask personas, I had been able to penetrate the mystery of his invisible play. However, learning about Eddie's play, as important as it was, was not in itself transformative. That would take place in the next phase of therapy that followed from Eddie's leap of trust. This ushered in the mourning phase of therapy. Mourning is the process by which Eddie would face and digest his pernicious attachments so that he could truly move on. Within that safe harbor of trust, Eddie took the risk of letting himself face the truth about Cathy and what he felt about her. He knew for the first time that he was angry at Cathy. He felt the anger. And he began to know why.

With the leap of trust, Eddie let me in through the wall of stone, the wall of thorns. And with that, Sleeping Eddie awakened. This had never happened in his life. Eddie retracted the sadistic Abuser off of me, and he took the aggression back inside of him as his own. He saw Cathy as the Abuser, and he began to face and mourn their relationship. Remember, the sadomasochistic story that originated with Eddie and his mother ended up projected onto the screen of Eddie and Cathy, where it had invisibly played itself out as the self-fulfilled prophecy of his ogre play. She had been a perfect fit and was the suitable carrier of his internal scenario.

Eddie had access to his anger at having been the object of cruelty, rejection, and humiliation. His anger was good aggression, not sadistic aggression. Abuse was, of course, the major issue of his play and consequently of his life. Rather than being understanding, dependent upon, and protective of Cathy, Eddie felt his legitimate rage at being mistreated. It previously had been taboo to face the truth of the actualities of his relationship with her. It had been too dangerous to challenge his intense emotional dependence on her, which was the only attachment he had ever had in his life. His attachment was supercharged, compensatory for the absence of a reliable trust with his ogre mother.

This was to be the paradigm for all the mourning that would take place in the rest of the therapy. Due to the evolution of trust with me, Eddie explored and mourned the truth of what actually happened in his life and what he felt about it. He also mourned what should have happened and didn't. He mourned his pernicious attachments. He fully faced his relationship with Cathy. He explored his teenage years. We dealt with the enactments of his current everyday life. We explored the major issues as well as minor incidents, like the fight with the professor and his subsequent dream, with which we began this book. Most important, the mourning explorations focused on his mother, his father, his sisters, and his brother—the very pain that had warped the writing of his play. All were faced and digested with me by his side. Many threads were followed to weave a whole cloth.

Eddie went back to his secret and private past. He said, "You know, she spanked me every day."

"How's that?"

"Actually, spanking was the family term. But it was more than that."

"What do you mean?"

"It was a beating."

"Tell me more."

"Okay, here's an incident … I must have been four. Margie and Clara had gone off to school, and my brother and I were looking out the window, watching them walk to the bus. He grabbed me, and I pushed him back. And he said, 'I'm gonna tell on you.'

"So I said, 'Go ahead,' and knocked him over. He cried and screamed, 'Eddie hit me!' My mother stormed in with that look in her eye. She was yelling and hitting me wherever she could. 'I told you to leave him alone!' Her hits felt distant and didn't bother me. They kept coming. When she was done, she grabbed me by the arm and dragged me to the corner. 'You stand here 'til I say so!'

"'No, I won't!' I said, and pulled away.

"She grabbed me and threw me back up against the wall, 'What did I tell you?'

"I said in an even tone, 'You said, "You stand here 'til I say so."' I was thinking, *What an idiot. You don't even know the stupid question you just asked?*

"She got madder and hit me on my back. 'Don't you talk to me that way! You think you're so smart.' I pulled away again, and she slammed me back into the corner. This time, I stayed there. She continued, 'You should be more like him. He's such a good boy,' and on and on. She went back to the window and continued to mumble under her breath. I stood there. And I stood there for what must have been a half hour. At this point, she was reading to him.

"She turned back to me and said, 'What do you have to say for yourself?' I didn't answer. 'I said, what do you have to say for yourself?'

"'Uhmm ... He started it.'

"Okay, this is it. You apologize, or you're going to reform school. What do you have to say?"

"'I said, he started it.'

"'Okay, wise guy, I'm calling right now.'

"She went to the phone and dialed what I thought was the reform school. I didn't know what 'reform school' was, but I knew I didn't want to be there. I assumed it was jail. I was sure I was going, and they were coming for me. So I panicked and started to cry. 'Don't send me to reform school. I'll be good.'

"She waited for a while and then said, 'Okay, I won't send you—this time.' And she picked up the phone again and told them not to come."

In addition to the exploration and mourning of Eddie's past, the most crucial arena in Eddie's psychotherapy was about our relationship. This was interwoven with all the other explorations. It was only possible for Eddie to mourn his pain anew within the trustworthy emotional arms of our holding relationship. This made the exploration and digestion of his projected play beliefs about me essential. The hovering personas of his sadomasochistic play had settled onto me as its projection screen. As we know, Eddie had seen me as the sadistic judge who was judging him as bad, disgusting, and fraudulent, and who rejected him on that basis. While he thought he believed what he saw, Eddie actually saw what he believed. He was suspicious (i.e., certain) that I didn't like him. He believed that he was boring me, that I was critical of him, that I was angry at him, and that I was exploiting him. His exploitation beliefs ranged from the idea that I was feeding my ego at his expense and aggrandizing myself as a superior know-it-all, to putting him down as inferior and lacking, all the way to his fear and belief that I had sexual motives and was interested in molesting him. Each time he addressed any of these out loud, he absolutely believed I was insulted and mad at him. We explored these beliefs over and over, as Eddie bumped into discrepancies between his projection of me and my actuality. These collisions were always bumpy. They were, however, the avenue by which Eddie ultimately tested his play beliefs for himself. The real establishment of trust wasn't a one-time leap. It took place by increments as he faced and tested his actual beliefs about exploitation on his own terms, in his own way, and in his own time. The heart of his therapy would turn on our evolving human relationship.

With all the back-and-forthing, the work of therapy happened. Eddie's projections of the sadistic and rejecting persona continued to peel off of me as his old maso-sadistic identity simultaneously peeled off of him. His problematic inner play was in the process of being dismantled. Through the transformative process of mourning his inner play, Eddie was no longer immersed in and inhabiting the endless war of relentless sadomasochistic fighting, As a result, his characterological symptoms gradually subsided all on their own. His anxiety had begun to evaporate and eventually ceased to be present. I no longer felt the presence of anxiety in my own chest when I sat with him. And in addition, the debilitating self-hatred of his so-called depression began to lift as well.

When these processes were well under way, Eddie had another dream, which was a status update on the changes taking place in his internal play:

"I was sitting at a table in a restaurant with an attractive girl and another guy. He had slicked-back hair and acted quite cocky. He was course, aggressive, and pushy. I felt intimidated by him. She was choosing which of us she was interested in. I was trying to show her how sensitive I was, that I was the opposite of him. Surely she would be put off by his macho and crudeness and especially his overt sexual intent. She would find me pure and innocent. And of course, that would be desirable to her. I wanted to protect her from even being subjected to him. She would find me a relief. I was certain she would value me, that my position would please her, and he would turn her off.

"All of a sudden, they got up from the table to go off together. She was visibly attracted to this slimeball! I was shocked and sick. I couldn't believe it, but I kinda knew it all along. As I sat there alone, rejected and forlorn, something changed inside me. I stood up and kicked my chair away. 'I will never take a backseat again.' I'm not gonna hide my strength, my power. I don't have to be a jerk, but I'm not going to hang back from being a player in life. I will stand up for myself and not let anything stand in my way again. I will take my due. I will take my rightful place. Never again!"

This dream represented the changes that were taking place inside Eddie. With access to his good aggression, he was shifting away from masochism. He had, in fact, begun to operate on his own behalf in the world. Eddie's pilgrim dream had foretold his beliefs about the exploitative and sadistic world of his play. In the actual therapy, these beliefs had been explored and tested in the living moment of our relatedness. This allowed Eddie to see for himself and authentically believe that I was not the abusive and rejecting persona of his play.

Eddie now began to move toward facing the most damaging element of abuse—maternal emotional deprivation itself, the absence of respectful loving. This had the greatest formative impact on Eddie's play. It had caused him to remove his Authentic-Being from the stage for protection. Eddie had thereby joined the available substitute avenue of relatedness, sadomasochism, through which his play was written. As the reservoir of reliable holding increased, the accent of the therapy shifted to the pain of the absence of love. Eddie told me the following story,

"When I was in first grade, my parents took a two-week trip to the Holy Land with our church. We stayed with my grandparents, my mother's parents. Before they left, my mother said to my grandmother, in my presence, 'Make a record of what he does while I'm gone.'

"It hadn't been a bad time. I don't remember much of my sisters or brother. I actually spent a lot of time alone, outside, up in the apple tree. I also worked with my grandmother in the garden, weeding. I remember sitting at the edge of the garden, snapping the snapdragons over and over—you know, between my forefinger and thumb.

"At some point, I felt super homesick. I had this sick feeling in my stomach and really missed my parents. Where were they? My grandmother and I were in the den, and she asked me what was wrong. I broke down and cried, and told her, 'I don't know what to do.' I was sobbing. 'I know that I'm very bad, and my parents don't love me.'

"She kept telling me, 'That's not true. They do love you. And you are a good boy.'

"'No, I'm not, and you don't understand. Mommy doesn't love me.' She kept trying to reassure me, but I knew what was true. Her protestations didn't mean anything to me. I was inconsolable. The sobbing went on for a long time This was actually the last time I ever cried. Eventually, I got control back and wandered upstairs to my grandmother's bedroom. I sat on the floor and looked at the patterns in her Oriental rug.

"Later, the long-awaited day finally came that my parents were coming home. But I went into a panic. Now, I knew my grandmother had made a record of all the bad things I had done. Understand, I was sure this meant a record that you would put on a record player. So I had to find this record and smash it, so my mother wouldn't be able to play it. I kinda thought the record-making machine was in the upstairs hall closet so that was probably where I'd find the record. I combed through everything in the closet, but I couldn't find anything.

Feeling really desperate, I began searching the rest of the house for that damned record. But it wasn't anyplace. So I resigned myself to the fact that I was really going to get it when they came home."

We can clearly see through the "record" story that Eddie did have deep attachment to his mother, but the attachment was sadomasochistic. She was his mother, and Eddie was bereft as a result of her absence. Even though his grandmother was a much more benign and loving figure, and she did have some emotional importance to him, she couldn't displace or be a substitute for his primary attachment. His grandmother was not able to comfort or reassure Eddie for two reasons. The coldness of his world was already so established that he couldn't derive any warmth from her or anybody. And when she tried to reassure him, Eddie knew her words were empty. As well-meaning as she was, by overriding the truth, she made Eddie feel even more hopeless and alone. When Eddie broke down and cried, it was because he couldn't contain his pain any longer. He cried and cried until he could cry no more, as he sank back, one more time, into a state of apathy.

At this point in the therapy, Eddie did face and mourn the pain of these events, with me in his corner. He reopened the apathy and allowed himself to feel the pain in the living moment of our discussion. As he mourned his sadomasochistic attachment, he began to relinquish it. This led him to truly challenge his deeply held identity—as bad. As this took place, something new began to emerge from the shadows. It was the feeling of Eddie. And along with it, a new and precious resonance materialized. I felt an alive fullness in my heart. I felt sweet sadness and tenderness. This all-important resonance was the feeling of my Authentic-Being touched by Eddie's Authentic-Being.

The new resonance reflected the presence of Eddie's Authentic-Being having awakened from its hundred-year sleep. We can't necessarily call it the recovery of Eddie. It wasn't like a fully formed Eddie had retreated and then re-emerged. He emerged and formed, in a sense, anew. We'll have to made up a word and call it the "covery" of Eddie. Nonetheless, Eddie was here, and I felt a real engagement with him.

This ushered in the healing phase of therapy. Eddie continued to emerge and solidify who he was, with me now reliably well entrenched by his side. As a result of this experience, he was writing a new play, in which his persona of self was infused with his Authentic-Being. Likewise, his persona of other was infused with the presence of the Loving Other. This opened his potential to give and receive love.

Eddie was now well on his way. In his life, things started to go quite well. He acted in his own behalf and did not hang back. His love of nature and biology had informed his graduate school interests in biological research, and by the time he got to his dissertation, Eddie was no longer a copier. He listened to his inner voice. He began his own research in a genuinely authentic and true direction. It was original work, intriguing, and cutting-edge at that time. His dissertation delved into the interplay of neurotransmitters in the brain. It's important to recognize that Eddie's fulfillment came from being true to himself. His emerging authenticity did not have reference to any influence from me. My value to him was from emotional holding, not my beliefs. It was of no import whether his political, scientific, or religious ideas or values were similar to mine or different.

For a long time, Eddie continued to follow his regular predilections in relationships—seduce, conquer, devalue, lose interest, reject, and abandon. Then he met Barbara. This was at a time when there was available Authentic-Being and Loving Other from which he could draw. Eddie was ready. Barbara was attractive, as was his wont. However, she was warm and caring, with an intelligence that was commensurate with his own. Hers was different from Eddie's. She had a comprehensive aesthetic sensibility, which Eddie came to value. And most important, she loved Eddie. And Eddie found his way to loving her.

Throughout the psychotherapy, Eddie had some degree of discomfort with the intimate emotional closeness with me because we were both male. He was certainly more comfortable now that he had settled in with a woman to love. As a result, in the latter part of the therapy, Eddie had two sources of nurturance: Barbara and me. Both of us contributed to the provision of love through which he now flourished. Her presence contributed to the therapy as well as to his actual life.

Eddie continued to have an occasional bout of anxiety or self-hate. When these symptoms reappeared, however, they were short-lived, and the familiar explorations exposed bits and pieces of the old play dynamic. His symptoms, when dealt with, dissipated, usually by the following morning. Likewise, an episode of suspiciousness and distrust would periodically arise and turn into a fight with Barbara. His emotional paranoia continued to lurk in him as a potential. But Eddie was no longer living from there as his primary self, relationship, or plot. When he dipped into suspiciousness and distrust, this too was explored, dealt with, and recovered from.

The good-enough solidification of Eddie's authenticity and our trusting relationship was the harbinger of the end of therapy—but not immediately, for there remained a final chapter in the therapy before Eddie went off on his own. It was for Eddie to mourn and digest our relationship. The point of therapy in the first place was for Eddie to flourish and prosper in his self, his life, and his relationships in the world. Therapy is much like a parent loving and raising a child. The parental relationship, so central and important to both parties, is in the service of raising a child to become an independent, autonomous, responsible, loving person in his own life. And so it was with psychotherapy.

Our solid and trusting relationship was not grounds to continue to meet, as it would be in a regular social friendship. Therapy is about recovery from damage, in the service of developing a full life. Like child rearing, it's about roots and wings. Deep emotional attachment is an intrinsic and central element for the establishment of roots. As opposed to the common notion that dependence is a dirty word, it is actually a necessary and inherent ingredient of a loving attachment. Eddie's need for me was essential for the establishment of roots. Toward the end of therapy, the all-important dependence had morphed on its own accord into mutual feeling. He gradually ceased to need me to be there for emotional holding. As Eddie grew and solidified, he naturally spread his wings. The good-bye period was one of sweet sadness and loss. This final mourning fostered his freedom to be on his own. Eddie no longer needed me with him, for he carried me inside. What he carried wasn't really my words or our explorations but my presence, as an "Eddiophile."

Therapy was over. It was time. In the psychotherapy, Eddie mourned and digested his mask figures, which freed him from their predetermination of a life of endless sadomasochistic relating, and eradicated his symptoms. In the course of this, he recovered his Authentic-Being, which allowed him to be himself and to love.

There is a footnote. A few years after therapy was over, Eddie wrote me a letter. Things had gone well, and he and Barbara were married. He had fallen into a pit of suspiciousness and jealousy, and he wanted to check in with me. His letter continued: "Here's what you would say to me ..." He then spelled out quite accurately what I would, in fact, have said. Then he concluded the letter: "I don't really need to come see you now. As I wrote this letter, it allowed me to remember you remembering me, and that was what I needed. I just needed to touch base with that, and I just did."

What was happening in Eddie's brain as he discarded his old problematic play and wrote a new one for the cortical top-down processing of life? We have seen Eddie re-establish a new top-down cortical circuit for the B7 chord in chapter 3. Those processes of simple relearning is a paradigm for the processes of the brain to deactivate old mappings and re-establish new circuits for cortical top-down functioning in general. The rewriting of the play of consciousness was a far more complex enterprise. Eddie's play was established through the limbic system, and, as such, the pain of change operated through feeling. Mourning the emotional pain of attachment was the agency of change for Eddie to relinquish and rewrite his internal play. And not surprisingly, the operations of mourning followed the same specific biological pathways as those that created his play in the first place.

In fact, mourning operates as the process of repair for trauma for all the limbic plays of relatedness, not just the principal play of character in psychotherapy. This includes death, loss, abuse, abandonment, rejection, sexual molestation, and others. Before we explore its specific biological operations in Eddie's cortex, as he mourned his play, we will first address it in its conventional reference—grief in the context of death.

Let's say a man's wife dies. He might say, "What is the point of mourning? It can't bring my wife back." Mourning, of course, will not bring her back. Nothing will. Mourning is for the mourner to recover from the loss so that he can resume living. The death of his wife was a jarring trauma, an event sufficiently powerful that it wrote a new play. In this newly written play, she is dead and gone, and he is alone. This new play is discordant with the old deeply held play of their life together, where his ongoing attachment was intact. Her death did not compute in his cortical world. In his consciousness, the old top-down cortical play overrode the new one.

This traumatic loss is much like the phenomenon of the phantom limb. Despite the fact that the amputee's arm isn't there anymore, it continues to live on in his consciousness due to its activated mappings in his cortex. Despite the fact that our widower knows cognitively that his wife has died, his marriage play continues to live on in the mappings of his consciousness. Mourning her death is the process by which the older play of his wife will cease to be his activated play. The process of mourning will allow him to inhabit the new play—that she is gone. Then she will take her proper place in memory.

The basic elements of mourning a death are similar among all cultures. The specific nuances and style may differ, but the processes are universal. Cultural traditions recognize that the husband remains connected to his wife and doesn't want to leave her. Take the rending of clothes. This is where, in Jewish tradition, the mourner rips open his clothing—in a symbolic gesture of killing himself. By this, he symbolically leaves his own body to be with his wife in death, which allows them to continue to be together. He retains his old play of active attachment.

Right after a death, all cultures provide a circle of loving others—family and friends—who surround the widower. At the funeral or wake or sitting shiva, they tell stories about his wife, share their feelings about her, and revisit who she was and their life with her. The major import of family and friends is to provide a holding circle around him. After this, the real work of mourning begins.

Elisabeth Kubler-Ross's five stages of grief—denial, bargaining, anger, sadness, and acceptance—accurately describe the processes involved in relinquishing the old play to accept and inhabit the new one. *Denial* means that the widower continues to inhabit the old, deeply held play as he keeps the new traumatic play at bay. Denial can't really work because the truth inevitably begins to creep in. Then he attempts to hold onto the old play and toss the new one away by *bargaining*. He employs magical thinking as he bargains with a personification of an all-powerful fate or God or death. "I'll do whatever you want if I get to keep her." When it becomes apparent that this doesn't work either, he gets *angry* at the inexorable truth that his wife has been taken from him. Eventually, this gives way to the *sadness* of losing his attachment. And finally, he *accepts* the new play of death and loss and absence. The old play finally recedes and is no longer in ascendancy, and the new play takes its place. He then carries her in memory.

In order to disconnect from the old play, the mourner must face and go through the pain of all the feelings of his attachment to digest the loss. The feelings are about whatever defined the actual story of their relationship (love, sadness, anger, envy, hate—whatever it was). To face and digest their deeply held story and mourn those feelings takes a long time. Typically, with death, the major work takes a year. To lay the relationship to rest, the mourner must deactivate the old play in his cortical theater. This allows him to accept the new play and for him to come back from the dead to go on in his own life.

Mourning is never really complete. The mappings of the old play remain in the cortex, like those mappings of the phantom limb. When walking down the street, I occasionally see a face in a crowd, or familiar hair, or a familiar gait, and I think, "Oh, it's Karen!"—a friend who died many years ago. My benign visions of Karen reflect, with feeling, that her persona lives on as a play potential within me, and remains available to be activated as a top-down cortical projection.

In Eddie's psychotherapy, the play that was mourned, digested, and deactivated was his primary characterological play. In its place a new play was written by Eddie through his experience during the therapy. The characterological play is the most deeply held story of all, even more so than our story of the death of a wife. In psychotherapy, Eddie mourned the story of his life, the attachment to Cathy, and more profoundly, the mask figures of his life—the attachments to his mother, father, sisters, and brother, through whom he wrote his play in the first place. Remember, for the stories to be relegated to memory, sadomasochistic attachments need to be mourned just the same as loving attachments.

The mourning of Eddie's play was the specific biological operation for the repair and healing of his suffering. Biological psychiatry, neurology, and neuroscience in general have preempted a claim on what is biological. They have defined biology as the domain of physical brain structure; brain organization, brain anatomy, and functional brain centers; neurotransmitters; hormones; information learned from studying brain lesions; and activated patterns of neurons that can be seen in brain scans associated with certain localized functions. There is a great deal of knowledge to be appreciated from these approaches. Unfortunately, their orientation has mistaken the parts for the whole. They have ignored the brain's most important biological manifestation of all: the play of consciousness.

When scientists study the brain, they break it down into its component parts. However, the component parts don't exist for their individual operations, as it sometimes seems when they are studied in a vacuum. Tinkering with the parts not only misses the boat, but can be misleading and destructive, with unintended consequences. It is like the story of the blind men and the elephant. Each blind man touches a part of the elephant and comes to his false conclusion as to its nature: the leg suggests it's a pillar; the tail means that it's a rope; the trunk suggests a tree branch; the ear is a fan; the belly is a wall; the tusk is a pipe. This book has been an attempt to grasp the whole enchilada. It is not defined by its component parts. There is an elephant in the room!

The component parts of brain functioning all work together in concert in the service of the central biological creation of the human genome—the play of consciousness. This specific production of the human brain is the unique adaptational feature of our Darwinian evolution—the defining characteristic of what it is to be human. It is the central organizing function of our biological lives and the fulfilled manifestation of our biology. We have seen that Eddie inhabited his play, unaware, throughout all his various trance states. This is what he was biologically programmed to do. And likewise, to attend to Eddie's suffering in psychotherapy was to repair Eddie's play itself, not its component parts. Eddie's psychotherapy dealt with the whole elephant.

Remember, Eddie came to me, inhabiting his theater of consciousness—this biologically generated, illusory, synthetic re-creation of the world through which he lived and experienced his life. His play was a brain-created representation of the world, superimposed on reality. As such, his very theater of consciousness itself was art. We have seen that the "art-ifice" of his theater was a biological production of his cortex. We now discover that art and biology are one. And to finish the circle, psychotherapy itself is, likewise, an art.

We have seen that Eddie's original play was written in his cortex through the adaptations by his temperament to his inhospitable maternal environment—the ways that his genetic temperament digested his mother's specific abuse and neglect. We saw in chapter 8 that his play formed and operated in his cortex similarly to the biological world it represented, and, as such, it followed the regular biological processes. We will now address how the processes of mourning in Eddie's psychotherapy are consonant with the way his play was created in the first place.

(1) In the context of the newly awakened emotional holding with me, Eddie came out of hibernation. The trusting engagement allowed Eddie to awaken from his coma. He reversed the withdrawal, or "flight," of his Authentic-Being for protection from harm. The new, trustworthy holding with me was mapped through the oxytocin pathways of his limbic system rather than the fight/flight avenues of serotonin/adrenaline of his traditional mappings. This was no longer an extension of his old play but the beginning of a new one.

Within the new circle of emotional holding, Eddie broke down (i.e., re-digested) the established scenario of his play—the personas of self and other with their maso-sadistic relatedness. Eddie reversed the extroverted and observer projection that the anger was coming from me. He took it inside himself and identified it as his own. With access to his own aggression, he shifted away from identifying as the object of anger but as the possessor of aggression. Likewise, this broke down his internalizer adaptation, and he relocated the source of attack as coming from the outside, coming from Cathy.

(2) He then recombined these features anew. As a result of this, he literally reformed his images of self and other. He identified with new attributes as *self* and designated the remaining attributes over to *other*. He knew himself as legitimate rather than as bad and deserving of attacks. Likewise, he recognized Cathy as abusive, rather than as innocent and good and special. He ceased hating himself but directed the anger at Cathy. He was no longer locked into the maso-sadistic enactment.

(3) He redistributed the images of personas and retained some inside and ejected others outside him. He carried a lovable and good-enough Eddie inside of him. In place of the passive response to attack, he mobilized an active stance, to harness his anger on his own behalf. Thus, Eddie became a participant rather than just an observer. He shifted to an active, participatory potential to fight back and protect himself in a self-respecting manner from the Abuser. His sense of other people became more benign and safe—he no longer felt himself under an attack that passive Eddie could not stop. He now had an active capacity. All of this was mapped in his cortex.

Eddie's first foray into mourning his play was just the beginning. Throughout the rest of the psychotherapy, this paradigm of mourning repeated itself over and over. With leaps of trust, Eddie continued to peel his projections off of both of us. This led to deactivating the old play and writing a new one in his cortex, flowing from the oxytocic limbic mappings of his Authentic-Being. As we went along, his Authentic-Being began to infuse a new sense of self.

Just as the mourning of a death takes place within the circle of emotional holding, so does the mourning of the characterological play. Without it, no mourning could take place. It is only possible to mourn in the presence of genuine caring and real human engagement. Mourning in therapy can happen only authentically. There cannot be an "as if" therapeutic enterprise, with posturing, pretending, or falsity. In the course of therapy, Eddie entered into my inner circle. And with his leaps of trust, a special intimacy grew in our therapy relationship.

Thus, Eddie mourned the abuse and deprivation of his life and faced the pain anew. He slowly digested, deactivated, and laid to rest the mappings of his old play. Obviously, his incipient new play did not initially displace the deep mappings of his old play. There was a lot to do. Eventually, with sufficient mourning, the balance between his old and new plays shifted. His old play was increasingly deactivated, and his new play became increasingly established in his cortex. By the time Eddie had the dream of kicking the chair, he was no longer depleting the serotonin in the synapses of those old circuits of an ongoing play of sadistic aggression because he wasn't inhabiting those activated circuits. As a result, Eddie deactivated his endless war. His anxiety and so-called depression lifted all by themselves. This was a built-in and inevitable by-product of the work.

And the mourning continued. And Eddie continued to map the trustworthy experience between him and me. Eventually, this was sufficient for the emergence of an Eddie self in his newly mapped play, who was infused by his Authentic-Being and love. This created the conditions when I began to resonate with the tender and loving feeling of his being. He was there. This was the marker that Eddie had emerged as an authentic person.

We have seen what it took in psychotherapy to deactivate Eddie's damaged play and form a new one in his cortex. The old one was relegated to memory, where it belonged. We have seen the scope of this process and what it took to repair the damage done to Eddie's play. We have seen that the processes of mourning in psychotherapy addressed the same processes that had formed his original play in the first place.

The time it took for recovery reflected the damage in his world. Eddie's therapy took four years, meeting multiple times a week. The idea that there could be a quick fix for Eddie's suffering is an absurdity. The necessary time for digesting his pain reflected the nature and degree of damage that created his characterological drama. Let's say you were baking a cake that took fifty minutes at 350 degrees, but you decided you wanted it in ten minutes instead of fifty. Here's an idea: Why not cook it at 1750 degrees for ten minutes? Sounds like a plan—the only problem is, you'll get soot. It cannot work. You cannot override Mother Nature.

No one lives in a pure Authentic-Being state. We all live from our cortically created representational selves. This is the way consciousness is organized. Eddie now operated from an authentic self, which was infused by his Authentic-Being. This is the source of genuine vitality and the capacity to love. He no longer identified as a maso-sadistic self, empty of authenticity and alone. The recovery of—or the "covery " of—his authentic self was the fulfillment of his psychotherapy.

When Eddie wrote his new play, it was purely his. His values, his self, his personas, his sexuality, his politics, his religious beliefs, his aesthetics, and the landscape of his world were his own. They all flowed from his Authentic-Being. I did not shape it or control it, and it was not imitative of me or my characterological world.

Eddie's original play was still there in his cortex. It was susceptible to being activated, and it occasionally was. Therapy didn't transform him into a different person. It fostered the best authentic potential within him. Trauma affects us. It always leaves scars. No one is immune from that. Psychotherapy helped Eddie recover. Character is destiny. The repair of Eddie's character freed him from that destiny.

Eddie's development and his psychotherapy are prototypical, but his is but one story. The creation of his play derived from his particular temperament, processing the degree and specifics of his deprivation and abuse. The resonance and mourning in his psychotherapy, likewise, were specific to his play. The rest of us have our unique stories, filtered through our particular temperaments. Each of us has our character. The full range of character worlds reflects different degrees of formative trauma on our varied temperamental dispositions.

My field, psychiatry, has strayed from its careful and caring clinical grounding, in its mission to ameliorate human suffering. The very idea that human struggles can be reduced to a biochemical disorder; that billions of us are hardwired to be pathologically diseased and a pill can cure what ails us; and that politically correct social pressure can pass as science and redefine and eradicate certain forms of human struggle is an embarrassment and an insult to the intricacies, complexities, and mysteries of the human story. In our time, with the promulgation of the psychiatric diagnostic manuals, DSM IV and V and onward, we see an ever-expanding list of so-called psychiatric conditions that have been constructed to fit the narrow, wrongheaded theories of biological, pharmaceutical, neurological, genetic, and politically correct interests.

The diagnostic manual should not be the product of making the data fit the theory; rather our theories should fit the data, the human story. The manual's ever-growing Byzantine complexity reflects work-around solutions to make theories seem to work that cannot account for real life. As Arthur Conan Doyle said, "I never guess. It is a capital mistake to theorize before one has data. Insensibly one begins to twist facts to suit theories, instead of theories to suit facts." It is likewise true that the collective body of older psychoanalytic theories were off base, Byzantine, and incomprehensible as well. Do they not know of Occam's razor? (Roughly translated, the simplest explanation for some phenomenon is more likely to be accurate than more complicated and convoluted explanations.)

I would suggest the following as an alternative to the DSMs. (Please note that I do not use the demeaning term *psychopathology*.) We can break down the degree of formative trauma on the development of character into roughly three groups:

(1) In the context of moderate problematic mothering, with some good-enough mothering, we have four major types of character worlds, depending on which temperaments are in ascendancy—obsessional, phobic, compulsive, and dissociative characters.

(2) In the context of severe maternal damage, the different array of temperaments generate schizoid and paranoid characters, sadistic and masochistic characters, narcissistic and echoistic characters, borderlinism, affective characters, anorexia, germ phobias, psychopathy, and psychotic depression.

(3) Finally, we have the psychotic character worlds in which there is a fragmentation of the intactness of the self persona and a rupture of the cohesion of the play itself. This derives from a damaged Authentic-Being, due to some combination of extremely early maternal damage, with some genetic predisposition, and possibly epigenetic effects, all still forged through the different temperamental orientations. The psychotic character worlds are hebephrenia, catatonic schizophrenia, paranoid schizophrenia, schizoaffective schizophrenia, manic depression, and paranoid state. We don't even see hebephrenia and catatonia mentioned much anymore because they don't fit contemporary models. But they did not disappear and are still there.

It is not the focus of this book to elaborate on the full range of human character worlds. The summary above is designed to indicate something of its scope. The full range of problematic human character presents a host of different symptoms that generate very different experiences of suffering. The varieties and types of plays show an unrecognizable contrast to Eddie's play and internal landscape. And they generate their own specific resonances in psychotherapy. However, in the context of engagement and trust in psychotherapy, the processes of mourning are universal and similar. Psychotherapy is the specific responsive avenue for repair and healing for the whole spectrum of human character worlds.

It is the essential spirit of this enterprise that every patient is an individual and not a label. The particular story of a life with one's temperamental adaptation is always unique. Nobody is defined as a pure-breed category or a spot on a graph. Every person has his literal story and makeup. Eddie presented a mixed picture. He had obsessional and phobic features anchored in a masochistic and echoistic character. And finally, his LSD use generated a temporary dissolution of the intactness of his self, creating a transient psychotic terror, which was not schizophrenic. This description does not let us know Eddie. To know him was to engage with him in a genuine way. Knowledge of his character was but an aid in the service of engagement with him and his play, in the living theater of therapy.

Sadly, there was a more honest and rigorous study of the human condition during the previous hundred years than what passes for psychiatric literature today. Although Emil Kraeplin could not account for the causes of schizophrenia, his descriptions were far more accurate and uncontaminated than contemporary paradigms, which ignore inconvenient facts. There were elegant characterizations of psychiatric conditions, beautifully elucidated throughout those years. And human character itself has been understood and beautifully illuminated for thousands of years in art, literature, theater, philosophy, and music. Here's a sampling of some of my top picks: we have Lao Tzu, Homer, Chaucer, Shakespeare, Vivaldi, Bach, Mozart, Beethoven, Michelangelo, da Vinci, Jane Austin, and Dickens. There are, of course, thousands more, and I'm sure you have your own picks. The centrality of understanding human nature and human character has been a meaningful part of the human quest in every tribe and culture in history.

As we have shown, the proper subject of psychiatry is human character and its vicissitudes. This book's $E=mc^2$ for psychiatry is—human character, for every individual, is forged by the degree and particulars of abuse and deprivation, as processed by one's constellation of temperament through the cortical image-ination. Psychiatry can only redress human suffering by mourning our internal plays in the context of the responsive emotional holding and boundaries of psychotherapy.

ON THE BIG STAGE

17

DELUSION, ILLUSION, AND BELIEF

OUR FINAL SUBJECT GOES WELL beyond the scope of psychiatry. I would be remiss if I did not address the inescapable conclusions that follow from what we have learned about the theater of consciousness as it sheds its light on the human mystery itself. This has to do with the issues of belief and illusion in general, as well as the broader implications of the built-in dissonance between the Authentic-Being and the characterological self. This turns out to be a difficult subject, because it challenges some of the deepest beliefs we hold dear, including our religious beliefs.

We humans are purely biological creatures, like all other creatures. There is only a 4 percent difference in the DNA of a human and a chimpanzee, which accounts for our species uniqueness. We even have a 60 percent overlap of our DNA with that of a fruit fly. A cheetah has its exquisite muscular physicality. An eagle has its feathered predatory arrogance. The unique and distinguishing feature of our biological adaptation is the human theater of consciousness. We live in the characterological drama of this body/hormone/brain synthetic bubble of consciousness twenty-four hours a day, awake and asleep.

All brain functioning is grounded in illusion. The brain operates by creating functional representations of reality, which are not reality itself. To take the simplest example, if you touch your leg, you take for granted that you feel the touch and that this takes place at the moment of contact. In fact, the sensation of touch is an artifact of the nervous system. The nerve ending sends an impulse down an afferent nerve through a series of depolarizing electrochemical reactions going to your spinal column and brain. The brain then synthesizes the body sensation of your leg being touched and projects it back onto your leg as its projection screen. In fact, you don't actually even feel the touch at the moment of impact. The nerve impulse reaches your brain a beat after the actual contact takes place. The touch is an illusion created by the brain. Brain illusion works very well—when you touch your leg, your experience is simply that you touched your leg. Illusion is absolutely adaptive and allows all biological creatures to function in reality. Everything we experience is a brain-created illusion. Everything. It is the adaptational function of biological evolution that synthetic brain productions are experienced as real.

The theater of consciousness is a vastly more complicated form of the same thing. All of consciousness is a brain-created representation of actuality. All images, all ideas, and all persona representations come from our theater of consciousness. Our cortical image-inations give form to every element of our consciousness. Everything we see and think and believe and know and feel and imagine comes from the fountain of images in our waking trance. There is nothing outside of this. All ideas, persona images, dreams, culture, art, music, dance, theater, novels, poetry, design, architecture, myths, mathematics, discoveries, religion, and inventions—from cave drawings to $E=mc^2$—came from the human image-ination in our cortical theaters.

The illusions of consciousness, as well as every other representation of the brain, are art-ifice. Our entire consciousness evolved to serve the functioning of the organism. Human consciousness is our medium through which we engage and live the human life. We survive, live, and propagate through the characterological world, integrated with the rest of the brain-body. What we see and experience and feel within the synthetic cortical illusion of consciousness is taken to be just true and real.

As we have seen, consciousness begins at about six weeks old. That is the point in time when a high enough level of order from sufficient limbic-cortical mappings take place, through morphogen-esis and experience, to create the feeling of our being. Throughout the book I have called this the Authentic-Being and capitalized it to underline its importance. Remember, this is purely a synthetic cre-ation of the cortex. And it should not be seen as a reference to a liv-ing entity of some kind. Likewise, the later representational images of consciousness, our characterological self and its stories, also are purely synthetic illusions created by the brain. There are two sources in the construction of our top-down representational plays. First and foremost, they are created in our formative years as we process our experience of good-enough loving, deprivation, and abuse by our specific temperament. Second, we take in images from our culture through communication (art) that deepens and enriches and gives specific imagery to our plays.

Let us begin our exploration of beliefs and illusion through an examination of delusion in the psychotic character worlds. As a med-ical student in 1970, I did a psychiatric rotation at the old Boston State Hospital, when it was still pretty much a snake pit. The inpatient ward was in an old and rundown red-brick building, oddly set in an unusually beautiful landscape. I felt uneasy as I stepped into the bowels of this new and unfamiliar setting, where I had been assigned a patient on the ward. Clearly, there was a lot of strange history in-side those walls.

After a nurse unlocked the forbidding metal door to the ward, I walked into a large room filled with staff and patients. Strangely, everybody was hovering against the walls of this great hall except a large black woman who stood alone in the center of the room in her bare feet.

Unbeknownst to me, there had been an altercation in which she had just clobbered an attendant with her shoe. I also did not know that she was to be my patient. As I walked up to her, she stared in-tently at me. Then she lifted her hands in front of her, holding them forth, fingers up, palms out. I sensed this as some kind of greeting, and for some reason, I mirrored her gesture, lifting my hands in a similar fashion.

She squinted and looked at me intently. Then she reached forward and took my hands in hers. She peered at me again and then slowly turned my hands over. She scrutinized me once again very carefully. Then, with some resignation and disappointment, she dropped my hands, pointed at an attendant, and said, "He took my shoes. Will you get them for me?"

I said that I would check it out. So I went up to a burly attendant who was holding her shoes and asked him about them. He knew that I didn't know what had transpired and said, "Sure, you can have her shoes." He was hoping this young naïve student was going to get his. But I gave her the shoes, and she said, "Thanks," and walked away.

The next day I saw her sitting quietly with a group of patients. I asked her if we could meet and talk, and she agreed. As we sat together, she told me the following story:

"I'm Florine, black earth mother of the sweet white Lord Jesus. You see that glass [of water]? Where would the water be without the bottom of the glass? You see this room? Where would these people be without the floor? You see the earth? Where would we all be without the ground, the floor of the world? Where would we all be without Florine, black earth mother of the sweet white Lord Jesus?"

It seemed like she had a point, so I asked her to tell me about what happened that brought her to the hospital. Florine told me that she'd had a terrible journey of going down to the forty levels of hell and back many times in her life. It happened again and was happening now. She'd come from New Orleans and was raised in a voodoo/ Catholic culture. She said she was tired, and that was enough for today. Tomorrow, she would tell me about the levels of hell in her descent.

The next day I found Florine on the ward. When I approached her, she glared, turned her back to me, bent over, let out a giant fart, and angrily stomped off. So much for our second session.

With some trepidation, I held my breath and approached her chair on the ward for our third session. This time, she accompanied me to a private therapy room, where she began describing the various levels of hell and the torment she had experienced and was experiencing. I listened.

The fourth session was the same as the second session. As it turned out, we had alternating sessions—tales of hell terror and then the farts! She did, in the course of time, describe to me her journey down and her journey back up. Eventually, the flatulence no longer played a role in our relationship. During this time, she was medicated with Thorazine. After about four weeks, she was back to her self, a warm, funny woman who was ready for discharge.

A week later, I was scheduled to see Florine for follow-up as an outpatient. Just prior to my meeting with her, I was to do an evaluation with a new inpatient. I introduced myself to my new patient, a tall, clean-cut, well-dressed man in a suit and tie, who carried a well-worn Bible in his hand. I didn't know why, but as soon as I sat down in the therapy room, I felt a terrifying feeling in my bones, and the hairs stood up on the back of my neck. I realized I had made a mistake. I had taken the chair farthest from the door, with his chair in between me and the exit. I wanted to get of the room, but I didn't dare get up to walk past him, for fear I would agitate him. So I tried my best to override my inner response and attempted to do an evaluation interview. He sat quite still, staring straight ahead, formal-looking and silent, with his Bible on his lap. He didn't answer any of my questions or introduce any conversation of his own. He didn't acknowledge that I was saying anything to him or that I was in the room.

I nervously kept at it, asking more questions. He began to get agitated and opened his Bible. He thumbed through it furiously, reading and mouthing certain passages silently. Still overriding my terror, I tried again to engage him. I didn't know what to do, but then I got an idea. Maybe he would talk to me if I asked him about what he was reading in the Bible. Perhaps it had some meaning as to what was going on inside him. I asked him what chapter and verse he was reading. He started turning the pages even more furiously and began reading aloud with an agitated voice. Then he leapt straight up into the air—it seemed at the time to be about ten feet off the ground—and charged out of the room (much to my relief!), where he was tended to on the ward.

Meanwhile, I felt shattered inside. I had a visceral feeling of fright throughout my body, and my mind was not working very well. I tried to calm down, but I couldn't—and I was about to conduct my follow-up appointment with Florine. I was in no condition to be a junior psychiatrist. What was I going to do?

I simply pushed on and met Florine in the waiting room. I suggested we talk while walking around the grounds of the hospital. As we walked, she said, "You might be wondering what happened on the day I first met you."

Indeed I did. Since I was hoping to hide my desperation, this subject worked for me. In fact any subject would have worked. It was "any port in a storm." Florine went on, "I knew that the sweet white Lord Jesus was going to come to me, black earth mother Florine, there on the ward. So when you walked through the door, I thought, *This is him, the sweet white Lord Jesus. He's come!* I would know it was him when he showed me a certain sign. When you lifted your hands in a certain way, that was the sign, and I knew you was the sweet Lord Jesus. Then he was going to take my hands. And when you took my hands, I knew you was the sweet baby Jesus. Then he was going to turn my hands in a certain way. And then you turned my hands ... But you didn't do it quite right. So I knew you weren't the sweet Lord Jesus. But you're the closest to him that I've met."

As we walked and she talked, I gradually calmed down and felt better. The terror abated, and I felt more intact and whole—not so fragmented. I could think clearly again. She had no idea that she was providing for me what I had provided for her—trustworthy, holding, being there. This, of course, had nothing to do with the content of what she was saying. I was not confusing myself with a Messiah. I was actually just hanging on.

I later learned that the way she incorporated the gestures when we first met was an active process of consciousness called "ideas of reference." Each occurrence in the moment was incorporated in an alive manner and referred to the content of her thinking. She interpreted the happenstance of the living moment through her projected fantasy. It was actively defined by her play of consciousness, with no reference to reality outside of that.

I learned about ideas of reference from my patient Peter, a schizoid individual who was in a paranoid state. He was hospitalized because he believed the CIA and the KBG were after him. He was, in fact, a nuclear physicist with a high security clearance. He had been running around the streets of Cambridge in a state of terror. The last straw had been when a leaf fell from a tree where he was walking. This terrified Peter, because it clearly had come from the KGB agent who was spying on him from the tree and who had inadvertently knocked off that leaf. Peter was brought to the hospital.

Over the next couple of months, Peter came out of his state of terror and was ready for discharge. That state of frank paranoia had diminished to a high vigilance, then vigilance, and then to his routine guardedness. On the day of discharge, he said, "I want to thank you for our talks, which helped me a lot. Will you thank the staff for me? They worked very hard to make me comfortable here on the ward. In particular, I want to thank the other half of the staff who dressed as patients for my benefit."

At first I thought, *Hmm, I'm not so sure he's ready for discharge.* But then I realized that he always lived in delusion, but because he never talked to anybody, nobody knew.

About six months later in outpatient therapy, due to the stresses of a growing intimacy with me (I was the only person he had talked to in years), he got frightened again. In the midst of a session, he jumped up and pointed to a painting on the wall. I asked what was going on. He just said, "I see the red!" And he ran out of the room. He meant that the color red in the picture referred to the Communist menace, and I was their dangerous representative.

In case you were wondering what was going on with the Bible reader, it turned out to be my first occasion of resonance with catatonia. In a catatonic state, one seems, from the outside, to be kind of frozen. People in a catatonic state tend not to move their bodies at all and remain mute. I have seen patients with classic "waxy flexibility," where the individual stands perfectly still. If you lift his arm, he will keep it there until you move it back.

One patient, after he came out of a catatonic state, explained to me that he believed that if he voluntarily moved a muscle or spoke a word, this would cause a nuclear explosion, and we would all be atomized. His believed image of nuclear bombs was a projection of his barely contained nuclear rage impulses and the terror of that annihilation. This image was an accurate measure of the intensity of his rage, along with the terror from the dissolution of the intactness of his self.

On another occasion, I evaluated a man in a catatonic state in the emergency room. He sat motionless in his chair, disarmingly so, with his hands neatly folded on his lap the entire time. When he decided to talk, there was no human inflection in his voice. He didn't move at all or gesture while talking. I had the same resonance as with the Bible patient—the same chilling, creepy body feeling of terror. He said, in a quiet voice, "I was going kill my mother with a knife. At the last minute, I decided not to, so I shredded the couch and killed the cat." His vocal attitude would have been more suited to "Will you please pass the salt?" As you can see, the resonance with this catatonic state was to a primal rage/terror that was consonant with what was actually going on inside of him, even though he showed no outward signs of rage or terror. It was diagnostic.

Now, we know that Peter was delusional when he thought a KGB agent was up a tree, spying on him. And for sure, Florine was delusional when she thought I was Jesus. And it is delusional to believe that intentional muscular action or intentional speech would cause a nuclear holocaust and destroy the world. Clearly, paranoid schizophrenics are delusional when they hear voices that are not there or have religious ideas that they are God or Jesus or the devil, or that God is talking to them, or that they have to follow command voices, or that they are space aliens with mental powers, or that they can hear radio waves from their teeth, or that their thoughts are being broadcasted, or that they have microchips implanted in their brains.

We have seen, through the story of Eddie, that the damage to ordinary plays of consciousness stem from the limbic consequences of deprivation and abuse, creating sadomasochistic plays. Without going into great depth, we must say a few words about these psychotic character worlds. In the psychotic worlds, there is a additional disruptive dimension to maternal deprivation and abuse. In the context of major emotional deprivation, the damage to these plays derives from an unmanageable limbic nuclear rage. The cortex cannot encompass this powerful rage in a cohesive way. It fragments the cohesion of the intactness of the play itself and the intactness of the self persona. When the self and its primal play flies apart, it generates a state of terror, the dimensions of which are far more powerful than regular anxiety. This terror/rage is the central characteristic of all of the psychotic character worlds.

Although the self and the plays are fragmented, consciousness continues its ongoing process of playwriting. Consequently, the cortical image-ination now writes new plays that are anchored in this limbic rage/terror experience. Disrupted plays of a fragmented self and terror-filled feeling and otherworldly plots are written and inhabited. The feeling of these otherworldly plays are captured by words like awe, dread, or horror.

Schizophrenia has, as its foremost feature, the rupture of the self. It is important not to romanticize schizophrenic psychosis, as was prevalent in the 1970s and has endured. There was a school of thought that saw psychosis as a breakthrough of the true self. This reflected the fact that the prepsychotic character world of schizophrenia is, in fact, problematic, hollow, and not sustainable. The prepsychotic characterological self of schizophrenia is a false self, like a cardboard cutout. And the eruption of psychosis is a built-in inevitability. However, the psychotic fragmentation is not anchored in the Authentic-Being and is always unmanageable. The resultant terror/rage is the worst and most unbearably frightening state of all potential human experience.

There is an another tragic feature of schizophrenia—the Humpty-Dumpty factor. Once the plays and the self are fractured, they cannot fully be put back together again. In addition, due to the powerful limbic rage and terror, they are more vivid and compelling than nonpsychotic plays.

As a result of the fragmentation, what would be regular thoughts in an intact play are experienced as literal, heard voices in the plays of paranoid schizophrenia. These auditory hallucinations are given form by the cortical image-ination, as voices of otherworldly figures who generate terror and awe. Since the psychotic world is an invisible play of consciousness, just like nonpsychotic plays, voices are heard, but no personas are ever seen. Psychotic personas operate invisibly, as do our personas, yours and mine. There are no visual hallucinations in schizophrenia. Visual hallucinations come exclusively from toxic states, tumors, drugs, seizures, or incomplete mourning.

In manic depression, the central feature is that limbic feeling cannot be contained by the ruptured play. It spins out of control without limits. Manic flights of feeling are likewise not to be romanticized. A patient in a manic psychosis can be quite humorous in his early mood-elevated phases. It feels ebullient. Like all mood states, it is contagious, and manic people make us laugh. It, however, always escalates out of control, and, in its final and inevitable form, shows itself to be a terror/rage state. At that point, it is almost indistinguishable from a catatonic state.

In the diagnostic manual, manic depression is now unfortunately referred to as bipolar. I do not use this terminology. And it is quite common nowadays for many people to be given a bipolar diagnosis. This ubiquitous diagnosis seems to be worn by many, as a badge of honor. Despite the presence of some marginal mood shifts, most of these people do not have manic depression. The lion's share of this diagnosis is incorrect. Mania is a very serious and debilitating psychotic character world, which always generates the disintegration of the personality and results in repeated hospitalizations throughout life.

Paranoid state, like with Peter, is also a psychotic character world, meaning the characterological play is fractured, generating the limbic terror. It produces extreme but intact images of dangerous and murderous, persecutory, sadistic personas. These are not projected onto otherworldly figures, as they are in paranoid schizophrenia. In this case, actual people and organizations, like the FBI, serve as its projection screens.

None of the psychoses operates as stand-alone states. They each reflect severely damaged characterological plays. The various bizarre plays of otherworldly characters and terror/rage feelings are in the potential cortical image-ination of all of us. This is recognizable in the broad appeal of the genre of horror movies.

Despite the bizarre elements of the psychotic character worlds, psychotherapy remains the appropriate and effective avenue to heal these damaged plays. The plays of the psychotic worlds operate no differently from yours and mine, with the exception that their play has been fractured. Due to this, these patients warrant the judicious use of medications to contain the wrecking ball rampage of terror/rage—in schizophrenia, to diminish the terror of a fractured self; and with mania, to rein in the rampaging mood. For repair and recovery, the emotional holding of psychotherapy is the central provision. Paradoxically, in a psychotherapy with a person with a psychotic character world, the advent of closeness is always potentially disruptive, due to the formative deprivation issues, like with Mike in chapter 14. Nonetheless, patients with fractured plays can recover enough to lead fruitful, meaningful, and satisfactory lives.

The uninitiated might ask, "Do people really believe the bizarre ideas of the psychoses?" The answer is yes. Clearly, we are talking about delusions, typical manifestations of the aforementioned psychoses. Conventional psychiatric knowledge teaches that we reality-test our beliefs so that they are rational and evidence based. And the problem with schizophrenics is that they have somehow lost this capacity to reality-test. But this is not the case at all. In fact, as we shall see, all kinds of bizarre things that don't stand up to reality-testing are routinely believed by nonschizophrenic people, more commonly than not. What people believe simply follows from the content of their invisible play. Belief in the play of consciousness is *not* unique to the psychoses. We all do it.

The play's the thing, and consciousness is king. Belief, for all of us, means inhabiting the cortical top-down projections of our limbic-cortical plays within a trance state of consciousness. When we dream, we believe it is reality. When awake, Eddie and you and I believe our invisible plays are reality. The difference in psychosis is that the play that is believed is a horror movie, with its built-in, characteristic, horrific imagery and horrific feeling. We have seen this in the psychotic plays of Florine and Peter. Rather than seeing the content of an obviously deluded belief as a disorder of belief, it should be understood as routine belief in a distorted play. What distinguishes psychosis from non-psychosis is not the issue of belief, per se, but only the characteristic content of the play in question. The salient issue is not that bizarre things are believed. The startling fact that psychotic delusions are believed actually illuminates the synthetic nature of belief in general.

The crucial time for the formation of beliefs is age four. This is when cultural ideas and images are taken in and join the stories that are building from the inside. These images are, of course, supplied by the parents as the representatives and carriers of the culture around them. As four-year-olds develop their plays, their cortical constructions draw from the mixing of internal and external images.

Let's look at an example of the developing theater of consciousness in my son Gabe, of George Washington fame, when he was four. One day Gabe came home from nursery school. He was sitting at the kitchen table having a snack of Oreo cookies and milk. He turned to me and said, out of the blue, "Daddy, do you know what God is?"

This took me aback, as I don't believe in any god and had never talked to him about such a thing. So I said, "No. What is God?"

"God is the sun, and there is a little of God inside each of us," he answered, pointing to his solar plexus.

Now, what in the world was this? Was Gabe some kind of precocious religious seer? Was he a Ptolemaic Egyptian who worshipped a sun god? Was he a yogi who interpreted the solar plexus as the location of the third chakra? Did he know the scientific fact that the sun is the source of life on earth? Did he know, perhaps, that the earth is a planet in its orbit around the sun? Or maybe he linked the etymology of "solar" plexus with "sun"?

There had been, in fact, a discussion at nursery school that day about God. His teacher said that God lived in the sky. God created life. And God was love. Gabe heard this information from an adult authority. He comprehended it through his four-year-old consciousness. Adults often take for granted that children comprehend the words they use in their regular, literal, adult meanings. But their consciousness is very different from ours. They are still anchored in magic land. At four, he had one foot in top-down representational images and ideas and one foot still in the sky. Wonderful (full of wonder) four-year-old consciousness is still connected to the corre-spondences of nature and image-ination. This is the context through which Gabe wrote his God play.

Since there had never been any God talk at home, Gabe didn't have any preconceived idea of God. He didn't picture the typical old man with a beard in the sky. He pictured the sun in the sky. What-ever he understood as creating life, aliveness, and love, he pointed to the body location where the Authentic-Being is felt. I don't know why this is the body location of the Authentic-Being, but nonetheless it is so. Whenever patients in therapy feel themselves come alive in therapy, they locate a feeling of breathing free as this spot in their mid-chest. Likewise, this is the same location patients often point to when they refer to a feeling of emptiness and constriction.

Gabe, at four, had not yet become estranged from the direct feel-ing of his Authentic-Being and its correspondences with the world around him. He linked this God in the sky—the sun—to this sense of his own aliveness and love, to the feeling of his Authentic-Being in his body. Fear not; Gabe did not grow up to be a religious mystic. He would soon enough, as we all do, plant both feet in the representa-tional world and be a regular kid.

I want to underline that this God discussion did not mean that Gabe was in touch with the presence of God. He was writing a corti-cal story through his image-ination. He was certainly in touch with the resonant presence of his Authentic-Being. In fact, this momentary God discussion from my avatar son didn't hold a candle to his be-lief in the Santa play. We never heard any more God talk from him, but he was a true believer in Santa. He talked about Santa a lot and, without question, he heard Santa and the reindeer on the roof many times. Does this mean he was in touch with the presence of Santa?

Gabe's four-year-old consciousness was a way station where his Authentic-Being was relatively unvarnished and remained a distinct, resonant part of active consciousness. This coexisted with Gabe's characterological self and world. He remained grounded in his magical image-ination. He was unconflicted that in his Santa story, the laws of nature didn't pertain. His play belief bore no relation to reality-testing. Gabe absolutely believed that Santa was in the sky and flew on a sled pulled by flying reindeer. This rotund man came down the narrow chimney, which he couldn't possibly fit through, with a huge bag of toys and went back up by putting his finger aside his nose. No problem. Be circumspect if you think a four-year-old's beliefs are sacred. Remember, this was the same kid who believed I could pull Snickers bars from his ears.

As we know, our plays are organized as stories. The basic stories of consciousness in four-year-olds reflect the foundational imagery of the family and are still grounded in magic. The Santa story is a big Daddy-in-the-sky story of judgment between goodness and badness and reward. Specific cultural information is taken in that gives form to these stories. The stories that we retain are the ones that parental and cultural authority validate.

Stories are the organized units of consciousness, the way the cortex is organized. How does the Jesus story compare to the Santa story? Three days after Jesus was tortured to death, he was alive and well, walking around, his wounds having disappeared. Then, he rose up into the sky in his body. There is no mention of putting his finger aside his nose. And he flew up to heaven, without the aid of reindeer, to sit at the right hand of God, who is him. Now, Jesus doesn't just leaves us gifts of sleds and sweaters and stuff. Jesus leaves us the gift of redemption and forgiveness from our sin, bad boys that we are. He also leaves us the gift of eternal life, where nobody dies. In the Jesus story, if you are bad and don't believe in him, you won't go up to heaven in the sky; you'll go down to hell, which is down there in some undesignated place. As with Santa, you better not shout or pout or cry—or no gifts. So you better watch out.

The point is, with deference to the importance of this belief to so many people, this is the same story as the Santa story—of judgment about goodness and badness with punishment and reward. Obviously, this magical story bears no relationship to reality-testing. It is simply not credible. It is no more plausible than the Santa story. Both are similarly created by the cortical image-ination, using images supplied by the culture. While the Santa story is discredited in childhood, the story of Jesus and God is believed by between one and two billion adults. Gabe believed in Santa until it was mocked out of him by a neighbor at age six or seven. Now, it certainly is true that the Santa play was fostered by the carriers of his cultural environment— my wife and me. And the God story was not. If the rest of our culture validated Santa as real and God as an invention, it would not have been Santa who was discredited by Gabe's naysayer, and we might have a Santa religion.

How does this pertain to Florine? The imagery of her Jesus-and-the-earth-mother story derived from her New Orleans cultural context. The Christ story was fed into her consciousness by her adult authority. This incorporated story was used, in turn, as the imagery for her schizoaffective play. If her great-great-grandparents hadn't been kidnapped and taken to Louisiana by French slavers, she would have grown up in Africa. Most of the slaves brought to Louisiana came from the slave coast—Ghana and the Ivory Coast. They were Ashanti. As such, she would have been fed the cultural images of the Ashanti religion. Those images, in turn, would have been incorporated as the personas of the dramatis personae of her inner plays, not the persona images of the Christian story.

And then, in this imaginary situation, her schizoaffective schizophrenia story would not have been about Jesus at all. Nyame would have been her God. She would have been Asase Ya, Nyame's wife, fertility goddess and mother of Bia. I would have been Bia. These would have been the persona images of her cortical image-ination as she created her schizoaffective delusions. In fact, her Catholicism was probably mingled with the Ashanti personas as it was. The Ashanti gods were passed on from parents to children in New Orleans slave culture, and mingled with Catholicism. Nyame probably played a role in generating the black-earth-mother image in the first place. Africa is the actual source of Creole voodoo. People all over the world believe the cultural images they are fed. Yet each person thinks the believed cosmology of his play is real.

We all have an intimation of our Authentic-Being underlying our characterological self, which morphogenetically supersedes it. Our Authentic-Beings shine through our characterological selves like a pentimento. A pentimento is created when an artist paints a picture on a canvas. He then covers it over by whiting it out and paints another scene on top of the original one. The hidden and inaccessible original painting shines through the new one on the surface.

As we saw, four-year-old Gabe was not yet estranged from his direct knowing of himself as the formless feeling of his being. It is built into morphogenesis that inevitably, the direct presence of the Authentic-Being recedes. Soon enough, Gabe, like all of us, came to know himself as his characterological self. This is the functional self of consciousness through which we go about the business of living a life—surviving, working, marrying, raising children, and relating to our families, friends, and tribe.

Each of us has a resonance that our deepest self is not encompassed by our ordinary sense of self. This dissonance generates a built-in and understandable confusion about our nature. Every person feels the presence of his hidden Authentic-Being, one way or another. It is generated by established circuits of cortical limbic mappings, an artifact of the morphogenesis of consciousness. These circuits remain throughout life as the agency that generates the feeling of our being. It is the anchor of our loving. It is the quiet voice inside of us. It is our innocence. It is the source of our creativity. It is the source of our conscience. It is the fountain of our aliveness. None of this is mystical or magical. It is just the way consciousness is organized in the brain.

Once we consolidate our adult selves, we all have a restlessness that something is fraudulent and missing inside. This follows from our built-in estrangement from our Authentic-Beings, and it haunts us. Deep down inside, we all sense the hollowness of the characterological self. Likewise, we all have an intimation of something deeper and more authentic.

This dissonance from our Authentic-Being also derives from the fact that our characterological self forms, to one degree or another, through the ordinary deprivations and abuses of life. At best, there is only good-enough loving, and there are no perfect characterological selves. In all of us, our characterological selves fall short of perfection. There are no perfect people.

Yet the Authentic-Being inside always makes its presence felt. This element of human nature creates a quest for wholeness in the individual. There is always an avenue in every culture to address this quest. This accounts for the religions and spiritualisms in every culture, every tribe on earth today, and throughout history. All of them try to address something that is ineffable and formless through the cultural images of their time and place.

We all carry the feeling of our Authentic-Being. Because the intimation of our Authentic-Being is such a powerful and compelling presence, it is a natural process of mind to give it representational form, to create an invented image of this formless presence. As the agency within us of authenticity, conscience, and loving, it lends itself to images of a perfect persona—a perfectly moral persona, a perfectly loving persona. You can probably see where this is going. This lends itself to an invented persona image that people would see as God. It is understandable that people tend to believe that this persona image is real. The persona of a perfect, unvarnished being is a projected image of the Authentic-Being. Every culture or tribe gives form to this intimation of the Authentic-Being.

And over and above this, an elaborated religious story gets written about God as a characterological persona. A God play is written. All cultures adopt magical stories of spirits and gods and devils. These are representational stories generated by the cortical image-ination. These spiritual and religious stories are experienced as real and inform what is believed. Different religions from diverse cultures give form to and validate representational persona images and stories, such as Jesus or Buddha or Vishnu or Yahweh or Bia. Hindus have an elaborate play of characterological personas, with a huge dramatis personae—supernatural creatures who are all believed to be manifestations of God.

The ancient Greeks had a different cast of characters in their dramatis personae, with their pantheon of gods and goddesses, all of whom were all magical figures with supernatural powers. For centuries, the Greek gods—Zeus, Hera, Mercury, Artemis—were believed to exist and be real, just as we believe in our religious stories today. They are now relegated to myth or fairy-tale status and are considered to be quaint stories. It's almost unimaginable that people deeply believed in that cosmology.

In Judaism, God is believed to be formless and ineffable, like the Authentic-Being itself. Nonetheless, this formless presence of God is likewise given a characterological self personification. Throughout the numerous Bible stories, this God, whose name must not be spoken, has all the characteristics of a regular, old, characterological persona, who is somewhat less than perfectly moral or loving. So many Bible stories depict the God persona as jealous, petty, dominating, controlling, sadistic, murderous, and even genocidal.

Religious beliefs derive from the natural process of incorporating cultural stories into top-down cortical plays. But they are purely cortical creations from the theater of consciousness. These magical stories are not real. All is believed story. There are no exceptions to this—none, zero. There is no soul—no eternal spirit somehow separate from the body. There are no spirits of any kind. There are no angels; there are no ghosts; there are no space aliens; there are no goblins; there are no devils, no Satan, no incubi, no Beelzebub; there are no gods; there is no God; there is no Jehovah; there is no Jesus; there is no Vishnu. There is no heaven. There is no hell. There is no afterlife. There are no visitations from the dead. All our dead ancestors are dead. They don't exist somewhere in spiritual form or spiritual body or in another dimension. There's no such thing. These are all synthetic representations from our theaters of consciousness, fused with images fed by our culture. They are not real entities. There has never been one instance of simple, straightforward validation in regular waking consciousness of any supernatural spirits, souls, or personas of any kind floating around out there—ever. It seems that reality-testing doesn't apply.

When we die, consciousness ceases, and we are no more. When my living bubble of consciousness is gone, I am no more. My theater is closed. It's over. I do not live on in any form. There is no spirit persona of me separate from my brain-body. There will be images of me that those who may love me or hate me will carry in their theaters. The actual me is not there. I will no longer exist, except as somebody else's imaginary friend or enemy.

In the history of man, it has always been believed that persona images are real spirits. And this continues to be true today in every culture around the world. It is as natural to believe this as it is to believe that when you touch your leg, it is just real, rather than an artifact of consciousness. We all inhabit our bubble of human consciousness created by our body/hormone/brain webs and believe the images created from our image-inations. And we believe the cultural images we have been fed. However, they are synthetic brain illusions. These creations of consciousness are all there is. No unseen spirit personas, gods, or devils exist outside the stories of our internal theaters.

Religion is a very powerful and compelling authority because it addresses the deepest issues of existence—life and death, suffering, morality, and our intimation of a deeper sense of self, which derives from the dissonance between our Authentic-Being and our characterological self. But religion is just a codified story that teaches that there are spirits, and souls somehow separate from our bodies, and that we are not subject to the laws of nature.

Reborn Christians believe that since their characterological self is hopelessly corrupt, the only path to salvation is to literally take Jesus inside and live from him. This could be seen as a kind of metaphor for recovering one's Authentic-Being. However, the metaphor is believed to be literal and not symbolic. Instead of deepening one's authenticity, they believe the source of love and morality comes from Christ, this reified persona image, not themselves. Thus, instead of fulfilling their own innocence, creativity, morality, integrity, and love, and becoming more authentically themselves, they merge with the Jesus persona and become *Christ*-ian.

In the Catholic mass, we have the same story in different form. One also takes Christ inside oneself to become pure. It is believed that the wafer that is eaten and the wine that is drunk are transformed into the body and blood of Christ. By eating his body and drinking his blood, the person then possesses Christ inside him. This is not intended as a metaphor. This miraculous transformation is called transubstantiation, and is meant as literal and real. This phantasmagorical story is so real to people that it has inspired some of the most beautiful music in the world, which I happen to love very much.

I heard an interview with a Major League relief pitcher who lost a baseball game. His comment after the game was that God knew the opposing pitcher could not handle a loss, and God knew that a loss would be a good trial for him. So God willed it that a pinch hitter hit his fastball for a game-winning home run. This ball player believed that there was a real, albeit invisible, persona, God, who was watching him from the sky. He was testing him, punishing him for being bad, and rewarding him for being good. This pitcher belonged to a church where everybody professed, witnessed, and supported the same belief. This was a projected belief in a big Daddy persona in the sky, watching him. How much does this differ from Peter's belief that a KGB agent was spying on him from a tree and watching everything he did? And does this have any resemblance to ideas of reference?

Three out of every four Americans believe that prayer can help people recover from medical problems. In this belief system, thoughts travel outside the individual mind where big Daddy in the sky will hear you and magically intervene, if you've been good. How is this different from the schizophrenic belief in thought broadcasting?

At this very moment, the Vatican is teaching more priests to do exorcisms. They believe and promote that there are truly such things as actual devils. Satan is not a metaphor. They believe this evil disembodied spirit takes possession of your body. And the priests possess secret knowledge to get these evil spirits out. How different is this from the delusions of horrific creatures and devils in paranoid schizophrenia?

Christianity is the dominant religion of our culture. But the same applies to all the other religions and the beliefs in their magical stories—Judaism, Islam, Hinduism, and Buddhism, as well as all the minor ones. And the illusions of beliefs is not limited just to religion. Humans operate within belief systems all the time, religious and secular. There are Marxists, Freudians, believers in channeling, believers in reincarnation, believers in past lives, believers in ADHD, believers in biological depression, believers in all kinds of ideas about sexuality, believers in statistical science ungrounded in specific mechanisms, and believers in all kinds of ungrounded health and dietary ideologies. Once these stories are embraced, they all operate as any other cortical top-down play story.

Top-down cortical plays and *belief* are the same thing. The great blindness of human consciousness is that we do not know that our rocks-under-water images are illusion. This is universal. When authoritative ideas and images and stories are fed into the plays of children, they become part of their play, and are experienced simply as real. The play is *belief*. With such reified beliefs, reality-testing does not pertain and of course goes right out the window. Images transmitted from the culture are *not* known to be false illusions. When anyone bumps into another person's different beliefs, there is always trouble. In general, it is not possible to have a conversation about beliefs.

Why is this issue so important? The quest for truth is very important. Once something is clear, we cannot go back and fog it over. It is inescapable that the stories in our theaters are synthetic. All belief stories are metaphors. They aren't literally true. We can't pretend that there are exceptions, because more people than not are attached to the stories. We need to follow the quest for truth wherever it leads.

What matters more than anything is to raise our children well. Our job as parents is to facilitate good-enough adult plays in our children—for them to become responsible, capable, self-sufficient, protective, caring, loving, respectful, moral, and kind; for them to take their place in society, respect their place in nature, fulfill their authentic predilections, and raise their own children well. This central theme underlies all of psychiatry. I have tried to show that the raising of children is all about boundaries and love. Above and beyond this, we, as parents, provide the cultural beliefs for our children, which have such enormous influence on their plays.

It is natural and adaptive for children to learn about the world from parental authority. Just as a mother bird introduces flying to her fledging young, humans introduce the culture into their children as they learn how to live and survive. This encompasses the skills for survival; the particulars of clothing, housing, food acquisition, language, art, values, and sexuality; and all the cultural rituals of growing up. Cultural indoctrination provides answers for the scary mysteries of existence as well. It becomes the fabric for belonging to their society.

However, all cultural indoctrinations are not equal. There are problematic cultural plays, just as there are problematic character plays. The defining characteristic of a problematic character play is the presence of sadomasochism; the same applies to problematic cultural stories. The defining characteristic of a problematic culture is, likewise, the presence of sadomasochism. Athenian children turned into Athenian adults. Spartan children turned into Spartan adults.

Christian cultural myths, taught to our children, promote that we are born bad, in original sin, and need to be controlled. Similarly, the Jewish belief is that the world is *traif*, or dirty. And a follower has to submit to a comprehensive set of rules from God to be clean and kosher. If you don't, then you are dirty and bad. In Islam, if you do not prostrate yourself and submit to its dictates, you can be dismembered, or stoned to death, or even beheaded. Do these beliefs have sadomasochistic elements? Is it narcissism to believe the only way to have salvation is by believing in the Jesus story, or to believe that the Jews are the chosen people of God?

Many people think that if a false belief gives someone comfort, then this is a good thing—no harm, no foul. But it is not so simple. For many people, false beliefs can be benign. However, there are many dangerous problems that customarily follow from false beliefs.

To believe in something that is not true is sustained by something called faith. Faith means to believe a story, despite the fact that there is no evidence (never mind that the story defies the laws of nature). Faith promotes belief in a story that is patently untrue. And to have faith is held as the highest virtue. People have great pride in believing in things that are not so, and have great scorn for others who don't buy it.

It is unfortunately built into reified image-inings, or faith in a lie, that it inevitably generates an evangelical impulse. When someone buys a lie through faith, he will insist on selling it to you if you do not believe. Deep inside, a believer has to disavow the obvious. It is a mark of faith to not doubt his false beliefs. Consequently, he projects his doubt onto others, onto nonbelievers. Then he is compelled to convert the nonbelievers in order to keep his own projected doubt from coming home to roost. But this cannot work. Once he has achieved a conquest of a nonbeliever, then the doubt will get re-projected onto other nonbelievers, because it is really his own. And he has to convert others, over and over, until every last nonbeliever is converted.

One's own projected doubt cannot get eradicated by converting nonbelievers. It's really one's own denied knowledge of the lie. Faith in a false belief cannot sit still. It is much like Lady Macbeth, who cannot wash her hands clean because the blood on her hands is a projection screen for the truth of the blood on her hands, inside her. Washing the projective surface will not eradicate the truth inside. The doubt about a false belief cannot be eradicated by convincing a nonbeliever projection screen to renounce the doubt that is really his own.

But not only that, false reified beliefs lead one to be a follower of the authority that professes the lie. People become sheep. The problem here is that people interested in leading faithful believers tend to be wolves or Pied Pipers. Of course, this is not always the case. But the wish to have control and power over other people, in general, serves the narcissism of those in power, not the well-being of the followers.

And finally, once people are indoctrinated into believing false images, they make these false beliefs sacred. Once images are reified and sacred, people will die and kill for them. Salvation by God becomes easily transformed into a salvation army. There has been more killing and brutality in the name of God or cultural beliefs than all the other causes of war put together—the crusades, pogroms, the Holocaust, and 9/11, just to name a few.

When people lived in tribes or monolithic cultures, their belief system was consonant and uniform for everybody. In today's world, we no longer live in a unified tribe or culture. The world has grown very small, and the Tower of Babel of beliefs out there bump into each other all the time. And unfortunately, differences in beliefs have always had a hard time coexisting.

To provide the best holding environment for our children has always been our parental imperative. The provision of good-enough boundaries and love in childhood by parents, family, friends, and village creates the foundation and reference inside to come through the precarious trials of adolescence. This includes the provision of a good-enough cultural story and cultural boundaries, all in the service of fostering the development of responsible, moral, and loving adults.

We as a society must promote cultural stories for our children that are dedicated to promoting the best of humanity. Our beliefs (i.e., our culture and its stories) need to encompass the full scope and grasp of the forces of life as accurately as possible. Life is difficult, and its exigencies must be appreciated. I do not pretend to be the arbiter of the best set of cultural myths. While I am not saying that there aren't some good, caring, and valuable aspects to some of our belief systems, it is constructive to peel back false and outmoded beliefs. I trust that facing the truth and dispensing with false gods is the best possibility for the human quest. Mourning old beliefs is the most difficult thing in the world. It is always scary. Psychotherapy is the quest to mourn personal problematic plays; the same applies to our cultural stories as they inform our plays. They are not sacred.

These implications from the theater of consciousness and its stories are inescapable. It illuminates the nature of belief itself and questions the promulgation of false beliefs. This is a good thing. The more we seek the truth and accept it, the better off we are. Over the millennia, old paradigms, like the Greek gods, have atrophied and died out. New ones come in to take their place. We saw that after Eddie mourned his old play, he wrote a new play that was more grounded in love and authenticity; the same possibility applies to our cultural stories at large.

Many people fear that the absence of the moral strictures of our religions would promote immoral and hedonistic licentiousness. I certainly do not subscribe to either licentiousness or rigid control. The stories of the human quest have always reflected a grounding in the Authentic-Being. It has always been the actual source of morality and love. By appreciating the implications of the theater of consciousness, we can find our way to cultural stories that comprise the best holding environment for our children.

Some would argue that this is promoting some kind of new ideological belief system. This is not the case. Not believing in something that doesn't exist and recognizing that an old belief is not true is not a belief. It is simply negating a falsehood. I have done my best to illuminate that the Authentic-Being and the characterological self describe biological processes that literally take place in our morphogenic development. This is not a belief. It might be wrong. And if so, then quest for the real truth. We should never be attached to any false belief.

I want to underline that these explorations about belief and illusion are a broader subject than our focus on psychiatry. In fact, religious, political, social, ideological, and scientific beliefs have no place in therapy at all. Differences in beliefs between my patients and me have no bearing on the therapy whatsoever. I have treated patients who were Catholic, including priests; fundamentalist Christians, including evangelical ministers; and Hindus, Buddhists, Jews, vegans, scientists, Freudians, Marxists, political ideologues, and sexual ideologues.

I have treated Catholic patients who were estranged from their church and God because they became angry at God due to a life tragedy. After they mourned and recovered themselves, they reestablished their relationship to Jesus and God and returned to the richness of their church and community. I've treated patients who, knowing I'm not religious, conclude, "You don't know it, but you are doing God's work." I've treated patients who donate money to monasteries to pray for my family, because they feel grateful for the psychotherapy. I receive and value loving thoughts, in their terms, even though I don't share the beliefs.

In psychotherapy, the patient challenges his own beliefs in his personal play about his self-persona and its relational plots. The therapist provides the necessary emotional holding and respect for the mourning. As I have tried to show, the mourning process in therapy is the hardest thing on earth. A patient will challenge his play in his own way and in his own time. I cannot challenge his beliefs. They are his, not mine. When patients mourn and rewrite their characterological plays, they do so in relation to their own lights, not mine.

To try to change someone's beliefs has absolutely no role in psychotherapy. If one tried, one couldn't do it anyway. Even within the therapy, I could not have convinced Eddie that he was angry at Cathy before he challenged his own belief. If I had tried to persuade Peter that the KGB was not actually after him, he would have concluded that my motive for saying that was because I was in cahoots with the KBG. Such is the nature of belief.

In closing, we have seen that the story of Eddie has been the vehicle for the many confluent themes of this book, all of which follow from the central one: the plays of the theater of consciousness. We have addressed the biology of consciousness as it is organized in the brain to create the theater and that it is the defining expression of the human genome. Our consciousness is organized as plays, with characters, relatedness, plots, and landscape written by our image-inations in the cortex, through the centrality of the limbic system and feeling. Once established, the plays operate in a cortical top-down fashion. We have seen that dreams are the enactment of consciousness in the trance states of sleep, and that myths and fairy tales are codified dreams for different cultures. Art and theater communications are the vehicles to transmit stories between people.

We have addressed the nature and nurture question through our understanding of how our temperaments process our maternal environment. The pertinent environment is the actuality of good-enough mothering, responsiveness, and loving versus the presence of the trauma of abuse and deprivation. It is the latter that creates sadomasochism in the plays of consciousness. The damaged characterological play is the source of human suffering. And we have seen that psychotherapy is the specific form to heal suffering, consonant with the way it gets established. Psychotherapy repairs the damaged play and promotes the recovery of the Authentic-Being through genuine engagement and emotional holding for the mourning of trauma. This allows the Authentic-Being to more fully infuse the newly written characterological self. Furthermore, mourning has been shown to be the literal biological process in the cortex for the rewriting of the play.

We have seen the centrality of love versus abuse and deprivation in child rearing, child development, and personality development. And finally, we have seen the importance of the illusory nature of our beliefs and their synthetic contents for our cultural stories. And we have explored how powerfully beliefs inform our top-down plays through the indoctrination of our cultural stories. We have seen as well the import of the dissonance between the Authentic-Being and the characterological self regarding the human mystery.

I have had the uncommon opportunity to be allowed into the hidden worlds of so many patients over the last forty years. To be let into their inner life, to give whatever clarity I could, to provide the circle of emotional holding, and most important, for them to thrive and flourish has been precious and very rewarding. It has been through the engagement with my patients that my understanding of the theater of consciousness crystallized and took form. We have seen that psychiatry, neuroscience, dreams, myths, fairy tales, and art, as well as the religious impulse, are all encompassed in this unified paradigm.

This is certainly not the last word on humankind, but it is the best I can contribute. And in regard to anything that is off base in this presentation, throw it away and clarify it better. We must follow the quest for truth wherever it leads. Hopefully, our explorations will be informed by the most important value of all—responsiveness and good-enough loving. Without that, we have nothing.

The theater of consciousness is a new paradigm, derived from contemporary knowledge that encompasses the age-old human quest. Human nature has not changed over thousands of years. And we have shown that this paradigm is, as it must be, consonant with old wisdom, love, and the human struggle. It is my hope that its implications will help to reinvigorate psychiatry, as well as serve society at large.

Acknowledgments

I AM DEEPLY INDEBTED TO so many people for their contributions to *Psychotherapy of Character*—my family and friends, my professional influences, my personal mosaic of influences, and those who have worked with me on the book. First and foremost, my wife, Nancy. She is the love of my life, a shining figure of caring, integrity, intelligence, beauty, and virtue. I am a very fortunate man. Her example taught me about motherhood, the underlying theme of the book. And my three children, Joshua, Gabriel, and Lily, who taught me depths of love I never could have imagined. I learned, as well, through raising them, the central principles of psychotherapy— boundaries and love.

My Professional Mosaic

The writings of W. Ronald D. Fairbairn, MD, who, as a fellow outsider, put it all together in earlier form. He had the courage to think for himself, dispense with dogma, and stay grounded in the essence of the therapeutic process. Harry Stack Sullivan, MD, was also a model for the courage to be true to himself. His writings illuminated the nature of schizophrenia, including its responsive treatment environment and psychotherapy. He wrote with honesty, caring, and humor. Antonio Damasio, MD, demonstrated the centrality of feeling in the neuroscience of consciousness and the biology of judgment. V. S. Ramachandran, MD, demonstrated the illusions of consciousness.

And Eric R. Kandel, MD, established the technical mechanisms of memory in the brain.

William B. Rothney, MD, was an early unsung teacher who taught me about failure-to-thrive infants and early mothering. Elvin V. Semrad, MD, was a psychiatric teacher who embodied the pure heart of therapy and the therapeutic relationship. Howard Wishnie, MD, has been my friend and colleague for forty years. Our regular meetings during this time have been invaluable to me. Through the deep trust between us, we could be open, vulnerable, and honest when issues in our own characters were stirred in the work. I have always been able to rely on his caring, integrity, and incisiveness.

Finally—and most important—I am indebted to my patients. It is you who have taught me about the play of consciousness itself and the full scope and range of human character. It is a privilege to be entrusted with your deepest vulnerabilities in the special intimacy of therapy and to be part of your recovery to fulfillment and love. Long after our psychotherapy is over, and for the rest of my life, you continue to populate the inner circle of my own heart.

My Mosaic of Influence

Lewis Thomas; Charles Dickens; Johann Sebastian Bach; Christopher Hitchens; Marc Chagall; Lao Tzu; Charles Darwin; Ali Akbar Khan; Walt Whitman; Beethoven; Pamela Gien's play *The Syringa Tree*; Robert Johnson; Colin W. Turnbull, for his incredible grasp of culture; Aeschylus, Sophocles, and Euripides; Frank McCourt; the Mozart *Requiem*; William Shakespeare; John, Paul, George, and Ringo; Gregory Bateson; Homer; Notre Dame and Chatres; the Band; Elizabeth Kubler-Ross; *Les Mis*; Red Auerbach; Plato and Socrates; Ray Charles; Claude Monet; Jane Austin; Vivaldi's *Four Seasons* performed in Sainte-Chapelle; Margaret Mead; Monuments; Harper Lee's *To Kill a Mockingbird*, book and film; Saint Sulpice; Brahms; Nietzsche; the Rolling Stones; Joseph Campbell; Laurence Stern (*Tristam Shandy*); Ravi Shankar; Bill Russell; Van Gogh; Richard Dawkins; Bob Dylan; T. S. Elliot; Stevie Wonder; Alan Watts; Handel's *Messiah*; Gandhi; Barbara W. Tuchman for her *March of Folly*; Hermann Hesse; Jimi Hendrix; and Larry Bird.

My Other Life

My summers on Echo Lake, Maine, with family and friends were the heart center of my life. I learned so many of the secrets of nature—the winds of the lake, plants, wildlife, birds (with special thanks to Bill Townsend), sky, geology, and time; My extended family of Maine friends, especially Bob and Sonnie Goodman, who are most dear to me, and all the children (now grown) are in my inner circle. The spirit of Maine has invisibly infused this book.

Writing the Book

There are many people who have been so generous and invaluable to me throughout the writing of this book. My son Gabe has been my prime confidant, as well as my neuroscience consultant. He has given an inordinate amount of time to *Psychotherapy of Character*. Our endless discussions have sharpened and refined what I had to say. I have relied on him to critique the content and the writing all the way through. His resonance with the scope of ideas was remarkable. It has been a very rare gift to be able to entrust my innermost sensibilities and hash out the substance of this book with a son. Nancy has been my rock with the writing. Through her artful vision, her critique has always been spot on, most pertinently when I didn't want to listen. Through all of this, she has been steadfastly patient. My daughter, Lily, has been an invaluable editor with her forthright comments. She is a savant, like her mother, and always clear.

I am deeply indebted to my principle readers. Frederica Cushman has been a great source of sustenance from the beginning. Many thanks for her tireless generosity and support as a reader and her rigorous work on the manuscript as an editor. Likewise, Peter Van Etten has been incredibly generous with his time, attention, thoughtfulness, and friendship. The probing questions, suggestions, and critiques from his encompassing mind have been such a valuable contribution. And another thanks to Howard Wishnie for taking time from his busy life for his thorough and thoughtful commentaries. As always, he has been selflessly there, with clarity and encouragement. Finally, I appreciate Bob Goodman for his dedication and support.

He is a kindred spirit, and his broad-ranging mind has brought a unique perspective.

And finally, I am grateful to my partners at Wheatmark for their publishing expertise and care—Grael Norton, Atilla Vekony, and Lori Leavitt.

APPENDIX
Do No Harm: The Destructive History of Pharmaceutical Psychiatry and its Bedfellows—Electroshock, Insulin Shock, and Lobotomies

THE ONE THING WE LEARN from history is that we don't learn from history. This is never more pertinent than in the hidden story of somatic psychiatry. To fully appreciate the danger of its current incarnation, psychiatric drugs, we must take somatic psychiatry out of its state of amnesia. Its predecessors—insulin shock therapy, lobotomies, and electroconvulsive therapy—should serve as a reminder, a morality tale, for the excesses and depravity to which conventional psychiatric knowledge and practice can easily sink. The underling theory of somatic psychiatry is that the source of human struggle is considered to be the brain itself, rather than the person. Treatments that follow from this simplistic, mechanistic, and reductionist notion have been to act directly on the brain, always with violating and destructive outcomes. The real source of human suffering is not the brain. It is in the person, the human being, in the context of damage to the play of consciousness. My life's work has taught me that the art, the science, the discipline, and the wisdom of psychotherapy attends to this damage. Tragically, over the course of one generation, psychotherapy has become almost extinct and has been replaced by drugs. There are no miracles and no shortcuts, as drugs, like the

271

other somatic therapies, always promise. We have repeated the same mistakes over and over again, and we are doing so today.

Somatic psychiatry originated with seizure therapy, or its first modern incarnation, insulin shock therapy (IST). It actually had its roots in the sixteenth century and was used psychiatrically around the time of the American Revolution. It was refined in 1927 into insulin shock therapy, when insulin was used to induce seizures as a treatment for drug addiction, psychopathy, and schizophrenia, with claims of a 50 percent remission rate. Papers were published in the *American Journal of Psychiatry*, starting in 1937. IST was widely used through the 1940s and 1950s. Its founding etiological principle was the (false) idea that seizures were the opposite of schizophrenia. Induce a seizure, and you balance out psychosis. In the 1930s, a more refined scientific explanation was developed for the (phantom) curative power of seizures. Its science proclaimed that psychiatric problems came from the autonomic nervous system. IST was said to work by blocking the nerve cells of the parasympathetic nervous system, thereby intensifying their tonus and strengthening their anabolic force. This restored the nerve cell, and the patient recovered. The corollary theory was that patients were jolted out of their psychiatric condition.

Next, we have lobotomies, originally called leucotomies. Lobotomies came onto the scene in the 1930s, having been invented and promoted by Antonio Egas Moniz. When I was a psychiatric resident, lobotomies were still fresh in psychiatric memory. The practice had only ceased in the early 1960s, after over twenty thousand people received this "treatment." Let's see ... what was the science? The source of psychiatric problems was located in the brain, specifically the prefrontal cortex. The treatment of choice, then, was to ream out the prefrontal cortex with an ice pick. Respected MDs had a miracle cure and were the vanguard of the field. Science proved that lobotomies cured not only schizophrenia but anxiety, depression, low self-esteem, obsessive/compulsive disorder, and the unwanted behavioral problems associated with mental retardation (this is code for sexual behaviors). It was respected and celebrated in the psychiatric literature and validated in journals with documented studies and peer-reviewed scientific evidence. Lest you think this is an exaggeration, Moniz won a Nobel Prize in 1949 for his great and wonderful discovery.

Eventually, the validating follow-ups were shown to be fabricated and deluded, with self-promoting lies and half-truths. Only after a great deal of harm were they debunked. And the ice picks were thrown into the trash heap of psychiatric history. We need to add that after lobotomies gradually attenuated, no one stopped and said, "What in the world did we just do?" How could sticking an ice pick in someone's brain ever have been even a remote consideration? What was going on that such a grotesque medieval mutilation was actually adopted as a good thing to do? And how could it have been publicly and professionally embraced? However, as always seems to happen, amnesia quickly set in, and we forgot the brutal inhumanity that was so recently celebrated. And the considerable body of discredited scientific validation was never scrutinized for its contribution to and for having promoted such harm. Instead, science moved on to support the next somatic treatment in exactly the same way.

Next, we have electroconvulsive therapy (ECT), which came along soon after IST, in 1938. ECT was still a part of the curriculum in my own psychiatric residency in 1971. Entire psychiatric hospitals, built exclusively for ECT, were still operating, with no empty beds. Scientific studies and respected journals provided documented validation for placing electrodes on patients' heads and applying huge jolts of electricity to generate seizures. Apparently, the jolt theory had gained traction. So we shocked the brain, instead of reaming it out. How humane. In addition to everything else, ECT also was touted as a cure for depression. It was allegedly proved that ECT was a safe, effective cure, with few, if any, drawbacks. The resultant memory loss not only was initially downplayed but was trumpeted as being therapeutic. (By the way, drugs are being developed today to chemically erase memories with the idea that this is therapeutic for trauma—same thing.) Later, under public pressure, ECT was refined to cut down on memory loss. The history of electroconvulsive therapy followed the same trajectory as lobotomies. Eventually, ECT showed itself to be the ineffective and violating practice that it is. But don't get overconfident. Incredibly, in recent years, ECT has made a comeback and is being promoted once again, when its progeny treatments, antidepressants, don't work.

Finally, we come to the current incarnation of somatic psychiatry, neurobiological psychiatry, and its treatment—drug therapy. Psychiatric drugs are next in the lineage of "treatments" whose focus is to act upon the physical brain. History is repeating itself. Our contemporary science has now apparently proven that human problems come from genetic or developmental neurobiological disorders of the physical, anatomical, biochemical brain. The somatic treatments for these neurobiological, genetic, synaptic hormonal neurotransmitter diseases are brain drugs—psychoactive drugs. Would you be surprised if the actual history of drug "treatments" has itself followed the very same pattern as the other somatic therapies?

The first psychiatric drugs were introduced in the mid-1940s — Thorazine, an antipsychotic for schizophrenia, and lithium, a mood stabilizer for manic depression. It is noteworthy that both Thorazine and lithium, as with the discovery of penicillin, were discovered by accident, not by research. They did not come from multimillion-dollar pharmaceutical labs or experts in scientific research with validating and substantiating studies in quest of psychiatric drugs. Phenothiazines (the drug family of Thorazine) were developed as antihistamines in the early 1930s and used as an aid to anesthesia for surgery. In 1947, Thorazine was given as an antihistamine to patients in a mental hospital, where it surprisingly showed its antipsychotic effects.

Similarly, lithium had a long and accidental history. It was initially developed for gout in the 1800s. It was even used as a tranquillizing ingredient in an early form of the familiar soft drink "7-Up Lithiated Lemon Soda," soon to become 7-Up, when soft drinks were still concocted to be popular medicinal cure-alls. Lithium was removed from 7-Up at about the same time as cocaine was taken out of Coca-Cola. Notice that their names purposely advertised lithium and cocaine as their active ingredient. Medicinals have always postured as an elixir of life, bringing eternal youth, happiness, no disease, physical strength, superior intelligence, sexual potency, etc. We can be gods. Lithium was found accidentally to work as a mood stabilizer for manic depression in the late 1940s, when an Australian psychiatrist injected mice with lithium urate when testing whether uric acid created mania. Instead, to his surprise, he found the incidental ingredient in his test—lithium—calmed the mice. It is a salt. Li is one row up on the periodic table from sodium, the prime ingredient of table salt. To this day, no one knows how it actually works.

Schizophrenia and true manic depression differ from all the rest of the psychiatric conditions because they actually manifest a brain disturbance embedded in a personality disturbance. Consequently, in addition to psychotherapy, a brain drug is a relevant component in the treatment of the personality of a person with these conditions. However, despite the claims of contemporary somatic psychiatrists, all the rest of psychiatric issues are not brain disorders. They are the result of damage to the personality. Whereas a damaged personality is, of course, reflected in the organization of the play consciousness in our brains, there is no actual brain problem. When the damage to the personality heals, this likewise is reflected in the brain. There has not been a positive contribution from psychiatric drugs since Thorazine and Lithium. There has been a great deal of harm. In the aftermath of Thorazine and lithium, there has been a continuous stream of allegedly curative psychiatric drugs. In each case, brain-based biochemical psychiatric diseases have been invented or co-opted to create the "need" for these pharmaceutical cures.

I will briefly review the hidden history of psychiatric drugs. They all follow the same trajectory as the other somatic treatments. Each drug arrives in the market with great acclaim. Each one is advertised to be efficacious, with no side effects, no addiction, no habituation, no drug tolerance (requiring higher and higher doses), and no high. Then, each in turn shows itself to be horribly addictive, with terrible side effects, with considerable drug tolerance, and significant habituation, while the highly acclaimed efficacy shows itself to have been fraudulent. And they end up being used simply for their considerable "highs." Keep in mind, when each drug gets discarded, new ones appear to take its place, with the same false promise—efficacious, no side effects, not addictive, no habituation, no drug tolerance, and no high. We move so quickly to the next new drug that we don't seem to remember the travesty that has just transpired.

In my lifetime, we started with bromides and chloral hydrate. Then Milltown appeared, with devastation in its wake. We then moved to the barbiturates—secobarbital (Seconal); street names are reds, red birds, and red devils; pentobarbital (Nembutal), known as yellow jackets; amobarbital (Amytal), known as blue heavens; amobarbital-secobarbital (Tuinal), called Christmas trees, and rainbows; and zopiclone (Imovane). They unfortunately turned out to create poor concentration, fatigue, confusion, and impaired coordination, memory, and judgment. They are highly addictive, with life-threatening respiratory failure during withdrawal. They have caused more deaths from overdose and have been used in suicidal overdoses more effectively than any other drug. Eventually, the once ubiquitous barbituates were relegated to the back shelf, except for their place in the ever-present street market for the purposes of drug highs.

Without a pause, in came the benzodiazepines with great fanfare—you know, efficacious, nonaddictive, no side effects, no habituation, no drug tolerance, no high—starting with Librium and Valium. The benzodiazepines were prescribed for anxiety (and still are). Unfortunately, these turned out to be as destructive and addictive as the barbiturates, with an even better high and greater habituation and major drug tolerance. In fairness, they are less lethal than barbiturates when you overdose. As always, the initial reports of problems were themselves discredited and scorned. Information about a significant psychoactive drug effect was suppressed for a long time—rage-reactions. When acknowledged, they were termed "paradoxical" rage reactions. Finally, the suppressed evidence came out and was irrefutable that Librium and Valium are extremely addictive and habituating, never mind creating significant highs. Valium turned into a nonentity. What ever happened to all the studies, all the papers, all the research that validated it? How could they have been so wrong? How can that be?

But fear not. Immediately new benzodiazepines popped right up to take their place—Xanax, Klonopin, Ativan, Versed, Serax, Restoril, et al. These, of course, are still touted as safe and efficacious. Worldwide sales in 2011 for benzodiazepines was $21 billion, never mind the black market (e.g., all over the Internet). I wonder why? Probably for that pesky neurobiological genetic brain disease, anxiety disorder.

Then we move onto the sedatives and hypnotics, also known as sleeping pills. Sales of prescription drugs alone in 2011 were $19 billion. Don't you want a full night's sleep with no insomnia? Don't you to wake up healthy, happy, and refreshed in the morning? We have Halycion (actually a benzodiazepine in disguise), Ambien, Lunesta, Sonata, and Rozerem, each with the promise of blissful tranquility, free and easy. Not so. Each gets discredited in turn—addiction, habituation, considerable drug tolerance, and very bizarre psychoactive side effects like sleep driving or sleep eating. But let's not learn from our mistakes. No need for concern; the new one is the real item. There never has been a safe prescription sleeping pill. But I'm sure the next one will be.

Now we'll turn to amphetamines, concocted by the Nazis for their pilots to fly all night when bombing England and their soldiers to need no rest for the Blitzkrieg: amphetamine (Adderall), atomoxetine (Strattera), dextroamphetamine (Dexedrine and Dextrostat), laevoamphetamine (Benzedrine), methamphetamine (Desoxyn, Methedrin), street names: crystal, meth, ice, speed, glass, chalk, crank; and methylenedioxymethamphetamine—street names Ecstasy, MDMA, E, or X.

Speed was touted as an "up," our first antidepressant, as well as an appetite suppressant for weight loss, with no need to diet or exercise. They were widely used by college kids for all-nighters. For the most part, they were used to get high, with massive addiction. Mental hospitals in the 1960s and 1970s were filled with amphetamine psychoses. Amphetamines were correctly discredited and pretty much disappeared from psychiatric and medical usage.

But then a strange thing happened. A new medical-psychiatric genetic brain disease got invented: ADHD. And what was the treatment of choice? You guessed it. Suddenly, speed was safe again, nonaddictive, no side effects, and it didn't generate psychoses anymore. Its sordid history went right back into amnesia. Apparently, the past didn't happen, so we certainly don't have to learn from it. I guess the significant percentage of inpatients suffering from amphetamine psychoses when I was a psychiatric resident was a figment of my imagination. We are currently doping a generation of our children with speed. Sales have reached $1.5 billion a year, never mind the black market. And the good news is, it's been discovered that adults have the same ADHD disease and should be on speed too. How is it that we can see the alleged ADHD brain disease disappear during any episode of the *Super Nanny* on TV? One witnesses a transformation of these genetically neurobiological diseased children into normal children every week, with no amphetamines.

Finally, we come to the latest and greatest, the antidepressants—the SSRIs, Prozac, and friends. "Clinical depression," of course, has now been transformed into a medical, biological, chemical brain disease. Any debate about this has now been settled and deemed to be conclusive. All the research, studies, and journal articles show, with irrefutable scientific proof, that this is real. And once again, it is accepted that the treatment is to act on the brain—no longer with ice picks, no longer with electricity, but now with psychoactive chemicals. It is a brave new world indeed. We have fulfilled Aldous Huxley's prophecy of soma, written eighty years ago. He took the name for his fantasy pill from the ancient Indo-Aryans happiness elixir, Soma. Prozac is the modern incarnation of the ancient human fantasy of a happiness pill. Legal sales of antidepressants topped $11 billion in 2011. We should mention that the black market for SSRIs on the Internet matches the frequency of black market Viagra offers.

Here's the list:

Selective Serotonin Reuptake Inhibitors (SSRIs)

- citalopram (Celexa)
- escitalopram (Lexapro)
- paroxetine (Paxil, Seroxat)
- fluoxetine (Prozac)
- fluvoxamine (Luvox), sertraline (Zoloft, Lustral)

Here are the rest of the antidepressants:

Serotonin Antagonist and Reuptake Inhibitors (SARIs)
- etoperidone (Axiomin, Etonin)
- lubazodone (YM-992, YM-35,995)
- nefazodone (Serzone, Nefadar), (Desyrel)

Serotonin-Norepinephrine Reuptake Inhibitors (SNRIs)
- desvenlafaxine (Pristiq)
- duloxetine (Cymbalta)
- milnacipran (Ixel, Savella)
- venlafaxine (Effexor)
- tramadol (Tramal, Ultram)
- sibutramine (Meridia, Reductil); these two couldn't get antidepressant clearance so they are marketed for other conditions, like weight loss and cigarette discontinuance

Norepinephrine Reuptake Inhibitors (NRIs)
- reboxetine (Edronax)
- viloxazine (Vivalan)
- atomoxetine (Strattera)

Norepinephrine-Dopamine Reuptake Inhibitors (NDRIs)
- bupropion (Wellbutrin, Zyban)
- dexmethylphenidate (Focalin)

Amphetamine Class Drugs Used As Antidepressants
- methylphenidate (Ritalin, Concerta)

And then there are the original antidepressants:

Tricyclic Antidepressants (TCAs)
- amitriptyline (Elavil, Endep)
- clomipramine (Anafranil)
- desipramine (Norpramin, Pertofrane)
- dosulepin [dothiepin] (Prothiaden)
- doxepin (Adapin, Sinequan)

- imipramine (Tofranil)
- lofepramine (Feprapax, Gamanil, Lomont)
- nortriptyline (Pamelor)
- protriptyline (Vivactil)
- trimipramine (Surmontil)

Never mind that these psychoactive drugs barely perform better than placebo. Never mind that suppressed studies are finally coming out that show the antidepressants are proven to promote suicides and homicides in children as well as young adults. I promise you it will come out that the same applies to older adults as well. It is even hidden that Prozac is hugely addictive. Commonly, when someone tries to discontinue Prozac, he feels "depressed" again. The conventional thinking is that his "biological" depression returns, so he has to get back on the drug. And this is used to prove the efficacy and necessity of the treatment. Looks like our patient will have to stay on Prozac for his disease for the rest of his life. What is actually happening is that the user has become habituated to the extra drug-induced supply of serotonin in his synapses. When the drug is discontinued, his natural ability to create serotonin is diminished and insufficient, due to biofeedback loops. Not only this, but users commonly have horrific withdrawal symptoms that are almost never publicized. An array of frightening neurological symptoms appear when trying to detox off this psychoactive brain drug—vertigo, lightheadedness, burning or tingling sensations in the skin, difficulty with gait and balance, blurred vision, tremors, twitches, and restlessness. Sometimes there are hallucinations. Patients, understandingly, get terrified from these symptoms and conclude that something really is dangerously wrong with their brain. As a result they don't dare to stop the Prozac. Thank God they are taking it in the first place and blocking these horrible neurological symptoms that are part of their brain disease. To discontinue an SSRI has to be done very slowly and carefully over the course of a year.

In fact, it is quite common that through drug tolerance, the serotonin-boosting effect attenuates, and its so-called antidepressant effect diminishes. The expert pharmacological psychiatrists then add one or two more specially selected antidepressants into the mix, and an antianxiety pill for good measure, or maybe even an antipsychotic. Sometimes, we even have to shock some patients when their "disease" is deemed simply too pathological. Prozac is the latest of these false and destructive psychiatric drug therapies. It too is following the same sad and tragic pattern as the rest of them. We never learn. Most important, despite the fact that our society is so acutely conscious of the dangers of drugs, our psychiatric drug epidemic is seen not only as okay but as a really good thing.

Sad to say that one of the great culprits in the sorry history of somatic psychiatry has been faulty science itself. Its brain theories have been substantiated by the science of today and validated in the professional journals. Scientific studies have apparently demonstrated their efficacy, while assuring there is little or no downside. The point here is that these practices are not only ineffective but harmful and destructive, almost 100 percent of the time. In the best tradition of science, one exception proves the rule. Once a theory is shown to be faulty, it is discarded. This never happens in the somatic psychiatry and pharmaceutical establishment. What kind of science can this be? How can the science be right when its outcomes are so wrong. A science that validates and promotes a lie is bad science.

The real history of somatic psychiatry shows the science to be faulty in method and fraudulent in its application. In addition, the multibillion dollar pharmaceutical industry and its influence peddling in academic psychiatry finally has been exposed as financially corrupted and manipulated. They have engaged in study suppression, falsification, strategic marketing, and financial incentives. Yet the methods and practices of this very deficient science are never questioned. Instead, it continues to get a free pass and remains the respected authority. We move right along. Our sacrosanct science continues to validate that the next new and improved drug will cure what ails us. Unless we learn from our experience, we are doomed to repeat it.

Made in the USA
Coppell, TX
12 May 2021